# Learning Airtable
*Building Database-Driven Applications*
*with No-Code*

*Elliott Adams*

Beijing • Boston • Farnham • Sebastopol • Tokyo

**Learning Airtable**

by Elliott Adams

Published by O'Reilly Media, Inc., 1005 Gravenstein Highway North, Sebastopol, CA 95472.

O'Reilly books may be purchased for educational, business, or sales promotional use. Online editions are also available for most titles (*http://oreilly.com*). For more information, contact our corporate/institutional sales department: 800-998-9938 or *corporate@oreilly.com*.

| | |
|---|---|
| **Acquisitions Editor:** Andy Kwan | **Indexer:** BIM Creatives, LLC |
| **Development Editor:** Jeff Bleiel | **Interior Designer:** David Futato |
| **Production Editor:** Jonathon Owen | **Cover Designer:** Karen Montgomery |
| **Copyeditor:** nSight, Inc. | **Illustrator:** Kate Dullea |
| **Proofreader:** JM Olejarz | |

November 2023:     First Edition

**Revision History for the First Edition**

2023-12-06:     First Release

See *http://oreilly.com/catalog/errata.csp?isbn=9781098133375* for release details.

978-1-098-13337-5

[LSI]

# Table of Contents

Preface. . . . . . . . . . . . . . . . . . . . . . . . . . . . . . . . . . . . . . . . . . . . . . . . . . . . . . . . . . . . ix

1. Introducing Airtable. . . . . . . . . . . . . . . . . . . . . . . . . . . . . . . . . . . . . . . . . . . . 1
   What Is Airtable?                                                           1
      Airtable and the No-Code Movement                                       2
   How We Got to Now: Spreadsheets and Databases Collide into Airtable        3
   Airtable's Primary Components                                              4
      Three Sections: Data, Automations, and Interfaces                       4
      Bases, Records, and Tables                                              5
      Fields                                                                  6
      Views                                                                   6
      Automations                                                             7
      Interfaces                                                              8
   Airtable Pricing                                                           9
   Airtable's Competitive Advantage                                           9
      The Airtable Community                                                  9
      Airtable's Backers                                                      10
      Design and Product Excellence                                          10
   Airtable in Context                                                        10
   What This Book Will Cover                                                  11
   Summary                                                                    15

2. Working with Records and Fields. . . . . . . . . . . . . . . . . . . . . . . . . . . . . . . . . . 17
   Records                                                                    18
   The Primary Field                                                          20
   Fields and Field Types                                                     22
      Input Fields                                                            25
      The Button Field                                                        31

Calculated Fields                                                      34

## 3. Linked Records and the Lookup Field. . . . . . . . . . . . . . . . . . . . . . . . . . . . . . . . . . . . 39
Why Use Linked Records?                                                40
  Define Relationships Between Things                        40
  Create a Single Source of Truth and Reduce Repetitive Manual Entry   41
Relationships Between Records in a Relational Database                 42
  One-to-One Relationship                                    42
  One-to-Many Relationship                                   43
  Many-to-Many Relationships                                 43
Aggregating Data from Linked Records                                   45
  Lookup Field                                               45
  Count Field                                                51

## 4. View Essentials. . . . . . . . . . . . . . . . . . . . . . . . . . . . . . . . . . . . . . . . . . . . . . . . . . . . 53
Configuring Views                                                     54
Getting Started with the Grid View                                    54
The Grid View's Configuration Options                                 55
  Filtering                                                  56
  Sorting                                                    61
  Hiding Fields                                              64
  Height                                                     66
  Summary Bar                                                67
  Coloring                                                   70
  Grouping                                                   71
Creating and Organizing Views                                         74
  Creating a View                                            74
  View Permissions                                           77

## 5. Importing Data. . . . . . . . . . . . . . . . . . . . . . . . . . . . . . . . . . . . . . . . . . . . . . . . . . . . 79
Importing CSV Files and Spreadsheets                                  79
  Importing Tabular Data from CSV Files                      80
  Importing Google Sheets and Excel Data                     81
Importing Different Types of Data                                     84
  Numbers, Currency, and Dates                               84
  Outliers When Importing Spreadsheet Data                   86
Sync                                                                  87
  Syncing an Airtable View                                   89
  Multisource Sync                                           95
  Security When Syncing                                      97
Form View                                                             98
  Setting Up a Form                                          99

Managing Form Access                                                                       103
Conditional Form Fields                                                                    104

## 6. View Types. . . . . . . . . . . . . . . . . . . . . . . . . . . . . . . . . . . . . . . . . . . . . . . . **107**
Visually Organizing with Cards: Gallery and Kanban Views                                   108
  Gallery View                                                                   108
  Kanban View                                                                    109
Visually Organizing Using Dates: Calendar, Timeline, and Gantt Views                       111
  Calendar View                                                                  111
  Timeline View                                                                  116
  Gantt View                                                                     120
  List View                                                                      124

## 7. Creating the Fall Tour Tracker Base. . . . . . . . . . . . . . . . . . . . . . . . . . . . . . **127**
Creating Relationships Between Tables                                                       129
  Connecting Cities to Lodging                                                    130
  Connecting Cities to Venues                                                     133
Creating the Shows Table                                                                    133
Creating the Regions Table                                                                  136

## 8. Formulas. . . . . . . . . . . . . . . . . . . . . . . . . . . . . . . . . . . . . . . . . . . . . . . . . . **139**
Basics of the Formula Field                                                                140
Formula Components                                                                         142
  Fields                                                                          143
  Operators                                                                       143
  Functions                                                                       143
  Numbers                                                                         144
  Text/String Data                                                                144
The Formula Editor                                                                         144
  Introduction to Operators and Functions                                        145
  Formula Examples                                                                146
Text Functions                                                                             149
  SUBSTITUTE()                                                                    149
  Shortening Venue Names Using SUBSTITUTE(), LEFT(), and FIND()                   150
  Using FIND() to Find the First Word                                             151
Date and Time Functions                                                                    155
  Calculating Weeks of the Tour                                                   155
Numeric Functions                                                                          162
  Calculating Ticket Revenue Estimates                                            162
Logical Functions                                                                          166
  Determining Whether to Buy an Insurance Policy                                  166
  Using SWITCH() to Calculate How Many Days Off Between Shows                      167

Using Nested IF() Statements for Data Validation     169

### 9. The Rollup Field................................................. 173
What Does It Mean to "Roll Up" a Field?     173
    Rolling Up Grocery Store Orders     174
    Setting Conditions for Rollup Field     175
    Choosing a Rollup Function     175
    Rolling Up Costs from the Fall Tour Tracker     177
Rollup Functions     178
    Arithmetic Rollup Functions     178
    Logic Functions     179
    CONCATENATE Text Function     180
    Array Functions     180

### 10. Extensions.................................................. 183
Three Major Categories of Airtable Extensions     184
    Extensions That Work with Data in Your Base     185
    Extensions That Connect to Third-Party Services     191
    Scripting Extension     193
Top Airtable Extensions     202
    Chart Extension     203
    Web Clipper Extension     211
    Page Designer     215
    Translate Extension     224
Keeping Track of Extensions     227
The "Manage Extensions" Dashboard     229

### 11. Airtable Automations........................................ 231
Airtable Automations Versus Other Connector Software     231
    Advantages to Connecting Airtable via Airtable Automations     232
    Disadvantages to Connecting Airtable via Airtable Automations     232
The Basics of Airtable Automations     233
    The If/Then Logic of Automations     233
    Simple Automation: When a Record Is Updated     234
    Simple Automation: When a Record Matches Conditions     243
    Advanced Automations     246
Triggers     272
    Airtable Triggers     272
    Third-Party Triggers     274
Actions     275
    Airtable's Actions     275
    Third-Party Actions     277

**12. Interface Designer.** . . . . . . . . . . . . . . . . . . . . . . . . . . . . . . . . . . . . . . . . . . . . . . . **281**
    Interfaces as a Frontend      282
      Why Use Interfaces?      282
      How Do Interfaces Work?      282
      What Makes an Interface?      283
    Creating Interfaces      284
      Creating Full-Page Layouts      284
      Creating a Dashboard Interface      293
      Creating an Interface with Multiple Tables and Buttons      299
      Interface Layouts      306
    Interface Elements      313
      View Elements      313
      Discrete Elements      314
    Interface Designer Permissions      316

**13. Platforms That Extend Airtable.** . . . . . . . . . . . . . . . . . . . . . . . . . . . . . . . . . . . . **319**
    Connectors      320
      Zapier      320
      Make      321
    App Builders      322
      Softr      323
      Stacker      324
    Summary      326

**A. The Web API and Blocks SDK for Nondevelopers.** . . . . . . . . . . . . . . . . . . . . . . . **327**

**B. Formula Functions and Operators.** . . . . . . . . . . . . . . . . . . . . . . . . . . . . . . . . . . . **333**

**Index.** . . . . . . . . . . . . . . . . . . . . . . . . . . . . . . . . . . . . . . . . . . . . . . . . . . . . . . . . . . . . . . . . **355**

# Preface

These are exciting times if you've never learned programming. Until the mid-2010s, there were essentially two types of knowledge workers: those who could write code and those who couldn't. The latter group was usually stuck organizing their data in spreadsheets. Now, the lines are blurred for the better. Anyone can build software tools with Airtable and other no-code platforms.

When I first taught my no-code course at Stanford, it wasn't clear which no-code tool would be most appealing to students. It didn't take long for me to find clarity. Semester after semester, Airtable is the tool that most students gravitate toward.

They love it because it's intuitive to get started. They love the design. Most of all, they love that whether they need to do things that would normally require some software background, like creating an interface for a team member or triggering email notifications, there's a clear path in Airtable that doesn't require any coding.

Around the same time the no-code course was offered, I was raising venture capital for a startup. I'd used Airtable with great success to organize small projects before, but now my team and I were effectively running the entire company on Airtable. We tracked potential customers and investors in Airtable, for example, but we also used Airtable to serve application data into our prototype—without any code. In other words, Airtable was effective for an incredible range of no-code tasks that helped our team do more faster, and it was even a temporary part of our product infrastructure for the prototype that led to closing the round of funding.

My students had spoken. So had my team and my investors. Airtable allowed everyone to do more faster without code. I hope it can do the same for you.

# Who Should Read This Book

The vast majority of people who wake up and spend most of their workday on a computer don't know how to write code. For these folks, the thought of building a custom application or software process might seem as achievable as scaling Everest in flip-flops. Is this you? Fear not; you're in good company. This book is for those often found juggling a dozen open tabs, wrestling with spreadsheets, and praying for miracles from the IT department.

# Navigating This Book

The first six chapters introduce Airtable and its core building blocks: records, fields, linked record relationships, and views.

The second half of the book starts with Chapter 7, which walks through building a larger and more complex Airtable base that's based on a real-world example of organizing a concert tour.

Chapters 8 through 12 build on this knowledge with formulas, the Rollup field, Extensions, Automations, and Airtable's Interface Designer.

Lastly, Chapter 13 discusses popular and well-regarded third-party platforms that extend Airtable. There are two appendices: a brief introduction on how a developer can integrate with Airtable and a glossary of formula functions.

# Conventions Used in This Book

The following typographical conventions are used in this book:

*Italic*
> Indicates new terms, URLs, email addresses, filenames, and file extensions.

`Constant width`
> Used for program listings, as well as within paragraphs to refer to program elements such as variable or function names, databases, data types, environment variables, statements, and keywords.

**`Constant width bold`**
> Shows commands or other text that should be typed literally by the user.

*`Constant width italic`*
> Shows text that should be replaced with user-supplied values or by values determined by context.

This element signifies a tip or suggestion.

 This element signifies a general note.

 This element indicates a warning or caution.

# O'Reilly Online Learning

 For more than 40 years, *O'Reilly Media* has provided technology and business training, knowledge, and insight to help companies succeed.

Our unique network of experts and innovators share their knowledge and expertise through books, articles, and our online learning platform. O'Reilly's online learning platform gives you on-demand access to live training courses, in-depth learning paths, interactive coding environments, and a vast collection of text and video from O'Reilly and 200+ other publishers. For more information, visit *https://oreilly.com*.

# How to Contact Us

Please address comments and questions concerning this book to the publisher:

O'Reilly Media, Inc.
1005 Gravenstein Highway North
Sebastopol, CA 95472
800-889-8969 (in the United States or Canada)
707-829-7019 (international or local)
707-829-0104 (fax)
*support@oreilly.com*
*https://www.oreilly.com/about/contact.html*

We have a web page for this book, where we list errata, examples, and any additional information. You can access this page at *https://oreil.ly/learning-airtable*.

For news and information about our books and courses, visit *https://oreilly.com*.

Find us on LinkedIn: *https://linkedin.com/company/oreilly-media*.

Follow us on Twitter: *https://twitter.com/oreillymedia*.

Watch us on YouTube: *https://youtube.com/oreillymedia*.

## Acknowledgments

I'd like to thank the dozens of students who have shown me the impact and creative potential that Airtable can have for non-developers, which inspired me to write this book. Thanks also to the team at O'Reilly for seeing the potential of the book and for their support throughout the process.

Additionally, I owe a great debt to the technical reviewers of the book, Kuovonne Vorderbruggen and Jeremy Oglesby. Their knowledge of Airtable is humbling, and their commitment to getting the details right has been a tremendous boost to the quality of the book. Similarly, Susan Lankford's editing of my early drafts greatly improved overall readability.

Lastly, I dedicate this book to my sister, Liz. Along with our parents, she's been a constant source of support and love.

# CHAPTER 1

# Introducing Airtable

Airtable is a tool for builders of all kinds. Like other tools in the no-code movement, Airtable democratizes the ability to create custom applications and software processes. And while there are many no-code solutions offering to widen the tent of software development, there are many reasons why Airtable is a popular choice in the increasingly crowded field.

In this first chapter, we'll start by looking at how Airtable fills an important niche by combining elements of a spreadsheet with a database. We'll then look at its primary components and what makes it special in comparison to other options, and then we'll have a brief primer on how Airtable thinks about, and structures, data.

## What Is Airtable?

Both Airtable newcomers and veterans can understandably struggle with how to describe it. As you create your first base, you'll see the Grid view (shown in Figure 1-1), which looks deceptively like a spreadsheet. While Airtable does share some properties of a spreadsheet, it is a full-fledged relational database with the same underlying principles of organizing data as the desktop standby Microsoft Access or the high-capacity databases that run much of the web, such as MySQL and Postgres. What may look like another tab in a freeform spreadsheet is actually a structured table of data.

Airtable's Grid view mirrors the visuals of a spreadsheet's multipurpose columns and rows of cells. Beware: these are not columns and rows of independent cells. Instead, each column represents a specific field that's defined by the type of data it holds (e.g., URLs, text, and data computed from other fields in that table). What might seem like an interchangeable row of cells actually constitutes a distinct record or entry in your database.

*Figure 1-1. In the Grid view, columns represent fields and rows are records.*

Specifically, it's a relational database. Why is that meaningful? A relational database has rules, such as what types of data are in your tables and how one table relates to another. These rules define a structure that can be easily interpreted, which enables your database (be it Airtable or another) to sort, filter, visualize, track, plot, and do many more things with your data.

Because the relational data model abstracts the user interface from the data itself, every user can have a tailored experience that lends itself to collaboration across teams. Airtable enables this with its specialized Views, which can be personalized for a task or user. Its Interfaces feature takes this a step further, enabling the creation of sturdy web portals that can simplify unnecessary complexity and restrict a user's access to data. In the Automations section of the platform, team members can design code-free logic to manipulate their data (by creating, reading, updating, or deleting it—what is referred to in software development as CRUD), whether for their own tasks or to enhance the workflow of a teammate. Importantly, Airtable allows you to achieve all of this by writing little, if any, actual code. It's a leader in the no-code movement.

## Airtable and the No-Code Movement

For decades, there's been a simple dichotomy inside organizations. Some people can write code, build products to access, and understand complex datasets. Others are not building software; this group often comprises most people in an organization. As we'll see later, spreadsheets have been a helpful middle ground between building applications and being dependent on developers. Still, this dichotomy is quickly becoming a fluid spectrum, thanks to no-code tools like Airtable.

No-code tools allow users to build software tools without using a traditional programming language. This can mean having a WYSIWYG builder to create interfaces, designing logic flows using a paradigm of "triggers" and "actions," or using a user-friendly way to approach relational data. As a result, no-code tools are closing the gap between software users and developers.

This democratization of software development has huge consequences. Colleagues of the dev team no longer need to sheepishly submit feature requests for internal tools. And instead of everyone who isn't a full-time software developer being a nondeveloper, people can ladder up. They can build their proficiency using tools like Airtable without necessarily taking the plunge into learning a full-fledged programming language. As we will see in the chapters ahead, Airtable offers many entry points to help teams be more efficient by allowing everyone to build their own tools and collaborate more quickly and easily than ever before.

## How We Got to Now: Spreadsheets and Databases Collide into Airtable

In the upcoming chapters, we'll see many reasons why storing your data in a rules-based relational database pays massive dividends in the potential for collaboration, analysis, and ease of use. But for now, it's helpful to understand how Airtable's popularity was accelerated not just by being a well-made collaboration tool but also by addressing a significant gap in the market of software tools for everyday users.

The relational database is tried and true. Corporations run enterprise databases from Microsoft and Oracle, while the web is powered by popular open source relational databases such as MySQL and Postgres. There is constant experimentation and boundary-pushing design for new types of databases that can improve performance and handle the world's mushrooming volume of data, but the relational database has endured.

All the while, spreadsheets have been the average knowledge worker's tool of choice for organizing data. This is not for no reason. A spreadsheet allows the user to store and manipulate data easily. That might sound elementary, but consider the alternative. Most software decouples those two things: it combines a data storage system and an interface.

It's a quantum leap forward to have the ability to put data into a spreadsheet and also manipulate it inside of the spreadsheet without having to build a software interface to interact with that data. This has brought huge productivity gains for any nondeveloper by mimicking the functions of database-driven software with the interactive spreadsheet.

Interacting with a database through a *web*-based application—something we now take for granted—ushered in the so-called Web 2.0 era. Web 2.0 applications were innovative because, for the first time, using a web app essentially mimicked software running on a desktop. It was a bona fide revolution. Salesforce proclaimed "No Software!" as its rallying cry while moving millions of salespeople from CRM systems run on an in-house server to Salesforce in the cloud. Google successfully introduced its suite of office products that run in the browser and has replaced MS Office in many organizations. GitHub created a multibillion-dollar layer of software version control that's web native. The world shifted to database-powered applications run in the browser.

But a funny thing happened as Web 2.0 began to pull practically every desktop application into a new iteration of itself on the web. The modern office produced invoices in Xero or QuickBooks. A sales team entered its new prospects into Hubspot or Salesforce. Marketing queued up social media posts in HootSuite. But where should we put ideas for conferences to sponsor next year? Where can we make a detailed list of our top competitors and our positioning against them? How can we collaborate on top priorities for retaining talent across departments?

The answer to these questions won't surprise you. Spreadsheets have been twisted and contorted to look and feel like a database without gaining the efficiencies that databases make possible. For example, spreadsheets don't allow viewing your data in different configurations based on user or task. They don't natively enforce rules on which types of data go where, and they don't innately consider your data to be a collection of things. Instead, they're flexible to the point of being flimsy. So people weren't repeatedly choosing the wrong tool per se, but rather they chose the best tool available. It's a mystery why no one made a credible software-as-a-service relational database until Airtable, but we'll see what the world was missing.

# Airtable's Primary Components

Let's get familiar with the components of Airtable as we begin to wrap our minds around the platform. We'll revisit each component later in the book in more depth. But, for now, having a passing understanding of these will reveal the contours of Airtable capabilities. (As a general note, because Airtable's interface evolves continually, we will focus more on the platform's fundamentals and not be overly concerned with the exact shape or placement of buttons and menus.)

## Three Sections: Data, Automations, and Interfaces

The table at the beginning of this chapter is an example of a Grid view (Figure 1-1), which initially looks a lot like a spreadsheet. Grid views, and the other six types of views, are part of Airtable's Data section. For many years, before Automations and the Interface Designer, there were only views in the Data section (though it wasn't called that—it was just Airtable).

It's worth getting oriented with Airtable by noticing the three sections atop the page: Data, Automations, and Interfaces, as shown in Figure 1-2. We'll start by discussing the concepts of bases, records, tables, and more, which are normally configured in the Data section. However, the structure of these elements is one part of what makes Airtable so uniquely powerful to nonprogrammers in Automations and Interfaces.

*Figure 1-2. The Data, Automations, and Interfaces sections of Airtable.*

## Bases, Records, and Tables

In Airtable parlance, databases are called bases. Each entity, or thing, you want to keep track of in an Airtable base is a record, similar to most database systems. So, for example, if you are producing a music festival, you would have a record for each musical artist performing. Likewise, a journalist keeping track of lawsuits would have records for each case, an auto shop might have a record for each customer, and a marketing department might have records to track the blog posts it's developing.

Airtable bases are comprised of one or more tables, and each table holds a specific type of entity (e.g., blog posts, court cases, and customers). For example, our Airtable base to organize a music festival, shown in Figure 1-3, might have a table of performers, a table of stages, and a table of vendors. Those tables can relate to each other in different ways, depending on the real-world relationships between those types of entities.

| | A Name | Stage | *f* Performance (time only) | Website photo |
|---|---|---|---|---|
| 1 | Cass McCombs | Grassy Meadows | 6:00 | |
| 2 | Steve Reich | Earwig | 6:00 | |
| 3 | Madlib | Grassy Meadows | 7:00 | |
| 4 | Vampire Weekend | Grassy Meadows | 8:30 | |
| 5 | Four Tet | Earwig | 9:30 | |
| 6 | Daphne | Earwig | 11:00 | |

*Figure 1-3. A base for a music festival, with tables for performers, stages, and vendors.*

If you're already familiar with relational databases, you know that the relationships of these records between different types of entities (represented by tables) give relational databases their flexibility and power. The relationships between records and tables in Airtable mirror these fundamental database concepts.

## Fields

Instead of generic columns in a spreadsheet, each of the columns (fields) you see in the Airtable Grid view has a defined type of data. Each field's type is a simple decision about what kind of data that field should store for each of the records in a table. For example, will each of your records have a date-formatted field to note its start and end dates? Will your base have an attachment field to store a headshot? Or perhaps a field to store a URL for each of the records in your base?

There are field types that calculate the date a record was created or modified. The Formula field is the bedrock of many of Airtable's superpowers; it has elements of Excel formulas and scripting. Any field you define holds the same data type for all records in that table. For example, if you have a field for email addresses named "manager email," as shown in Figure 1-4, that column can store an email address for each of the records in that table. These self-imposed constraints of what data fields contain make Views possible.

*Figure 1-4. Each field holds a specific type of data.*

So every table in a base has records and fields. Each record in a table holds a value for each field, which is contained in a cell in the Grid view.

## Views

Since fields define the type of data they hold, this enforced structure allows Airtable to offer purpose-built ways to view and understand the records in your base, as shown in Figure 1-5. For example, the Calendar view can place records on a monthly calendar grid. The Gallery view allows you to view your records as tiles across the page.

As you might guess, the Calendar view uses dates associated with your records. Airtable further leverages date data by allowing you to put your records in the Timeline view, where you can see when the events in your base begin and end. Project managers will be familiar with the Gantt chart, which, in addition to making a timeline from critical dates in your records, allows you to put dependencies between records. For example, you can visualize that item B needs to happen before A or C.

The Form view is a handy way to create simple, web-based forms that can be shared from Airtable with a public or password-protected URL. As with everything Airtable, as we'll see in the coming chapters, it's easy to get started building forms, but you can add near infinite levels of complexity as you get more familiar with the platform.

| | | | |
|---|---|---|---|
| ⊞ Grid view | | ☐ ⤢ | The PTA Disbands |
| | | 125 | 'Round Springfield |
| Create... ∨ | | 126 | The Springfield Connection |
| ⊞ Grid + | | 127 | Lemon of Troy |
| ▣ Form + | | 128 | Who Shot Mr. Burns? (Part C |
| ▦ Calendar + | | 129 | Who Shot Mr. Burns? (Part T |
| ▦ Gallery + | | 130 | Radioactive Man |
| ▭ Kanban + | | 131 | Home Sweet Homediddly-D |
| ▱ Timeline + | | 132 | Bart Sells His Soul |
| ☰ List + | | 133 | Lisa the Vegetarian |
| ▱ Gantt + | | 134 | Treehouse of Horror VI |
| New section + | | + ✎ Add... | 204 records |

*Figure 1-5. The left-hand sidebar gives access to all of the views in your base.*

## Automations

Airtable Automations is a tool inside the platform that allows you to set up conditions to automate things like creating a new record in a table, updating a record, sending an email, and other actions that rely on connecting with external software platforms. Each automation is defined by the trigger that instigates the automation and the resulting actions. For example, we can specify in an automation that if a record is updated in a particular way, a Slack notification with some select details about that updated record will be sent to a specified channel in our Slack workspace.

Since automations are quick and easy to learn without any coding, they can empower less technical team members to start automating processes inside your bases and processes that connect to other services. Automations currently has native integrations with the Google Workspace suite, GitHub, Facebook pages, Outlook, Microsoft Teams, and more. Depending on the service you're integrating with, you can create a calendar event once a record has been assigned to a collaborator in your Airtable base, add issues to GitHub when the status of a record changes, and engage with innumerable other scenarios.

If there is a third-party app service you'd like to interact with your data inside of Airtable but it isn't natively supported, you can connect to external APIs through Airtable scripting. We will cover Automations in Chapter 11. For readers who aren't software developers, Appendix A offers an overview of what their developers' counterparts can do with Airtable's web API and the Airtable software development kit (SDK) for building Airtable Extensions.

## Interfaces

While the different types of Airtable views offer common ways to work with data, such as Kanban boards and timelines, Interfaces (shown in Figure 1-6) is a quantum leap forward for the platform. You can create dashboards of your data, choose which fields to show, filter which records show up, and choose which fields to allow the user to edit. Essentially, you can quickly build web interfaces for your Airtable data without writing a line of code—creating your own database-driven web app for whatever your needs are. Keeping with our running theme of Airtable's power and accessibility, in Chapter 12 we will look at how anyone can get started building interfaces.

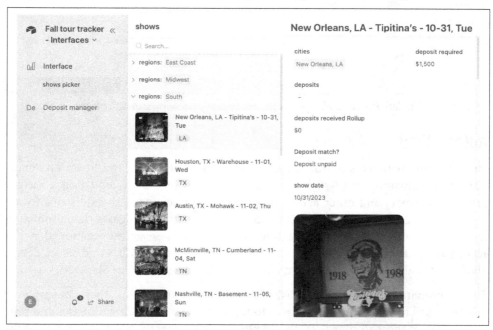

*Figure 1-6. Build web applications in Airtable using Interfaces.*

# Airtable Pricing

Like all software-as-a-service products, Airtable is subscription-based and offers progressively more features and functionality in each pricing plan. In the summer of 2023, Airtable overhauled its pricing into these four tiers:

- Free
- Team: $24 per user per month (or $240 annually)
- Business: $54 per user per month (or $540 annually)
- Enterprise Scale: custom pricing

The revised Free plan has far fewer records and automation runs, and it doesn't include Extensions or Sync. For the purpose of this book, we assume you'll at least be on the Team plan. (There is a free trial for this pricing plan.)

Airtable has traditionally shown restraint in changing feature availability and pricing. They've tended to do it usually when a new component is introduced (e.g., Automations), and they assign the availability to the different pricing tiers. Still, things can change. The pricing and plans are kept current at *https://airtable.com/pricing*.

# Airtable's Competitive Advantage

The no-code database, automations, and interfaces of Airtable give us the ability to leverage our data in highly productive ways. But aren't there other no-code products that allow you to build a database, connect to other platforms, and even construct your custom interfaces? Yes, but there are reasons why Airtable has become so popular and why it's so widely used.

## The Airtable Community

There are many considerations for adopting a piece of mission-critical software that may house some of your organization's most sensitive data. It's essential to assess the functionality of the product today and try to ascertain its longevity. Like open source software projects, web platforms can be judged by the activity and dedication of their communities. In the same way that a new JavaScript framework may die on the vine from a lack of contributors, a productivity software-as-a-service (SaaS) platform needs ardent users to advocate for the changes required for users working and building in Airtable every day.

The number of users that make up the Airtable community is not only large. It's fanatical. Given the platform's flexibility, there are endless edge cases and unique questions that arise, and most answers can be found in Airtable's voluminous community forum and on the many YouTube channels dedicated to Airtable. (Note to reader: Because of these edge cases, it's virtually impossible to account for them all inside this book. However, we will attempt to address the most common snags and potentially confusing orthodoxy of Airtable.)

## Airtable's Backers

Founded in 2012, Airtable has consistently grown. In its most recent round of funding, the press release announcing the company's valuation at more than $11 billion says that "over 80% of the Fortune 100 use Airtable." This high rate of corporate adoption by an independent software platform is no small feat. As the saying goes, "no one gets fired for buying IBM," which is as true today for Google and Microsoft as ever. Airtable has beaten the odds by gaining loyal users inside large, discriminating organizations with incredibly high security and data standards.

While venture capital funding alone is never a clear indicator of success, Airtable has raised funding from some of the most successful venture capital funds. These include Benchmark and Founder Collective and institutional funders like T. Rowe Price and JPMorgan in its fundraise of December 2021.

## Design and Product Excellence

If Facebook's infamous motto was "move fast and break things," Airtable might be the opposite. Every button, every menu, and every option exudes sophisticated restraint. Users are drawn in by its use of color and the thoughtful interplay of elements in its interface. Airtable has been known for carefully adding features that serve an acute purpose and do so sparingly.

# Airtable in Context

Airtable isn't a database that's suitable for an application with millions of users. Instead, the platform is a good match for projects with some complexity. This is specifically the case when you need collaboration among stakeholders at different levels but don't need to access massive amounts of web-scale data.

While an Airtable base has more limited storage than a production database, it is much easier to use and much harder to break. Airtable makes it easier than a large-scale database to undo mistakes, and it eliminates the pitfalls of a traditional database by abstracting away the crucial components. For example, in Airtable you can't see the actual unique identifier for each record, which is formatted something like `rec1234123412341234`, but you can enter anything you like into the cell for that record's primary field (more on this in Chapter 2).

Airtable has a similar trick for the names of bases (prefixed with appxxxxxxxxx), views (viwxxxxxxxx), tables (tblxxxxxxxxx), fields (fldxxxxxxxxx), and more. If you're interested in the actual identifier of your base or a given record, it's straightforward to find that data. These identifiers can be seen in the URL bar of the browser. Airtable structures a URL by listing the base ID, the current table, the view being accessed, and then, when a record is opened, that record's ID. Here's the format:

```
airtable.com/appxxxxxxxxx/tblxxxxxxxxx/viwxxxxxxxx/recxxxxxxxx
```

This convention of abstracting the editable names of Airtable components in your base from the actual identifiers allows for a broader spectrum of users to interact with the platform and have the advantages of the relational database model without the strict requirements that are needed for a burly production database that might store hundreds of millions of rows. (Airtable's Team plan allows for storing up to 50,000 records per base, and its Business offering allows up to 125,000 records.)

# What This Book Will Cover

Let's preview what we'll cover about Airtable in the rest of this book.

## Chapter 2: Working with Records and Fields

In this chapter, we will delve into the core of Airtable: records and fields. We will explore how tables in an Airtable database are made up of records and how each record represents a specific entity. We will also learn about the different field types, which represent each record's properties or attributes.

We will start by exploring the primary field and then dive into various field types that Airtable offers. We will cover input fields like text fields, URL fields, and Single/Multiple select fields as well as calculated fields like Autonumber fields, Date fields, and User fields. Later in the book, we will explore in more detail the most complex field types. Along the way, we will provide tips and tricks for using certain field types effectively.

## Chapter 3: Linked Records and the Lookup Field

Chapter 3 explores how Airtable establishes relationships between different items in our database, creating a relational structure. Using an example involving orders and wholesalers, we see how linked records improve efficiency and understanding of our data.

Linked records create a reliable single source of truth by centralizing and updating data consistently. Understanding one-to-one, one-to-many, and many-to-many relationships allows for effective linking of records. We also discuss two field types that offer insights related to linked records. The Lookup field cross-references data between linked tables, enriching records. The Count field efficiently tallies the number of linked records between tables.

## Chapter 4: View Essentials

This chapter explores the fundamental tools that make Airtable a powerful collaboration platform: Views. Think of Airtable Views as the different ways you and your colleagues can see and interact with your data. We'll begin by tackling the Grid view and will look at how you can filter, sort, and hide fields in your Views to focus on what's important to you. We'll walk you through examples and show you how to use conjunctions and nesting condition groups to create complex and precise filters.

Once you have your data filtered and sorted to your liking, we'll delve into grouping records within different fields. Grouping is a great way to understand patterns and similarities among your records. You'll discover how easy it is to collapse, expand, and organize groups to gain deeper insights into your data. We'll also explore features like changing row heights and using the summary bar. These options allow you to present and analyze your data more flexibly and efficiently.

## Chapter 5: Importing Data

Chapter 5 explores the practical aspects of importing data into Airtable. We'll discuss how to import CSV files and spreadsheets. You'll learn about importing data from Google Sheets as well as syncing data from other sources using Airtable Sync. We'll also delve into the Form view, which allows you to gather structured data from outside parties. Lastly, we'll touch on security measures for forms and the use of conditional form fields. This chapter will equip you with the knowledge and tools you need to incorporate into your Airtable base data from various sources.

## Chapter 6: View Types

Building upon our understanding of the Grid view and the options across views, we delve into other views that offer even more versatility and insights.

First, we dive into the Gallery and Kanban views, which are ideal for visually organizing projects. Next, we explore the Calendar view, which allows us to visualize our data over time. Then, we move on to the Timeline view—a powerful tool for planning and tracking projects. Next, we introduce the Gantt view—a specialized view for scheduling and tracking activities. Finally, we discuss the List view—an ideal choice for managing hierarchical data and complex projects by providing a comprehensive overview of project structures and relationships.

## Chapter 7: Creating the Fall Tour Tracker Base

In this chapter, we create a Fall Tour Tracker, which we'll use through the rest of the book to demonstrate new features and concepts in a practical form. We show you how to import and link records from CSV files and synced tables to build tables for cities, venues, and lodging. You'll learn how to establish meaningful relationships between these tables, from one-to-one to one-to-many connections. We cover the creation of a Shows table from scratch, linking it to the other tables for efficient data management. Additionally, we introduce the concept of a Regions table and demonstrate how to use linked records and a Rollup field to calculate the number of cities in each region. This chapter sets the foundation for concepts explained in subsequent chapters as we stick with the Fall Tour Tracker throughout the rest of the book.

# Chapter 8: Formulas

In this chapter, we explore the power and versatility of formulas in Airtable. Formulas allow users to manipulate, calculate, and analyze data in their tables without requiring any programming knowledge. We will uncover the different types of data that formulas can manipulate, including text, dates and times, and numerical values.

You will learn how to use Airtable's formula editor, which provides a user-friendly interface for building complex formulas. We will delve into the various formula functions and operators that enable you to perform calculations, manipulate text, and create conditional logic. Through real-world examples and step-by-step explanations, you will discover how to format data, calculate revenue estimates, and build a formula to determine whether to buy insurance for specific events.

# Chapter 9: The Rollup Field

The Rollup field allows you to extract valuable information from linked records. It has two main functions: it looks up data values from a linked record field in the same table, and it can answer questions about these values using various Rollup functions. This chapter explores the process of "rolling up" data, from choosing the linked field to setting filter conditions and selecting the appropriate Rollup function. With real-world examples and step-by-step explanations, you will discover how to calculate totals, find maximum or minimum values, and gain insights from linked record relationships.

# Chapter 10: Extensions

In this chapter, we delve into the world of Airtable extensions and explore an array of tools that can enhance your Airtable experience. Extensions provide a simple way to perform specialized tasks within Airtable. Whether it's cleaning up data, triggering text messages, importing data from platforms like GitHub, or finding stock photos, there is an extension available to meet your needs.

We then explore several popular Airtable extensions and provide examples of how they can be used effectively. The Chart extension allows you to visualize your data, the Web Clipper extension enables you to import data from web pages, and the Page Designer extension allows you to create custom PDF layouts. By the end of this chapter, you will have a clear understanding of how extensions can enhance your Airtable workflow and be equipped with the knowledge to make the most of the available extensions for your specific needs.

## Chapter 11: Airtable Automations

In this chapter on Airtable Automations, we explore the power and versatility of using simple no-code tools to streamline your workflow. With Airtable Automations, you can reduce the repetitive busywork that comes with managing data while minimizing the potential for human error.

We delve into different triggers and actions available in Airtable Automations, including options for integrating with popular third-party services and executing complex conditional logic. By automating repetitive tasks, leveraging conditional flow control, and syncing data across multiple platforms, you'll gain insights into how powerful and efficient your workflow can become with Airtable Automations.

## Chapter 12: Interface Designer

We explore the power of Airtable Interface Designer to create tailored web experiences for different users and streamline workflows within organizations. We begin by examining the different premade interface layouts. Then we look at the individual elements that unlock the ability for custom interfaces to provide a flexible and intuitive frontend to access and manipulate data effectively.

We delve into the practical applications of Airtable Interfaces through the creation of three examples: tracking a concert tour; creating a reporting dashboard for ticket sales and revenues; and constructing an interface for managing deposits from venues. These examples reveal how interfaces can be customized to meet specific business needs, control data access, and provide valuable reporting insights. With point-and-click no-code functionality, anyone can build powerful interfaces without code, putting highly accessible application development in everyone's hands.

## Chapter 13: Platforms That Extend Airtable

In the no-code realm of Airtable, where simplicity meets functionality, a host of external platforms have arisen to extend its power even further. This chapter explores two categories of applications that seamlessly integrate with Airtable: connectors and app builders. Connectors such as Zapier and Make open up a world of automation workflows, bridging the gap between Airtable and other software. Meanwhile, app builders like Softr and Stacker allow users to create customizable and user-friendly web applications that are built on top of their Airtable data and are especially well suited to building apps for external users.

## Appendix A: The Web API and Blocks SDK for Nondevelopers

If you aren't a developer, this chapter is a gentle introduction of Airtable's powers beyond the realm of no-code.

We start by explaining the essence of REST APIs and how the Airtable Web API follows its conventions to communicate with other platforms seamlessly. Delving further into Airtable's API, we discuss its flexibility in creating custom connections and advanced features that go beyond prebuilt integrations. Expanding on the enhancements that are possible through the API, we delve into developing custom extensions using the Airtable SDK. Airtable provides a toolkit that developers use for creating custom Extensions. Featuring descriptions of how integration and custom development work within Airtable, this chapter lays the foundation for nontechnical readers to converse fluently with developers.

## Appendix B: Formula Functions and Operators

This book concludes with a comprehensive appendix that serves as a reference guide for all the formula functions and operators available in Airtable. This appendix provides a complete list of these functions and operators, along with clear explanations and examples for each one.

# Summary

The world doesn't suffer from a lack of web applications; we are drowning in them. Airtable stands apart from the rest by combining a robust relational database with a multitude of tools for both the developer and the less technical user. Airtable can transform how you organize, view, and ultimately understand your data to make the most critical decisions. We will dive headfirst into all you can do with Airtable until we approach its very distant limits. In the next chapters, we will understand the role of records in Airtable and the many field types that can better structure the data inside each of your bases.

# CHAPTER 2

# Working with Records and Fields

As mentioned in Chapter 1, Airtable bases have three sections: Data, Automations, and Interfaces. This Data section is where almost all of the configuration of an Airtable database happens. (Once the database is set up, we can then do things like design Automations and configure interfaces.)

A relational database, like Airtable, is made up of tables that contain records. For those unfamiliar with databases, each table represents a certain type of entity, such as a task, project, or person. Each separate instance of an entity in every table is a record (e.g., every task in a table of tasks is a record).

For each table representing a group of things (e.g., tasks, appointments, and contacts), there are fields that each represent a property or attribute of each thing (or record). For instance, a field might hold a start time for the appointments in a table of appointments. In a table of project management tasks, there might be a text field with the name of each task and a number field to note how many weeks each task is expected to take. Fields can also perform a calculation, reference data in other tables, and more.

Depending on the field type, the data may be formatted in a specific way. The different types of fields and their properties are easier to digest if we break them down into two main categories: input fields and calculated fields.

Before field types, we'll start this chapter by looking at records in more detail. Then we'll consider the primary field, which has unique properties worth understanding. Finally, we'll walk through Airtable field types.

In Chapter 1, we learned that columns represent fields and that rows are records in the Grid view. In Figure 2-1, we have a freshly created base, where the examples of the primary field (always on the far left in the Grid view), a field, and a record are noted with arrows.

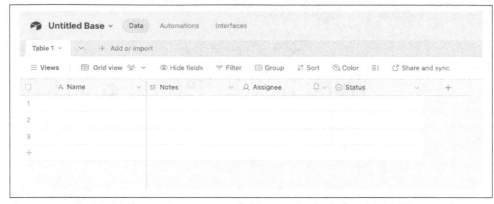

*Figure 2-1. In the Grid view, the primary field is on the far left, other fields are columns to the right of the primary field, and records are rows.*

# Records

Let's imagine we are creating an Airtable base about episodes of *The Simpsons*. To organize and catalog the episodes (each being a record), we will create fields for the different aspects of each episode. But to get started, we are going to create a new base and then create an Episodes table. In Figure 2-2, you can see we've started with some basic information like the name of the episode, which season it is from, the episode number, the date that it aired, and the link to that episode on Wikisimpsons.

| | A Episode | ⊙ Season | A Episode ... | Airdate | ⬦ Simpsons Wiki URL |
|---|---|---|---|---|---|
| 11 | The Crepes of Wrath | 1 | 11 | 4/15/1990 | https://simpsonswiki.cc |
| 12 | Krusty Gets Busted | 1 | 12 | 4/29/1990 | https://simpsonswiki.cc |
| 13 | Some Enchanted Evening | 1 | 13 | 5/13/1990 | https://simpsonswiki.cc |
| 14 | Bart Gets an F | 2 | 1 | 10/11/1990 | https://simpsonswiki.cc |
| 15 | Simpson and Delilah | 2 | 2 | 10/18/1990 | https://simpsonswiki.cc |
| 16 | Treehouse of Horror | 2 | 3 | 10/25/1990 | https://simpsonswiki.cc |
| 17 | Two Cars in Every Garage and Three... | 2 | 4 | 11/1/1990 | https://simpsonswiki.cc |
| 18 | Dancin' Homer | 2 | 5 | 11/8/1990 | https://simpsonswiki.cc |
| 19 | Dead Putting Society | 2 | 6 | 11/15/1990 | https://simpsonswiki.cc |

*Figure 2-2. Building our Episodes table in the Grid view of our new base.*

Once we've created our new base and go to the Grid view, we can see some default fields and columns, as shown in Figure 2-3. (We will investigate most field types in this chapter and a handful of the more complex field types in Chapters 8 and 9.) Airtable allows us to view and interpret the data in each of our records in countless ways with views via grouping, filtering, and sorting records, which we'll explore in Chapter 3.

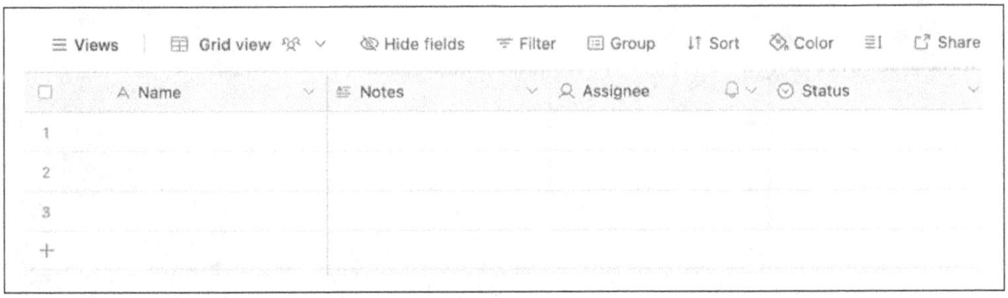

Figure 2-3. The default Grid view.

Airtable stores all the information that we enter about our records, even though we may not be able to see it all in a particular view. In the Grid view, we can click the two diverging arrows to the left of any primary field cell, and a pop-up will open and show all of the fields in that view. This is called the Expanded view, shown in Figure 2-4, where we can see all the details of a record. (You may also see a button labeled Hide fields; after you click that button, it will reveal the remainder of the fields not visible in that view.)

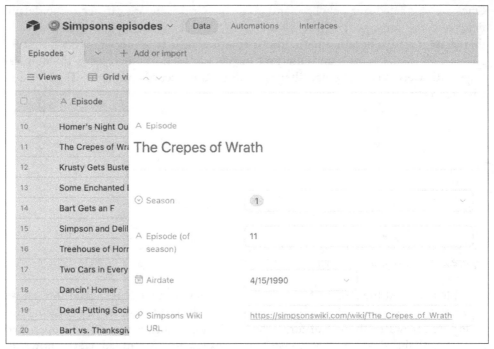

*Figure 2-4. Opening the Expanded view for a record shows all of the available fields, regardless of what is shown in a view.*

## The Primary Field

Every table has a primary field, and each record has a primary field value (which can be blank but is usually filled once the base is up and running). There is a primary field in each table that identifies each record. The primary field is always on the far left in the Grid view. You can't hide the primary field, move it between other fields, or delete it. The Primary field is a persistent element for every record in every table of every Airtable base.

Once we understand the primary field, we can better understand linked relationships (Chapter 5), a cornerstone of unlocking Airtable's power as a relational database. Here in Figure 2-5, we see the default layout of the Grid view, with the primary field's default title of Name.

| ☰ Views | ⊞ Grid view 🎭 ∨ | 👁 Hide fields | ⤳ Filter | ⊞ Group | ↕ Sort | 🎨 Color | ☰ | ⎘ Share |
|---|---|---|---|---|---|---|---|---|

| ☐ | A Name | ∨ | ☰ Notes | ∨ | 👤 Assignee | ⌂ ∨ | ⊙ Status | ∨ |
|---|---|---|---|---|---|---|---|---|
| 1 | | | | | | | | |
| 2 | | | | | | | | |
| 3 | | | | | | | | |
| + | | | | | | | | |

*Figure 2-5. The default when creating a new table in the Grid view, with Name as the primary field.*

In relational databases like Airtable, each record has a unique identifier. However, as previously mentioned, users can choose the data they want in the primary field. So Airtable hides its unique identifier as something called the "record ID," which is its system for assigning a unique identifier for each record (underneath the hood, it's a long string prefixed by "rec" that resembles recYRQKe56vO9U7mL).

Since the record ID actually identifies each record and is hidden, users can have the same values in the primary field for one or more records. This abstraction means that two identical values in the (visible) primary field don't "break" the database. That said, it's a best practice to have unique values in the primary field—otherwise, at minimum, this could get confusing very quickly! The Auto-number field, discussed later in this chapter, is helpful if you want to ensure that no records have identical primary field values.

The primary field can be a text field, a numerical field, or a variety of formatted fields that we will look at in this chapter, such as dates, phone numbers, and URLs. The primary field can also be the result of a calculation of other field data in a table. Using the Formula field, denoted by a small "fx" symbol, which we will look at in Chapter 8, your primary field values can combine data from your other fields. For example, as we can see in Figure 2-6, in our *Simpsons* episode base, we can have a primary field that puts the episode's name with the season and episode number in parentheses.

*Figure 2-6. Using data from other fields to create a unique value for the primary field.*

Now, let's look at some of the many fields that can be customized to store different attributes of our records.

# Fields and Field Types

Fields are the way to measure and classify the records in the tables of our database. A pair of shoes has color, brand, size, and other attributes, each of which can be a field for a table of shoes in an Airtable base. As another example, every shipment of houseplants from a plant nursery has an order date, a certain number of plants, a destination, and certain types of houseplants. Those houseplants are stored in their own table. Each has its own price, pot size, and country of origin, and each type of houseplant either will or won't be contained in a given order.

These attributes of our records are called fields in Airtable. Adding new fields to records in a table is easy and flexible. In the Grid view, you can click the plus symbol next to the rightmost column in the view. As we can see in Figure 2-7, this opens the dialog to allow you to name the field and choose its field type.

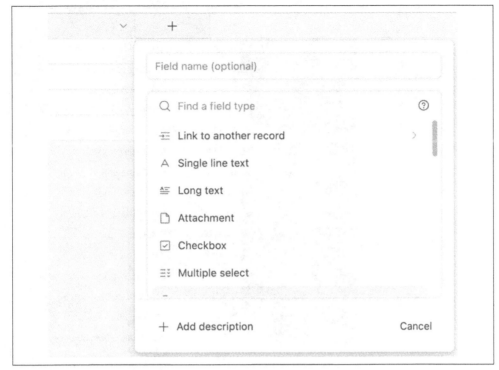

*Figure 2-7. Creating a new field in the Grid view.*

Another way to create a new field is to click the small drop-down arrow icon next to the name of a field to open the field customization menu. As shown in Figure 2-8, this offers a menu of options to modify the field, including inserting a new field to the left or right. Clicking one of these two options brings up the same menu we saw in Figure 2-7, allowing us to choose the name and field type of our new field.

If we choose the first option, Customize field type, this allows us to change that type of data in that field. Later in this chapter, we will look at when to use the different field types depending on the type of data we want to store.

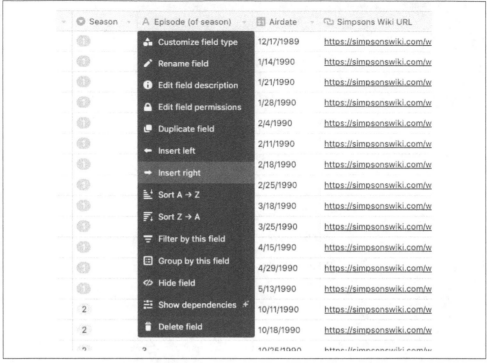

*Figure 2-8. Field customization menu.*

Of the more than 20 fields in Airtable, we can loosely group them into two primary buckets: input fields and calculated fields. Input fields are the most intuitive and straightforward, allowing for simple interactions between Airtable users and their data. Users can enter text, input a phone number, choose a selection from a drop-down menu, assign a due date, and more.

Airtable has a couple of input field types that are less like an empty spreadsheet cell and more similar to a UI element. Instead of entering a value, users can, for example, choose a star rating for a record or check a checkbox. Still, these fields ultimately hold measurable, modifiable data. (There's another field type that behaves like a UI element, the Button field, and we'll discuss its unique properties and powers in "The Button Field" on page 31.)

There are field types in Airtable that don't take direct user input in the way you'd enter a number into a spreadsheet cell. Instead, these give a value for the last time a record was changed or the last user who changed it, for example. These are examples of calculated fields. First, we'll discuss the many types of input fields.

# Input Fields

Airtable offers the following kinds of input fields:

- Text
- URL, Phone number, and Email
- Single select and Multiple select
- Duration
- Date
- Number, Percent, and Currency
- Rating
- Checkbox
- Attachment
- Barcode
- Button

## Text fields

There are two text field options, the Single line text and Long text fields. While both can hold 100,000 characters, or somewhere around 20,000 words, Long text has many advantages for dealing with big chunks of text. For example, a Long text field can visually "wrap" text to the next line so you can read more than just what fits in the width of the field. (Conversely, a Single line text field cannot contain line breaks.)

There are a couple of ways to format text in the Long text field: using Markdown or using a small pop-up menu inside the Long text field. Toggling on "Enable rich text formatting" in the field customization menu makes it possible to format text as bold, italicized, or hyperlinked. After selecting the text, a small pop-up menu appears with these options. The second method to format text in a Long text field is a pared-down set of Markdown commands, which rely on using simple characters to denote things like code snippets, code blocks, headings, quotes, lists, and checklists.

## URL, Phone number, and Email fields

Three common formatted field types are URL, Phone number, and Email. These field types will take any text data but will only format it if the data conforms to certain rules. For example, if you enter the word "frog" into a Phone number field, Airtable will not reject it. But when data is entered in the correct field type, it does make life easier.

The URL and Email fields add an interactive element to your base. For example, after you enter "oreilly.com" into a URL field, clicking on that cell opens a new window in the browser pointing to that URL. Similarly, clicking a properly formatted value for a record's Email field will trigger the default response from your computer's operating system when email links are clicked, such as opening your desktop email client.

The Phone number field can take a 10-digit number, and Airtable will format it like a US phone number. Airtable automatically inserts parentheses around the area code and a dash between the next three digits and the last four digits.

 Although users cannot click on a phone number inside the Airtable web app to open FaceTime or another browser-based phone service, it is possible to initiate a phone call using the Airtable mobile app by clicking on a phone number in the base that's stored in a Phone number field.

### Single select and Multiple select fields

The ability to easily create a list of items from a drop-down menu inside a table is one of the most appealing features to mainstream Airtable users. The thoughtful design automatically assigns a different color to each selectable item, and you can reassign colors in the field customization menu, as shown in Figure 2-9.

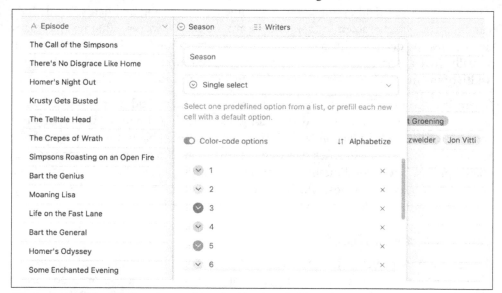

*Figure 2-9. In the Single select and Multiple select fields, colors are automatically assigned to each option.*

Using Single select and Multiple select fields helps categorize the attributes of records. These are best for data that lends itself to being categorized in a defined, limited set of options. The primary difference between the Single select and Multiple select fields is that, as the names suggest, you can select more than one option for the Multiple select field, as shown in Figure 2-10. In our *Simpsons* base, we expect that there will be multiple writers who worked on an episode. With the Multiple select field, we can choose as many writers as we need; the number can vary from just one writer to a dozen or more.

For example, in our *Simpsons* episodes base, there is a column for the season each episode belongs to. We know that there's a small, finite number of seasons, and we know that each episode only belongs to one season. This makes for a good candidate for a Single select field since we will reuse each option we add to the field and since we're confident that we don't need to assign more than one season to a given episode, as with a Multiple select field.

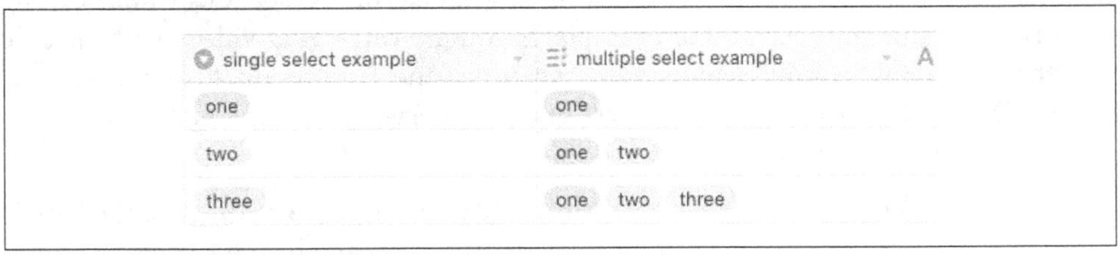

*Figure 2-10. The Multiple select field type can hold multiple options.*

Conversely, if we added a field to our Episodes table to track the length of each episode, a Single select field might not be the best choice. We might want to compare episodes by their duration, but it's unlikely that we would want to group them by their duration. As we will see later in this chapter, the Duration field can store values down to the millisecond, but even if we are measuring the duration only to the second, it's unlikely that many episodes will share the exact same value. So, if we were to use the Single select field, we would likely have as many unique values as episodes.

For our season Single select field, once we have input the correct season for each episode, we immediately have a visual, intuitive way of glancing at your base and knowing which season each episode belongs to. (As we will see in Chapter 4, we can filter, sort, and group records based on a Single select option for a field.)

The Single select and Multiple select field types share a unique characteristic: the order of the options listed in the field customization menu dictates the order the values are sorted in. To view the order of options in a field, we click the small arrow to the right of the field name, then click "Customize field type."

### Number, Percent, and Currency fields

The Number field type is an all-purpose container for numbers. It's often the best choice when inputting a quantity or measurement, whether you're measuring miles, hamburgers, or stitches on a baseball.

However, a few exceptions deserve a closer look. For example, if you're measuring the time duration of something, then you should use the Duration field. If you are measuring amounts of money, the Currency field provides formatting specific for that. Lastly, if you need to express a fraction of a whole number as a percentage, then the Percent field offers some built-in arithmetic to translate that number.

### Duration

The Duration field measures time in hours, minutes, seconds, and fractions of a second up to a millisecond. Airtable gives the option to display a Duration value in whatever resolution you specify, whether more granular or less specific, while keeping the original value untouched. For example, if you are cataloging videos with specific lengths measured in milliseconds, you can input the lengths up to three decimal places. Or if you just want to store a less granular measure, you might be fine just to measure minutes and seconds.

The Duration field also illustrates how Airtable can mask some of the data the base is holding. For example, with the duration of 2:03.079, we can change the resolution to only show hours, minutes, and seconds, which would display 2:03. Doing so, however, does not remove the 0.079 seconds entered into that cell. Whatever values are entered, changing the display resolution will not round or otherwise change the number.

### Date

It's important to understand what the Date field makes possible in Airtable. In future examples of formulas, we'll see how there's a dedicated group of Airtable formula functions to format and calculate dates.

In Chapter 6, we see that the Calendar view is powered by having one or more Date fields in a table. Similarly, the Timeline and Gantt views must have Date fields to pull info from so that they can plot records in a sequence.

From the field customization menu, we can see that Airtable's Date field can hold a few variations of date formats, including US, European, and ISO specification formats. Airtable also has a "friendly" format that lists the name of the month and day along with the year.

If you add time to your Date field, this unlocks more options. In addition to choosing a 12-hour or 24-hour format, you also can specify a Date field to use the same time zone for every collaborator, as shown in Figure 2-11. Airtable usually tries to determine your time zone and display it accordingly. As you can imagine, when different people in different parts of the world collaborate on a base, it is helpful to have a shared reference for time.

*Figure 2-11. Choosing for all base collaborators to view the datetimes in this field as Pacific Time ("America/Los_Angeles").*

## Rating

The Rating field allows users to choose from five different styles of icons through the field customization menu, including stars, hearts, flags, and a thumbs-up, which are available in 10 colors on a scale of 0 to 10. Users can also add a scale between 1 to 10. Airtable actually stores the rating as a number. In formulas and Automations, it will be worth remembering that we can use numbers to represent ratings when we're not directly editing with the Rating field.

## Checkbox

The Checkbox field is similar to the Rating field but slightly more straightforward. Instead of having a range of up to 10 hearts or flags, you can give each record a single star, heart, thumbs-up, flag, or checkmark. The Checkbox field sets a simple binary variable for your records. For example, in our *Simpsons* base, it may be necessary to keep track of which episodes feature Groundskeeper Willie, so a red star notes episodes where he makes an appearance.

### Attachment

The Attachment field is one of Airtable's most celebrated features. You can have many Attachment fields in a table and store a wide array of file types in any of those fields. You can also preview a surprising number right inside the Grid view. Airtable will generate thumbnails for image files, including Photoshop, Word, Excel, text, PDFs, and PowerPoint files. In addition, you can preview audio in the Grid view, and a pop-up video player allows you to view video attachments directly from the Airtable interface.

It's important to keep in mind that storage in Airtable is limited. Airtable's pricing tiers have different storage allowances. For example, the free plan offers 1 GB total, the Team Plan offers 10 GB, and the Business Plan has 100 GB. You can check how much of your attachment storage is in use in each base on our Airtable workspace page, as we can see in Figure 2-12. You can also check how many rows you have toward our row quota in the same section of the account page.

*Figure 2-12. Keeping track of limits on records and storage in a base.*

So how do you get attachments into our base? Airtable offers some reasonably simple manual ways, but several options are available for doing it with automation, too. For example, you can set up an attachment field to store headshots in a CRM base in the Grid view. After clicking a record in that field for a contact in the CRM, Airtable presents a pop-up screen after you hit the plus button that prompts "Select files to upload," as shown in Figure 2-13.

You can drag and drop attachments directly into this file uploader. Other options allow for uploading through this pop-up modal window. For example, you can also import a file via a URL, perform a simple image search, take a photo with your computer's camera, or import from various sources (including Google Drive, Dropbox, Box, and OneDrive).

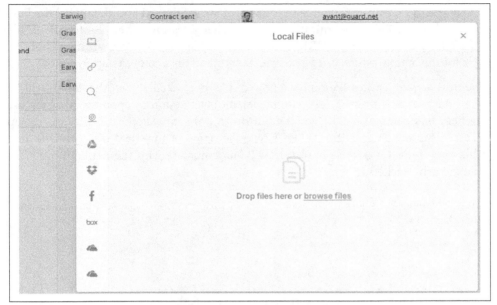

*Figure 2-13. After clicking into an attachment field in the Grid view, there are many options for sources of files to upload into the field for a record.*

You may find it faster to drag files directly into the cell to upload an attachment for a record. This action requires good dexterity with a mouse, especially when your rows of records in the Grid view are set to the most compressed height, but inserting files this way is slightly faster than triggering the pop-up dialog.

### Barcode

For projects when you're cataloging items in a store, for example, the Barcode field is invaluable. With the Airtable app installed on your smartphone, you can use your camera to scan over a dozen different barcode types (including QR codes and UPC codes) and import the data directly into the Barcode field for a given record.

## The Button Field

The Button gives a Grid view the feel of an application. It can also be conceptually confusing. While a database field, in *any* kind of database, is usually of a specific data type, Airtable's Button field isn't storing data. It's really a manual trigger that performs a specific action.

At its most basic level, users assign actions to the interactive Button field that are triggered when a user presses a Button field for a record. For example, as we will see later, we can configure a Button field to open a URL referenced from another field when the button is pressed.

When creating a Button field, we first need to name the field and then label the button itself in the field customization menu. When creating a new Button field, the default label is called "Open URL," but let's title it "Open wiki." We can then choose a style for the button, which can be colored text or text on a colored background.

The next step unleashes the button's power. We must decide what the action will be when the button is pressed. The simple default is an action to open a URL. Let's use the field that contains a URL for the button to point to. There's a URL field set up called "Simpsons Wiki URL." When I type the name of that field into the URL formula box of our Open wiki button, it will autocomplete with the name of our URL field in curly brackets (Figure 2-14).

*Figure 2-14. The formula box in the Button field configuration will autocomplete the names of other fields in the table.*

After clicking "Create field," any record with a valid URL in the Simpsons Wiki URL field can be opened in a new browser tab when my new Open wiki button is clicked, as shown in Figure 2-15.

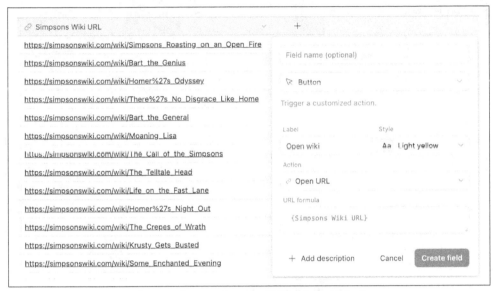

*Figure 2-15. Creating a button that can open a URL when clicked.*

As shown in Figure 2-16, Airtable also has Extensions available in its Marketplace that can be triggered using one of these preconfigured buttons. For example, we can configure a page layout to create a PDF from certain select information in our records. In addition, Airtable has preconfigured apps that can leverage third-party APIs, such as sending emails via SendGrid, sending SMS messages via Twilio, or finding stock photography with Pexels.

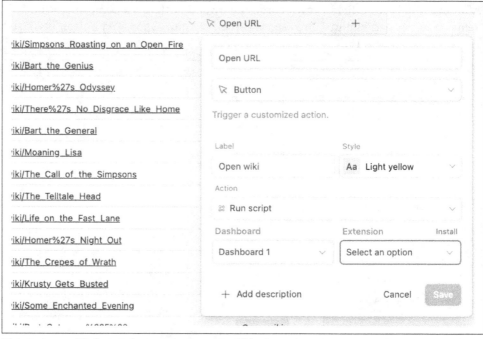

*Figure 2-16. Clicking a button to open Airtable extensions.*

The Run script option in the button configuration menu refers to the Scripting extension, a dedicated container for custom Java-Script. We'll look at the types of ways you can modify your base using the Scripting extension in Chapter 10, which discusses Extensions. For now, it is worth knowing that users can trigger a Scripting extension configured to connect with an external data source, process data in a record, or complete most any action on your Airtable data you can imagine with JavaScript.

## Calculated Fields

Airtable allows the following types of calculated fields.

- Autonumber
- Created time
- Last modified time
- Last modified by
- Created by and User

If input fields are about entering and interacting with data, these so-called calculated field types are more about understanding your data. For example, we can choose one of the input fields, the Rating field, to our table of *The Simpsons* episodes and choose a rating for each episode between 1 and 5 stars. However, if we also added the calculated field "Last modified time," we could see the last time the rating was changed.

These six calculated fields—Autonumber, Created time, Last modified time, Last modified by, Created by, and User—give us insight about either our records, a sort of meta information, or what actions we have taken for our records in our base. The actual field values for records, like the date an episode aired, can be significantly enhanced with these types of meta information. Furthermore, these fields can help us sort through our data, not only based on the field values of records but based on information calculated about the data with calculated fields.

## Autonumber field

The Autonumber field is a utility that provides a unique, sequential number for every record in your base. In the primary field, Airtable places no constraints on those primary field values being unique between records, but using Autonumber always creates a unique number for each record in a table. As a result, we can be assured that an Autonumber field will not have duplicate values like we might have in our primary field (whether intentionally or unintentionally).

Once a user creates an Autonumber field, the existing records in a table will be assigned a sequential number, starting with the number 1. New records will be given new sequential numbers, regardless of other records that had been deleted after the Autonumber was created.

For example, if we add an Autonumber field to a fresh base with the standard three blank records, those will be numbered 1, 2, and 3. If we then add two more records, those new records will be numbered 4 and 5, respectively. However, if we delete records 4 and 5 and then add two more new records, those records will be numbered 6 and 7. In other words, Airtable does not reassign sequential values and simply assigns new sequential numbers to any new row created.

If you want a start fresh with sequential ordering without gaps because of records that were deleted or added since an Autonumber field was created, an easy way to do this is to simply create another Autonumber field.

At first, new users might be confused by seeing records in the Grid view with small numbers on the far left side of the page. These numbers begin at 1 and are always sequential. You can think of these numbers as a temporary compass; they provide a shorthand for understanding how many records you have in that view and the context of where you are in those records. You can drag any record above or below its current, so long as you don't have sorting activated—another signal that visual order in a view is very subject to change. These ordered numbers on the left will change with every filter grouping, filtering, or sorting, which we will learn to apply in Chapter 4.

### "Created time" field

The "Created time" field is a timestamp of when each record in a table was created. This field can become one of your most trusted utilities for understanding your base data. For example, since we are collaborating with our friends to compile this base of *The Simpsons* episodes, we want to keep track of when someone has created a new record to start to build information on an episode.

Similar to Autonumber, the Created time field does not have many options. (But, like the Date field, you can choose whether or not to include time. You can also choose whether or not to have all of the base collaborators on the same time zone.)

### "Last modified time" field

While the Created time field is an unchanging value, the "Last modified time" field updates every time there is a change for a record. The default updates when a change is made to any editable field. You can also customize this by choosing which field, or fields, you want a Last modified time field to track. In Figure 2-17, we can see an example of using the Specific fields option to create a Last modified time field that only tracks changes that happened within the synopsis field.

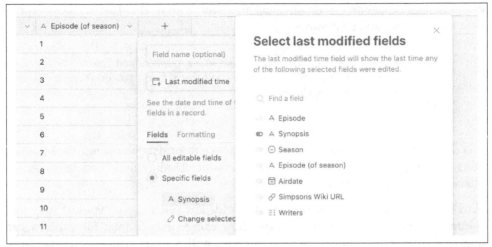

*Figure 2-17. Choosing just one field to trigger an update to this Last modified time field.*

### Last modified by field

Airtable was built for collaboration. You and your colleagues can share access to a base and make changes as you work together on a project. This brings us back to the dilemma of tracking who made changes to a spreadsheet.

The Last modified by field tells us who most recently made a change to a record. Similar to the previous example, where we tracked the most recent time the synopsis field was modified, "Last modified by" can track who modified any field in a record or a selection of fields. And we're not limited to just one "Last modified by" field in each table, either.

### "Created by" and User fields

The "Created by" field is another straightforward utility without frills or options. You can see which teammate created a given record or whether it was created directly via the API or an Airtable Automation. Down the road, we may want to filter, group, and sort our records by who created them, and this field leverages Airtable's metadata to do that with certainty.

When you and your team are divvying up work inside of Airtable, the User field can help track who will do what work on which records. You can configure a User field to allow for multiple people, or just one person, to be assigned to a field. Think of the User field as a "Single select" field where the options are the collaborators in your base.

This might be helpful, for example, in describing who is ultimately responsible for that record. Suppose you're using Airtable to track QA issues in your code. In that case, the single collaborator option could be useful to know that Jane is solely responsible for that issue and its resolution.

 If a bell icon is next to a User field's name, newly added base collaborators will be notified when you add them. But if you don't see it, this option is toggled off.

Calculated fields show how Airtable stores a wealth of data about our data that we don't always see. As you progress with your understanding and proficiency with a platform, you can tap into this data as needed.

Now that we understand how records and fields are much more than just rows and columns of data, we're ready to dive into how using views to their full capacity can unlock organizational superpowers for our data, both for ourselves and across teams. In the next chapter, we will explore linked records and computed fields, which allow for even greater flexibility and versatility in creating structured relationships with our data.

# CHAPTER 3

# Linked Records and the Lookup Field

We've seen some of the advantages of using Airtable to keep our data structured. We can define fields in Airtable; each record is a distinct item in that table. The next step is linking records, which creates relationships between tables. More specifically, we create relationships between different items in our database, where every table represents a single type of item. The Linked record field allows us to associate items in one table with items in another table. Suppose we are using Airtable to manage the inventory of our grocery store. There might be a table of the orders we place with the different wholesalers that supply our inventory. In this Orders table, we could start with a Single select field, which tracks which wholesaler fulfills that order. In that case, we could select the appropriate wholesaler from the drop-down menu. But what if we also wanted to see more info about the wholesaler itself?

We could have a few extra fields for the wholesaler's information in the Orders table, like its address and phone number. But if that information were living in just the Orders table, we'd have to copy and paste that information several times—every time we choose the wholesaler for the order. To solve this problem, we can use linked records to create relationships between the records in each table.

The orders and the wholesalers could each be in separate tables, as shown in Figure 3-1.

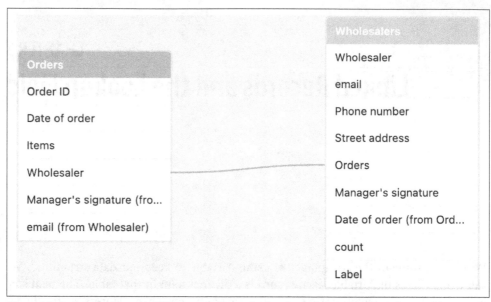

*Figure 3-1. Arranging two different things, wholesalers and orders, into two tables connected by linked records.*

We could start with the original table of orders, where each order comes from a different wholesaler. In the second table, we could store information just about the wholesalers. This leverages linked records for efficiency and a better understanding of our data: when a wholesaler is linked to an order using a linked record, we are now set up to easily populate wholesaler data in our Orders table.

In Airtable, records in one table can relate to records in another. This concept of relationships between entities, which the Linked record field enables in Airtable, is the foundational idea of relational databases. We have different tables of data for different things. There might be a table for the wholesalers we order from, for the orders we place with the wholesalers for our inventory, and for the produce available to order from the wholesalers.

# Why Use Linked Records?

Linked records introduce best practices for storing and retrieving data, which is especially important as the amount of data you track grows.

## Define Relationships Between Things

The power of Airtable's relational database model comes into focus when we use linked records to organize more than one type of thing: gadgets, records, gizmos, invoices, or whatever they may be. If you're organizing different things that are related, and this may be the case more than you realize, you'll benefit from having more than a single table of data.

The relationships between tables via linked records make Airtable a proper relational database, like well-known incumbents such as MySQL, Filemaker, and Microsoft Access. Airtable uses linked records to keep different types of things separate but connected. Our first base for the initial short tour was all stored in one table. We'll have many tables in the Fall Tour Tracker base we'll build in Chapter 7, and each table will be specific for a certain entity. Each table is fundamentally a place to hold different entities or entity types.

Until now, there hasn't been a modern relational database accessible to the majority of knowledge workers. It's likely that there are still some people in your organization who are used to working with spreadsheets to organize their work and share knowledge. The incumbent database tools are outdated or too technical or both, but Airtable puts the relational database's power in the hands of these users.

## Create a Single Source of Truth and Reduce Repetitive Manual Entry

In the grocery store base, information about the wholesalers is only stored in a table of orders. The data is static and has to be updated manually for each order. For example, we want a wholesaler's phone number in each order record so we can call if there's a problem, so we'd have to enter the phone number (and any other wholesaler info) again in each new order record. And what if a wholesaler changes its phone number? We would have to manually update every order record associated with that wholesaler.

Linked records eliminate this problem. They ensure that your data is stored in a single location, or "single source of truth," so any changes or deletions are consistently updated everywhere, which also reduces manual entry.

In the example of a table of orders and a table of wholesalers, both tables represent one type of entity or thing, so you can independently modify each table without disrupting data in another table.

For example, if we want to catalog each wholesaler's email, we can simply add a field to the wholesaler's table. If we want to find a wholesaler's email when reviewing an order, we can use a Lookup field after linking that wholesaler to an order in the Orders table, as shown in Figure 3-2. (We'll examine Lookup fields later in this chapter; they unlock a powerful way to reference data from another table through a linked record relationship.)

| ↕ Order ID ∨ | 📅 Date of order ∨ | ≡ Wholesaler ∨ | ≡Q email (from Wholesaler) ∨ |
|---|---|---|---|
| 1 | 2/17/2023 | Harvest Haven Distributors | tscullard6@china.com.cn |
| 2 | 2/23/2023 | Nature's Bounty Wholesalers | arehnb@so-net.ne.jp |
| 3 | 2/4/2023 | FreshField Foods Co. | athreadgoldi@tinypic.com |
| 4 | 1/14/2023 | Orchard Oasis Suppliers | dchasneyj@toplist.cz |
| 5 | 2/7/2023 | GreenGlobe Produce Partners | mlomaza@sbwire.com |
| 6 | 2/22/2023 | FarmFusion Distribution | fsymesh@abc.net.au |

*Figure 3-2. Using a Lookup field to pull an email address from another table.*

To take advantage of these benefits, it's helpful to understand the basic architecture of how entities in a relational database can relate to each other.

# Relationships Between Records in a Relational Database

There are three main types of relational database relationships.

## One-to-One Relationship

Some relationships between records and different tables can only be between two records, one from each table. For example, if only one order can be delivered during each delivery time, the relationship between orders and delivery times would be one-to-one, as shown in Figure 3-3. Every order has only one scheduled delivery time, and every delivery time only allows for one order.

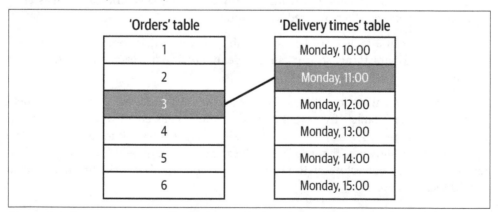

*Figure 3-3. In a one-to-one relationship, each record can only be related to one other record.*

## One-to-Many Relationship

In one-to-many relationships, one record in a table relates to one or more records in another table, as shown in Figure 3-4. For example, our table of orders linked to the table of wholesalers is an example of a one-to-many relationship. Every wholesaler has received one or more orders, and each order is specific to one wholesaler.

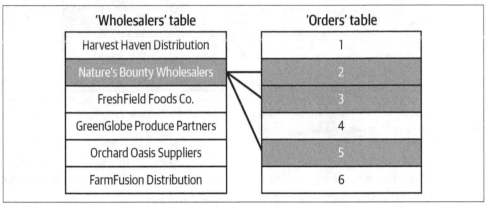

*Figure 3-4. In a one-to-many relationship, a record in one table can relate to one or more records in another table.*

## Many-to-Many Relationships

The last type of relationship between tables occurs when many items relate to many other items. In other words, one or more entities in one table can relate to more than one entity in another.

For example, let's imagine we have a table of produce items, as shown in Figure 3-5. We might order asparagus from Orchard Oasis one day and then order asparagus from FarmFusion the next day. Thus, asparagus has a relationship to many orders. And when we place the first order with Orchard Oasis, it also might include lettuce, so that order has a relationship to many produce items.

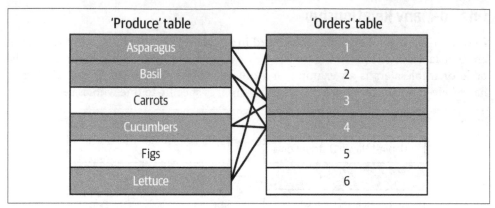

*Figure 3-5. A many-to-many relationship allows for an item in one table to relate to several items in another table, and vice versa.*

In Figure 3-6, we can use Airtable's Base Schema extension to visualize the linked record connections in our base. (This is one of the many Extensions available in the Airtable extension marketplace that we will look at in Chapter 7.)

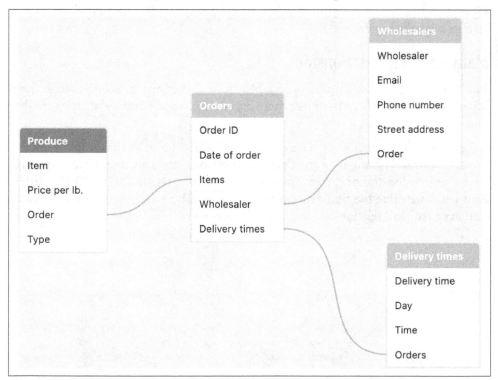

*Figure 3-6. Visualizing the relationships between tables using the Base Schema extension.*

Understanding the different types of relationships between our linked records equips us to start making these relationships effective and productive. When we create the book's primary running example in Chapter 7, the Fall Tour Tracker, we will set up different relationships like these between the records in that base. Before we do that, let's look at a few field types specifically designed to extend what linked records can do.

# Aggregating Data from Linked Records

In Chapter 2, we looked at calculated fields such as Created time, Last modified by, and Created by. Each of these calculated field types computes something about your base and its data, like when a field was last updated for each record in a table or which user created a record. Next, we'll look at two more field types that measure data related to linked records: the Lookup and Count field types.

## Lookup Field

The Lookup field works off a Linked record field. It allows you to cross-reference information between linked tables once you make a connection, or link, between a record in one table and a record in another. Linked records allow you to pull any piece of information from those records, from one table to another.

To illustrate the Lookup field, let's consider a simple example of wholesalers and orders. This is a one-to-many relationship because one wholesaler can have many orders, but each order can only belong to one wholesaler. If we have wholesalers in one table and orders in another, we can set up a simple linked record relationship between these two tables, as shown in Figures 3-7 and 3-8.

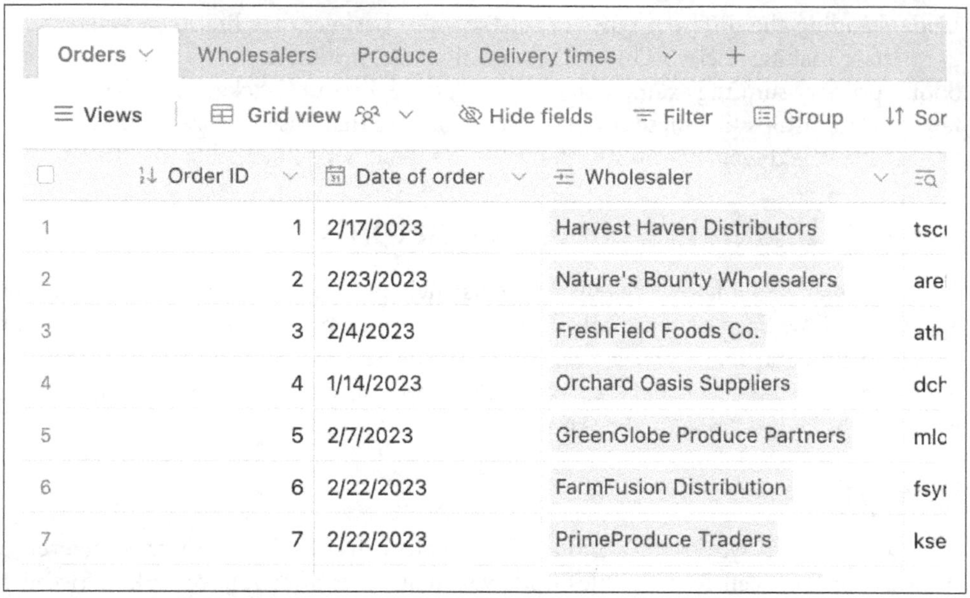

*Figure 3-7. Viewing the wholesalers linked to order via the Orders table.*

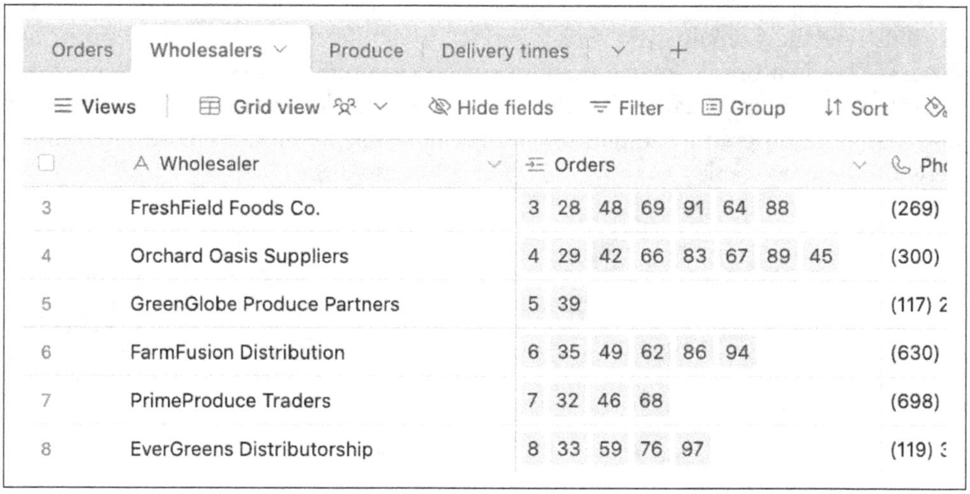

*Figure 3-8. Viewing the wholesalers linked to order via the Wholesalers table.*

## Creating a Lookup field

There are two ways to add a Lookup field (or fields) to a table with a linked record. The first way is how you might normally create a new field in the Grid view, by pressing the plus sign and choosing Lookup fields, as shown in Figure 3-9.

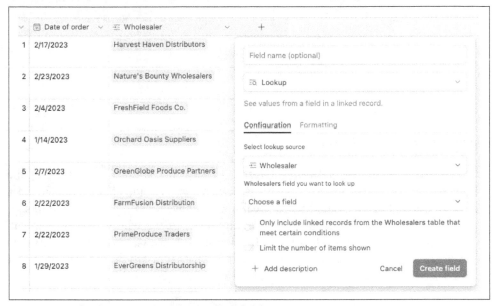

*Figure 3-9. The first way to add a Lookup field.*

Airtable also has a convenient way to add multiple Lookup fields at once. Next to the name of a Linked record field, click the down arrow, as shown in Figure 3-9. Then choose "Add lookup fields" to bring up a list of every field related to that linked record in its own table. As shown in Figure 3-10, you can choose multiple fields at once to bring into your destination table.

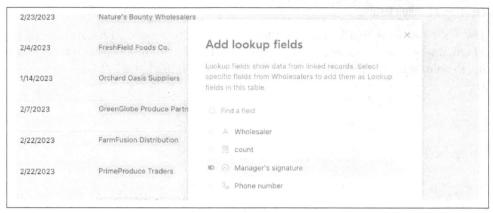

Figure 3-10. Adding Lookup fields.

In our Orders table, we might be interested in knowing about an attribute of the wholesaler fulfilling the order. This task is perfect for a Lookup field. We can use a new Lookup field to find out whether we'll need to have a manager available to sign when the order is delivered, as per the requirements of the wholesaler. We can call this information into the Orders table. In Figure 3-11, we can see the Wholesalers table is the original source of information on whether a wholesaler for an order requires a manager to sign for the delivery.

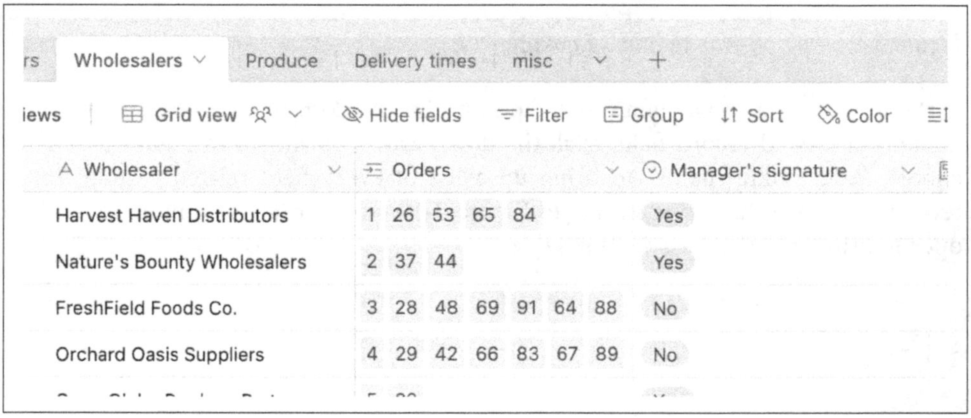

Figure 3-11. The source of the data that will be pulled into another table with a Lookup field.

We not only want to know if a manager's signature is required for any delivery made by a particular wholesaler, but we also want look at which orders require a signature. To achieve this, we can create a Lookup field in the Orders table that pulls information from the linked wholesaler record, as shown in Figure 3-12. We will call it "Manager's Signature (Wholesaler)." This Lookup field will display the value of the

"Manager's signature" field from the linked wholesaler record for each order, also shown in Figure 3-12.

By including both the original field name and the Lookup field in our Orders table, we can clearly see where the data is coming from and reassure everyone that the correct information is being tracked and displayed in our Airtable base.

| | 📅 Date of order | ⩨ Wholesaler | 🔍 Manager's signature (from Wholesaler) |
|---|---|---|---|
| 1 | 2/17/2023 | Harvest Haven Distributors | Yes |
| 2 | 2/23/2023 | Nature's Bounty Wholesalers | Yes |
| 3 | 2/4/2023 | FreshField Foods Co. | No |
| 4 | 1/14/2023 | Orchard Oasis Suppliers | No |
| 5 | 2/7/2023 | GreenGlobe Produce Partners | Yes |

*Figure 3-12. Pulling the information about the manager's signature into another table via a Lookup field.*

### Adding conditions to Lookup fields

We can also use a Lookup field to pull values of one or more fields from multiple records into a single Lookup field for a single record. For example, we have multiple items linked to each order in the Orders table. When we create a Lookup field for the price of each item linked to an order, the result is a group of values, each from a different record linked to that team, as shown in Figure 3-13.

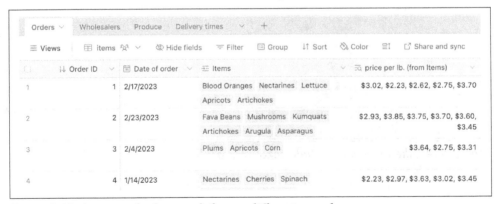

*Figure 3-13. A group of values, each from a different record.*

### Putting conditions on Lookup fields

Sometimes, we may want only to surface certain data from all the records linked to a record. For example, we may just want to see orders placed in the last week if we have a Lookup field in the Wholesalers table for dates of the orders we've made to each wholesaler.

To do this, we toggle the option to "Only include linked records," which filters linked records that meet certain conditions. We can then add conditions that are essentially the same as the filters available in Views. We can choose to filter by what is or isn't in a field or whether a field is or isn't empty. As shown in Figure 3-14, we can filter records to determine whether the order was placed in the past week.

You don't have to filter just the field that you've referenced in the Lookup field. You can set conditions on any field in the table of the linked record.

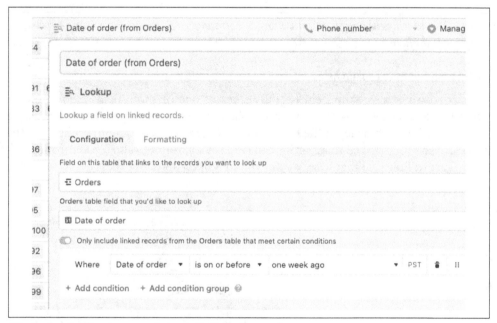

*Figure 3-14. Filtering to only include linked records.*

# Count Field

The Count field does just one thing: count linked records. As we'll see with the Rollup field, there are more sophisticated ways to count linked records, but the Count field is the quickest way to know how many linked records are linked to a record in another table, if that's your only goal.

To use the Count field, you simply specify the Linked records field in the table that you'd like to count. After clicking Save, you'll see a tally of linked records in that field. As shown in Figure 3-15, we can see the number of orders linked to a wholesaler.

| | A Wholesaler | Orders | count |
|---|---|---|---|
| 3 | FreshField Foods Co. | 3 28 48 69 91 64 88 | 7 |
| 4 | Orchard Oasis Suppliers | 4 29 42 66 83 67 89 45 | 8 |
| 5 | GreenGlobe Produce Partners | 5 39 | 2 |
| 6 | FarmFusion Distribution | 6 35 49 62 86 94 | 6 |
| 7 | PrimeProduce Traders | 7 32 46 68 | 4 |

*Figure 3-15. Using the Count field.*

In conclusion, linked records allow you to establish relationships between entities and organize your data effectively. By connecting different tables, you can access and associate information between records, creating a more structured, interconnected database. In the next chapter, we will dive into Airtable's views, which provide essential tools for working with your data in a way that precipitates collaboration and doesn't require any programming to filter, sort, and otherwise organize your records to understand your data.

# CHAPTER 4

# View Essentials

Views are an essential piece of what makes Airtable effective as a collaboration platform. Airtable Views offer more options for how data can be viewed than what you see in a spreadsheet. For example, you can put a filter on a spreadsheet column to see the tasks that occurred within the last year. But let's assume that your colleague opens the file a few hours later, clears your filter, and creates a different filter on a column. When you return to the file, the filtered rows you see are different, and the resulting rows of their filter is now in place. With Airtable, instead of just a single snapshot of the data, you and each of your collaborators have multiple customized views from the different Airtable view types (e.g., Grid, Calendar), each of which can have its own filter (and more).

Airtable gives you six kinds of views to configure for visualizing your data. For example, you might want to understand your data over a period of time. You can create a Calendar view, a Timeline view, or a Gantt view. Or you may need to see a more visual representation of your records, where an image from each record is enlarged on a movable card. This is possible with the Gallery and Kanban views. Views can serve these needs, and countless others, without changing the underlying data in your base. Among these six types, you can create multiple views of the same type.

When you first create an Airtable base, you are presented with a Grid view. This is the view in Airtable in which you'll lay the groundwork for configuring your base. After we cover the fundamentals of views with the Grid, we'll move on to the other views in Chapter 6.

It's critical to understand that each view always presents a table's data, but you can frame that data in many different ways depending on how a view is configured. And conversely, any changes to records in the table affect the data of all views.

Just like how a photo filter in Photoshop can transform the look and feel of a photo without necessarily altering the original image, Airtable views give you different ways to visualize your data without changing the underlying data itself.

And just as applying a filter to a photo doesn't actually modify the original image file, creating a view in Airtable doesn't affect the underlying data in your base. It simply presents the data in a different format or arrangement. You can toggle between views and explore your data from various angles without making permanent changes.

## Configuring Views

Users can configure the data that a view displays. Some of these controls are available in every view, such as the ability to filter records. However, some apply to only one or two views, such as the ability to change the height of rows in the Grid view. Of the seven views in Airtable, Table 4-1 notes which configuration option is present in each.

*Table 4-1. Each view has a unique mix of configuration options.*

| Name | Hide fields | Filter | Group | Sort | Color | Height | Share view | Customize | Summary bar |
|------|-------------|--------|-------|------|-------|--------|------------|-----------|-------------|
| Grid | ✓ | ✓ | ✓ | ✓ | ✓ | ✓ | ✓ | | ✓ |
| Calendar | ✓ | ✓ | | ✓ | ✓ | | ✓ | ✓ | |
| Gallery | ✓ | ✓ | | ✓ | ✓ | | ✓ | ✓ | |
| Kanban | ✓ | ✓ | ✓ | ✓ | ✓ | | ✓ | ✓ | |
| Timeline | ✓ | ✓ | ✓ | ✓ | ✓ | ✓ | ✓ | ✓ | ✓ |
| Gantt | | ✓ | ✓ | | ✓ | | ✓ | | |

## Getting Started with the Grid View

The Grid view is the default view for a new Airtable base and where most data entry happens in the Data section of Airtable (however, the increasing robustness of Interfaces is increasingly moving manual data entry/modification away from the Data section). Plus, it's usually where you will do the initial configuration of fields on your base.

You can customize the information presented in a given view via controls in the toolbar. Above the names of fields in a table is a horizontal toolbar with icons for Hide fields, Filter, Group, Sort, and other configuration options, as shown in Figure 4-1.

*Figure 4-1. The various options for customizing the Grid view via a toolbar of controls.*

Let's create another base we can reference as we move through these different views. This time, let's set up a base to organize a band's concert tour and call it "tour tracker."

Planning and scheduling a concert tour is a complicated endeavor. You need to book concert venues, find lodging, plan a route across the country that's efficient, and, of course, make sure that tour will be profitable. Airtable is great for planning projects of all kinds, and we'll be able to see how to leverage dates and times by working from a project-oriented base. To get started, we will have a base with just information about the band's small summer tour in 2022, as shown in Figure 4-2.

*Figure 4-2. A simple base with one table that keeps track of our summer tour.*

# The Grid View's Configuration Options

Airtable provides a handful of ways to control which of our records are visible for practically every view. For instance, most views have the option to Filter, Sort, Color, Hide fields, and Share your data. (The Share option isn't *really* a configuration option because it doesn't change what data it presents in a view, similar to how a Button field isn't *really* a field because it doesn't store data that can be accessed.)

# Filtering

Filtering allows us to customize which records are displayed in a view. A *condition* is the atomic unit of filtering, and it has three pieces, including 1) the field that you're filtering with that condition; 2) the operator, which is how you filter; and 3) the value, which is what you compare your records against with the operator. So the structure of an Airtable filtering condition is:

1. Field
2. Operator
3. Value

For example, as shown in Figure 4-3, if we set up a condition for a numerical field, we can use conditions like "equal to" or "less than." These two options would not be available to filter a text field.

*Figure 4-3. Filtering a set of records using a value from a Number field.*

In the previous example, the field we chose is Capacity, the amount of people a venue holds, and we want to use Filter to show us only the venues that can hold 900 or more attendees (900 is the value of the condition).

Now let's filter a text field. We can search to see which records contain certain text in a field. For example, we may want to know how many times we'll be staying in a Fairmont hotel. We can search the "Lodging" text field to see if it contains the word "Fairmont," then we can choose the operator "contains" to find records with that word in the Lodging field value (see Figure 4-4).

*Figure 4-4. Searching a text field with a fragment of text using the "contains" operator.*

As we've seen, fields holding text or numerical data can be filtered with operators unique to those types of data. Filtering a Multiple select field shows us another example of unique operators based on the field type we're filtering. Since a Multiple select field has a defined set of options, we can use conditions like "has any of" to specify that we want to filter records with one or more of the options. Or we can use "has none of," which ensures that none of the resulting records have any of the options we specify.

For instance, in our Instruments field, we can note whether the instruments the band will perform with at a show are either their own (Band), from the venue (Venue), or rented from an instrument rental company (Rental). In Figure 4-5, we can choose to filter out the shows where we are using rental equipment by using the "has none of" operator.

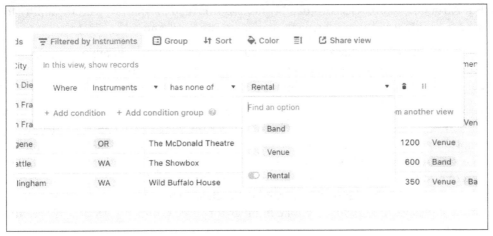

*Figure 4-5. Using the "has none of" operator on a Multiple select field.*

 Both "is empty" and "is not empty" are powerful tools to filter records. Since these two operators only check whether a field has a value or not, there is no value to specify in the third component of the condition—the condition only has two components instead of three. Filtering for whether a field is empty or not can be used on any field type. For example, if we want to check for missing phone numbers in the "Venue number" field, then we can specify that phone number field and choose "is empty" for the operator. As we can see in Figure 4-6, this condition will show every record missing a value in the Venue number field.

*Figure 4-6. The "is empty" and "is not empty" operators are available for any field type.*

## Conjunctions and condition groups

Using a single condition in a filter helps you understand what your records contain. But Airtable also unlocks considerably more powerful data analysis with the ability to specify multiple conditions using the conjunctions "and" and "or."

For example, while looking for records without a venue phone number, we might be especially concerned about the venues in California where the tour begins. Using a conjunction to combine two conditions into a condition group makes this task easy.

Let's use the "and" conjunction to find records in our table of California venues without a phone number. Our first condition for the venue phone number field is "is empty," and then we create a new condition connected with an "and" conjunction. The second condition begins by choosing the State field along with the operator "is" and our value of "CA" (one of the options in our Single select field State). The result, which we can see in Figure 4-7, highlights the fields where we've applied conditions, and it shows we are missing a phone number for three California venues. We see the result in Figure 4-8.

*Figure 4-7. The conjunctions "and" and "or" allow us to combine multiple conditions as a condition group.*

*Figure 4-8. The result of combining two filter conditions.*

Let's look at one more simple example before we combine a condition group with another condition. Instead of using the conjunction "and," let's try using "or."

We need to account for extra time getting to some of our performances early. For example, if a venue is large or the band is using rental equipment, those conditions require the band to arrive a few hours earlier. So we can simply set up an "or" conjunction to show us the records that meet the condition of either a capacity over 900 or the Equipment field, including the selection "Rental."

As we see in Figure 4-9, we have five records that meet the criteria. Four of them have a capacity of over 900, while one venue is smaller but does have instruments from a rental company. Using the "or" conjunction in this condition allowed us to ensure we understood every venue where we needed to be early.

*Figure 4-9. Using the "or" conjunction to show results for two different conditions simultaneously.*

But what if we only want to know which venues in California are either large or use rental equipment? If we try to add a third condition using the "and" conjunction to specify "CA" for the state, we cannot do that. We can only add another "or" conjunction. However, using nested filters is where Airtable's filtering can add layers of "and" plus "or" logic.

## Nesting condition groups

Using nested condition groups, we can combine a condition group with another condition or condition group. For example, when we want to understand when the band needs to arrive at a California venue early, nesting these conditions is the answer. First, we can click "Add condition group" to specify either a venue capacity over 900 or instruments from a rental company. Then, as shown in Figure 4-10, we combine that first group using the "and" conjunction with a condition that specifies only records that have venues in California.

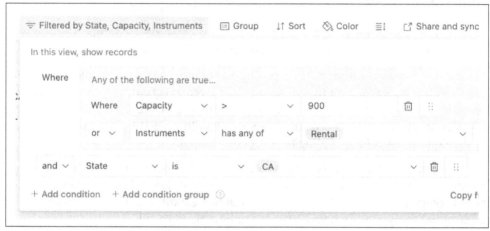

*Figure 4-10. Combining a condition group with a condition.*

Airtable offers the ability to add yet another level of nesting to a filter. For example, we can create another condition group inside of the condition group from Figure 4-10. In that filter, we have the condition that the state is California. We'll keep that. In the condition group, we specified that we were looking for records that either had a capacity of more than 900 or where we were using equipment rentals. We can add another qualifier inside of that condition group.

We will continue to filter for records with venues with a capacity of over 900. However, there's now an option to specify records with rental instruments and records for which we don't have a venue's phone number. Figure 4-11 shows that we are alternating "and" operators with "or" operators.

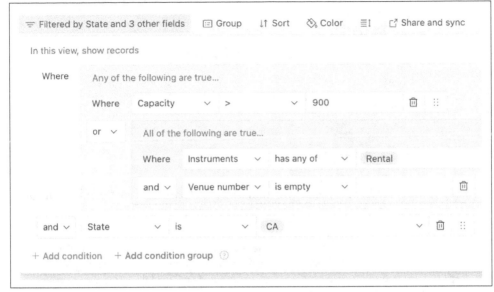

*Figure 4-11. A filter with a condition group inside of another condition group.*

Like many pieces of the Airtable platform, filtering is a very powerful tool, but it's easy to get started. Of all the views, filtering is the only control available for every view.

## Sorting

Sorting controls the order in which your data is displayed within a view. It's available in the Grid view and most other views. Just like with filtering (or any other configuration option), when we sort our data in Airtable, sorting is only rearranging the data we see in the particular view we are working in.

In the toolbar of configuration options above our records, you can choose fields to be sorted. Depending on the field type, the sort order has different options. Text fields, date fields, and numerical fields are sorted in ascending or descending order. Figure 4-12 shows an example of sorting our date field in descending order.

*Figure 4-12. Text fields, date fields, and numerical fields can be sorted in ascending or descending order.*

 As you may remember, the stars in a Rating field are actually numerical values. So records can be sorted in descending or ascending order by their rating value. The Checkbox field can also be sorted beginning with unchecked or checked records.

Single select and Multiple select fields have a unique way of being sorted. The order of options inside the field customization menu determines how they will be ordered in a sort. Airtable offers the options First–Last (meaning starting with the first option listed in the field customization menu) or Last–First.

We can also sort by more than one field at a time and change the hierarchy of how Airtable performs a sort. A larger dataset than the handful of shows in the tour tracker can better demonstrate sorting by more than one field, so let's return to our base of *The Simpsons* episodes.

We can start by sorting the episodes by season. Each season has over a dozen episodes. So while the episodes are sorted in the season they occur, as shown in Figure 4-13, within those seasons the records could be in some arbitrary order until we apply a secondary sorting.

*Figure 4-13. Applying the first layer of sorting.*

It's easy to add more sorting. In Figure 4-14, we've sorted Episode (of season) in alphabetical order.

You'll notice that there is a capital A icon next to the title of our episodes field. This represents the Single line text field. Since the number of the episode isn't a measurement or quantity, we don't need to use a number field. Since we've used a text field, we are sorting it A->Z instead of 1->9.

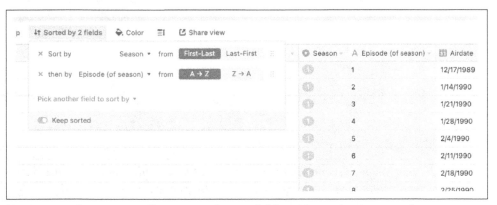

*Figure 4-14. Sorting records in a view by two fields, with one having precedence over another.*

When we sorted the Season field, you may have noticed it is a Single select field. Single select and Multiple select fields are ideal for working with data that essentially represents a category of your records in a table. In this case, there are a limited number of seasons, and we know that multiple episodes will go into each season. The Single select field is a good choice because each season is a larger container that contains the episodes for that season.

Single select and Multiple select fields are sorted uniquely: based on the order of the options. In Figure 4-15, we can see how the options in our Season field happened to be in numerical order. Because the option "First" is the first option in our field, it's the first in the sort. If the fifth season was first instead of last, our sort order wouldn't happen to be in numerical order—it would be 5,1,2,3,4 instead of the 1,2,3,4,5 order we'd instinctively expect.

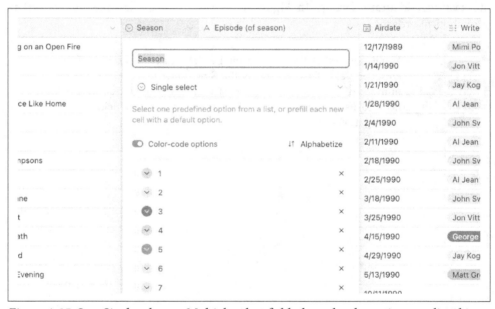

*Figure 4-15. In a Single select or Multiple select field, the order the options are listed in the field customization menu determines the order they appear in when sorted.*

## Hiding Fields

As your bases grow, you will inevitably have more fields that define the attributes of the records of the people, places, and things you're cataloging. You may quickly find there are many more fields than you can see on your screen at once in the Grid view, and "Hide fields" can narrow down what's important to see in a given view.

Located on the left side of the toolbar above your field labels, as we can see in Figure 4-16, the Hide fields icon opens up a drop-down list of every field in your table. (As a reminder, it's not possible to hide the primary field or remove it.)

A toggle switch to the left of every field name can show or hide that field. This drop-down menu is also a convenient place to change the order of the fields by grabbing the small group of dots (sometimes referred to as a "grab handle") to the right of the field names. The order of the fields in that drop-down menu (from top to bottom) mirrors the order of the fields in the Grid view (from left to right).

*Figure 4-16. The order of the fields in the "Hide fields" drop-down menu, except the primary field, is the same as whichever Grid view you are working on.*

 We can also change the order of the fields in a view without opening the "Hide fields" drop-down menu. You can click the down arrow icon next to each field's column and choose "Hide fields" in the field customization menu. Or, if you just want to move a field out of the way but not hide it, the most tactile way is to simply click on the title of the field and drag it to a new position.

"Hide fields" can allow us to scroll through all of the fields in a table in a compact list. But as you get closer to Airtable's maximum of 500 fields per table, scrolling through the list of fields can be a tedious way to find a field you want to hide or show. You can jump to the field you need by clicking in the "Find a field" dialog box. In Figure 4-17, we've started typing the first few letters of the field we want to find, which pulls up relevant potential matches.

*Figure 4-17. Typing a search query into "Find a field" at the top of the "Hide fields" menu.*

Though the "Hide fields" functionality exists in the other views, it's labeled "Hide fields" only in the Grid view. In other views, this function is labeled "Customize fields" and may add one or two extra options, but the functionality to hide fields is otherwise the same between different view types.

## Height

In the Grid view, it's possible to change the height of all rows in a view equally. For example, if we have a large number of items in a Multiple select field, we might want to increase the height so we can see more of those in the Grid view, as shown in Figure 4-18.

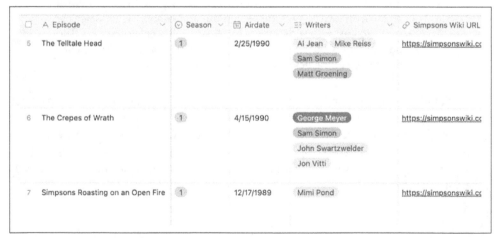

*Figure 4-18. Adjusting the row height in the Grid view to see more multiple select options for each record.*

# Summary Bar

In the Grid view, we see that field names are listed at the top of each column and the rows of records are numbered. At the very bottom of the page, there's a thin row with small text. It's easy to miss. This is the summary bar. Let's use it to understand the contents of records in a Grid view.

The summary bar highlights how using a database like Airtable instead of a spreadsheet does have some trade-offs. For example, because each record in a table is the same type of entity, we can't add another row in the Grid view just to sum up arbitrary values in a field column. To compensate for this, the summary bar offers a spreadsheet-like functionality to set up some basic analysis of our records by field, as shown in Figure 4-19.

| ⊙ Season | ⌄ | 📅 Airdate | ⌄ | A Episode (of season) | ⌄ | ☰ Writers | ⌄ | 🔗 Simpsꞌ |
|---|---|---|---|---|---|---|---|---|
| 1 | | 12/17/1989 | | 1 | | Mimi Pond | | https://sin |
| 1 | | 1/14/1990 | | 2 | | Jon Vitti | | https://sin |
| 1 | | 1/21/1990 | | 3 | | Jay Kogen    Wallace Woloda | | https://sin |
| 1 | | 1/28/1990 | | 4 | | Al Jean    Mike Reiss | | https://sin |
| 1 | | 2/4/1990 | | 5 | | John Swartzwelder | | https://sin |
| 1 | | 2/11/1990 | | 6 | | Al Jean    Mike Reiss | | https://sin |
| | Unique 9 | | Filled 100% | | Unique 12.32% | | Empty 190 | |

*Figure 4-19. The summary bar displays basic calculations of field values for records visible in a given view, such as number of unique records, percent of records filled, percent of unique records, etc.*

Four general summary functions in the summary bar offer information on how many records of a field are populated:

*Empty*
> Tells us how many records don't have a value in that field

*Filled*
> Tells us how many records have a value in that field

*Percent empty*
> Gives a percentage for how many records don't have a value in that field

*Percent filled*
> Gives a percentage for how many records have a value in that field

When we used filtering earlier to analyze the data in our concert tour base, we wanted to understand how many venues lacked a phone number in our records. Even though we could just count the records we see in the small dataset, the summary bar gives us tools to use with bigger datasets. For example, before applying filters, we can set the summary bar to the "Empty" function for the "Venue number" field. As we see in Figure 4-20, the summary bar gives a count of how many records in that view, presently unfiltered, don't have a value for the venue's phone number.

The summary bar is configured uniquely for each view in your base, and its calculations reflect any filtering for that view.

| A Venue | ⌄ | ☏ Venue number | ⌄ | # Capacity | ⌄ | ☰ Inst |
|---------|---|----------------|---|-----------|---|--------|
| Observatory North Park | | (619) 239-8836 | | 450 | | Band |
| The Troubadour | | | | 500 | | Band |
| The Fillmore | | | | 1200 | | Venue |
| The Chapel | | | | 400 | | Band |
| The Catalyst | | (831) 423-1338 | | 1400 | | Venue |
| The McDonald Theatre | | | | 1200 | | Venue |
| The Crystal Ballroom | | | | 1500 | | Renta |
| The Showbox | | | | 600 | | Band |
| Wild Buffalo House | | (360) 734-4206 | | 350 | | Venue |
| | | | | Empty 6 | | |

*Figure 4-20. Using "Empty" to get a tally of records without a value in a given view.*

Especially when working with large sets of data, the Unique and Percent unique functions highlight when we may have unintended duplicates in a field or need a running calculation of unique values.

Let's use another example from our tour base. If we want to know how many different cities we visited on the tour, we can use the Unique function. In Figure 4-21, we see that eight of our nine records in the City field are unique (i.e., we only played one city twice). In the State field, we can use the Percent unique function to see that, of all the records in the view, about one-third of the different values in that field are unique.

| rt | date | City | State | A Venue |
|---|---|---|---|---|
| | 7/14/2022 | San Diego | CA | Observatory Nort |
| | 7/15/2022 | Los Angeles | CA | The Troubadour |
| | 7/16/2022 | San Francisco | CA | The Fillmore |
| | 7/17/2022 | San Francisco | CA | The Chapel |
| | 7/19/2022 | Santa Cruz | CA | The Catalyst |
| | 7/20/2022 | Eugene | OR | The McDonald Th |
| | 7/22/2022 | Portland | OR | The Crystal Ballrc |
| | 7/23/2022 | Seattle | WA | The Showbox |
| | 7/26/2022 | Bellingham | WA | Wild Buffalo Hou: |

9 records        Unique 8    Unique 33.33%

*Figure 4-21. Using the "Unique" and "Percent unique" summary bar functions.*

Using your cursor to select records in the Grid view will change the output of the summary bar. Only the records selected will be part of the calculation in your summary bar when you have selected some arbitrary group of cells.

Similar to the Empty or Filled options, the summary bar also has an option for checkbox fields. For example, you can summarize the count of checked or unchecked records, or you can calculate the percent unchecked or checked.

There are also summary functions for numeric fields and date fields. When working with numbers, mathematical operators include:

- Sum
- Average
- Min
- Max
- Range
- Standard deviation

You can summarize date fields in the summary bar by choosing between:

- Earliest date
- Latest date
- Date range (in days)
- Date range (in months)

Histogram is a unique way to visually see the distribution of values in your records with a tiny set of bars instead of a number. Lastly, for an Attachment field, the summary bar allows you to see the total size of all the attachments in records for that view, as shown in Figure 4-22.

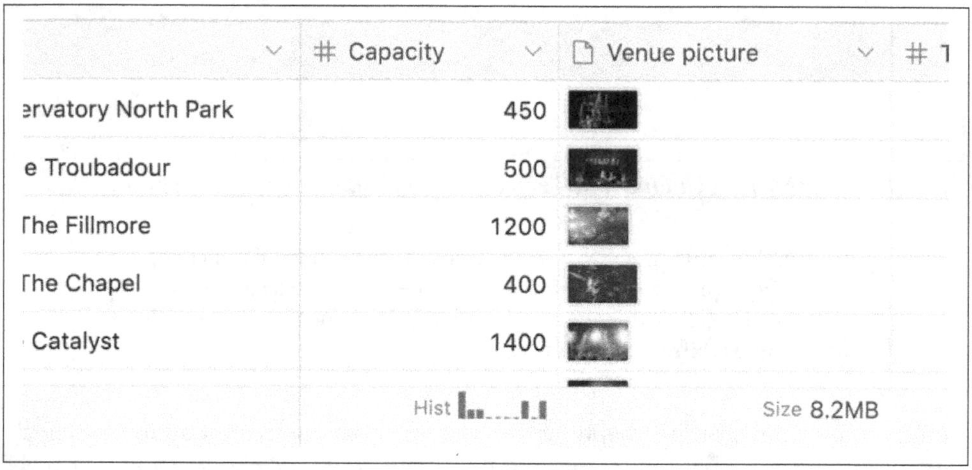

*Figure 4-22. Examples of histogram and attachments in the summary bar.*

## Coloring

Coloring records in an Airtable view is another powerful way to organize and differentiate your data between views. Like other view configuration options such as sorting and grouping, coloring provides a visual representation that enhances your understanding of your data.

Let's take a look at an example using episodes from our *Simpsons* base. In Airtable's Grid view, clicking the Color icon located in the toolbar above your field names will open up a color palette, where you can select a color to apply to your records based on the condition(s) you choose.

We can assign a different color to each season to make distinguishing the episodes from each season easier. For instance, we can assign a red color to the records from the first season and a blue color to the records from the second season, as shown in Figure 4-23.

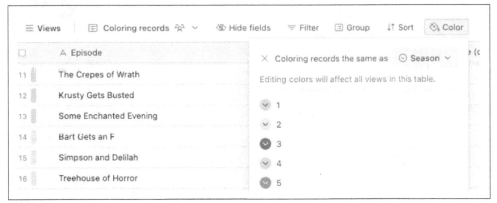

Figure 4-23. *By utilizing record coloring, we can quickly identify and group episodes based on their respective seasons.*

Coloring records can be helpful when you want to highlight certain types of data or identify specific categories within your dataset. For example, you can use different colors to signify genres, ratings, or any other criteria that are relevant to your specific use case. (Keep in mind that coloring records is specific to the view you are working in and does not change or impact the underlying data in your base.)

## Grouping

Grouping records helps us understand how records share characteristics. After clicking the Group button in the toolbar of the Grid view, Airtable will suggest grouping by Single select or Multiple select fields in your table.

Let's group records using the Season field in the Episodes table of our *Simpsons* base.

In Figure 4-23, we grouped the records by season, in order of First-Last. When we used sorting on this field, the order of the seasons wasn't dependent on the title of the Single select option but was based on the order each season is listed in the field customization menu—the same is true for grouping as sorting.

In Figure 4-24, we see that Airtable has moved records into visual groups, but we still don't have much insight into the characteristics of the groups we just created.

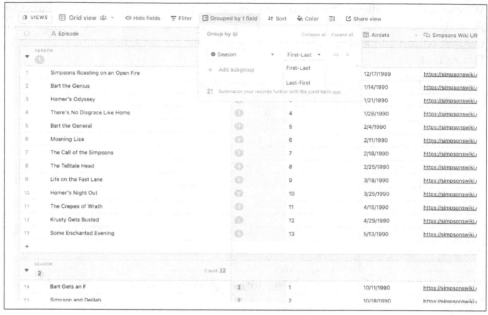

*Figure 4-24. Grouping records by a Single select field.*

Grouping records gives us tools we can quickly visually reference. For example, in the same menu where we chose the field to group by, we can click the "Collapse all" option to reduce all the records into bundles of groups where we can't see the individual records themselves, as in Figure 4-25.

*Figure 4-25. Collapsing groups of records.*

We can group additional fields into a hierarchy, similar to nesting condition groups in filtering. Airtable refers to grouped fields after the first group field as "subgroups." For a subgroup to be useful, the subgroup field should have duplicate values among the records in your grouped field. We can look at our *Simpsons* base for an example of when using a subgroup doesn't yield much insight.

First, we are grouping the records in the Episodes table by season. Next, let's add a subgroup for the field "Airdate." The examples you see in Figure 4-26 illustrate the issue with choosing Airdate as our subgroup. Since the value of the Airdate field is unique for every record, using this as a subgrouping simply puts each episode into its own subgroup. This is effectively the same as grouping them by season only.

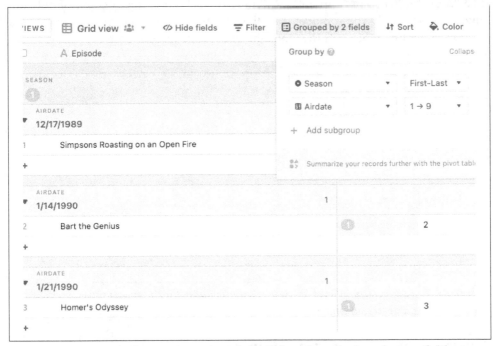

*Figure 4-26. Using a subgroup is not insightful if the values for the subgroup field are unique.*

Grouping in Airtable has the same sorts of flexibility as we've seen with other view configuration options. For example, you can move subgroups around, just as you can reorder different fields you're sorting by and different conditions you've set up in a filter. The "Collapse all" and "Expand all" options can condense or expand, respectively, everything you are grouping. And then you can individually expand or collapse subgroups or sub-subgroups.

Combining the summary bar with grouping offers unique insights. For example, if we use the summary function "Unique" on the Season field, we see the result for all records in that view in the summary bar, but we also see the values of that summary function performed on each group and subgroup.

Let's look at a more advanced example. In Figure 4-27, records are grouped by season, and the Unique % summary function is applied to the Episode (of season) field. For each group of records grouped by season, there is only one unique value in the Season field, so the Unique % value is 100%. However, the summary bar considers every field value for every record in the table across all seasons. It shows that only 12.32% of the 203 records are unique. Similarly, each group has a count of only one unique value. But in the summary bar, the Unique function returns a count of nine unique values that represents the nine different season choices from the Season field.

*Figure 4-27. Each grouping level displays a unique value for the function we've chosen for a given field in the summary bar.*

# Creating and Organizing Views

It's worth mentioning again that a view is just a unique way of looking at data; changing a value for a record in any view will change that value for the record in all views. You can have a section of views just for yourself, views for a specific purpose that a team may share, or views with a subset of data you may want to share outside your organization.

## Creating a View

Clicking on the "Views" icon in the left sidebar opens a list of the views present in a table and a menu at the bottom of the sidebar with many options. In this "Create..." section, you can choose any of the six types discussed in this chapter.

We can choose to create a new Grid view, Calendar view, Gallery view, Kanban view, Timeline view, or Gantt view, as shown in Figure 4-28.

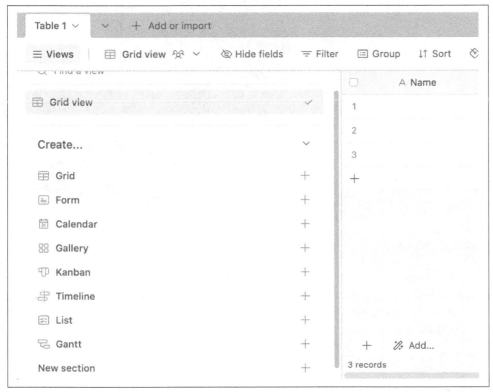

*Figure 4-28. The different options for creating a new view.*

Let's start with an example. In our tour tracker base, our first table is "2022 summer tour." We've added two new fields to this table: "Venue picture," which has an image of the venue, and "Contract status," which is a "Single select field" with several options to categorize the contract progress for each performance date. But let's assume we have too many fields in a Grid view to see everything without a lot of scrolling from side to side. Let's create a new view that displays only certain data.

If we click "+" next to "Grid" in the sidebar, a small dialog box appears that suggests a generic name for the view (such as "Grid 2"). It also has three radio buttons with options for "Who can edit." Let's leave the default option, "Collaborative," toggled on. But before we click "Create new view," let's change the name from the default Airtable suggests to "Venue information," as shown in Figure 4-29.

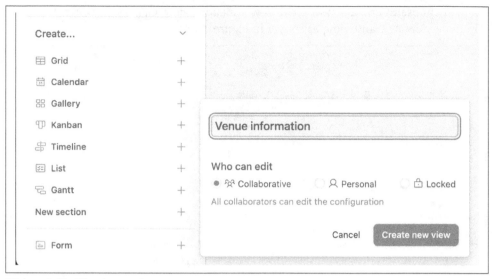

*Figure 4-29. Naming a view.*

Let's do one more thing with this view. If we hover over the name of the view in the sidebar, the Grid icon displays as a light-gray star. When we click that star, Airtable creates a section in the sidebar labeled "My favorites." As a result, any views we star in the same way will now be in the "My favorites" section.

We can also create a "New section." Sections are essentially folders of views.

## Naming Records

A general rule of database design is that each record should have a unique name. This is one reason why it's advisable to have dynamically generated names, and there are many ways to accomplish this (e.g., the Autonumber field type). Airtable does allow you to have records with the same name (e.g., the same value in the primary field), but that can very easily lead to confusion.

In Chapter 8, we will look at how to use a formula to dynamically generate a name for each record based on data from fields in the table. While that can be helpful in understanding which records you're dealing with among the various views, we can just as well name our records manually.

In this summer concert tour table, there are a few candidates for a quick and easy unique name for each record. We could consider using the name of the city, although we have two shows in Los Angeles, so those would be duplicate names. Those two shows in Los Angeles are at different venues, so we could use the venue name as the name of the record. However, we may not remember which venues are in which city, so this could lessen the potential of getting a quick understanding by glancing at a customized view. And while our date field is unique for each record, it doesn't give us any context about where we will be on the tour.

We can use a semi-manual shortcut since we don't have many records in this table. Let's start with the City field, then copy and paste those values into our primary field. Next, let's type a dash after the city name, followed by the day and month of the tour stop. This will give us a unique and descriptive name for each record, though we'll want to use a formula for this in the future.

Next, we can begin customizing this view, while our original view will keep its current layout. Since each of our records has a unique identifier, as we added in the sidebar, let's start by removing some fields from the view. We can toggle off Date, City, State, and Lodging. Now we have a more condensed set of fields, as shown in Figure 4-30, where we can see the venue's name, phone number, capacity, where to source instruments, a picture of the venue, and the status of the contract.

| | | A Venue | | ℭ Venue number | | # Capacity | ∷ Instruments | | ▯ Venue... | ⊙ Contract s |
|---|---|---|---|---|---|---|---|---|---|---|
| Buffalo House | | Wild Buffalo House | | (360) 734-4206 | | 350 | Venue Band | | | Negotiating |
| Chapel | | The Chapel | | (369) 828-0435 | | 400 | Band Venue | | | Awaiting leg |
| atory North Park | | Observatory North Park | | (619) 239-8836 | | 450 | Band | | | Gathering d |
| Troubadour | | The Troubadour | | (627) 926-8716 | | 500 | Band Rental | | | Contract se |
| owbox | | The Showbox | | (425) 272-1654 | | 600 | Band | | | Awaiting leg |

*Figure 4-30. A customized view, after removing some fields.*

# View Permissions

When we created our view, we had the option of making it either Collaborative (the default), a Personal view, or a Locked view. We've made Collaborative views in this chapter. Let's look at the other two options for defining who can access your views.

### Personal views

Personal views can be seen by everyone in a base, but only the owner of the Personal view can customize it using filters, grouping, sorting, etc.

By default, Airtable hides Personal views from your collaborators. However, the gear icon in the sidebar's upper right corner has an option to toggle on or off "Show everyone's personal views." When this is toggled on, you can see a subsection inside "All views" called "Personal views," which is a collection of the personal use of your collaborators in the base for that table.

Personal views are useful for having your own unique ways of viewing data in a table without creating lots of clutter in the "All views" section for everyone else in your team. It can also be useful to create a Personal view, which you solely have the ability to change, to share a particular analysis or vantage point with your colleagues.

### Locked views

The third type of view is the Locked view. Essentially, a Locked view is in a frozen state. Once you lock a view, no one—including the creator—can change that view until it is unlocked. As a reminder, just because we lock a view doesn't mean any of that data is prevented from being changed in another view.

Airtable gives you the option to put a small description on a locked view so your team understands why it is locked.

So why would we want to lock a view? You might use that view as a shared reference with your collaborators, and you don't want any changes made to its configuration. For example, you might have a Calendar view that is filtering for certain events applicable to your team. There isn't a need for anyone to change the data displayed for that purpose, so locking the view means that it will always have the same configuration until it is unlocked.

A Locked view is also useful when you're sharing data in a table using "Share view." We'll look at this functionality in the next chapter, but the use case is similar to automations. If you're publicly going to share some data in a given view, then you want to make sure no one inadvertently changes what data is in that view. Locking the view is a simple and effective solution.

Now that we know the different ways we can organize our data using views, we want to understand how to get data into our bases. In the next chapter, we will look at how we can import static files like CSVs, connect to other Airtable bases, and also make connections to third-party services to get that data syncing into Airtable.

# CHAPTER 5

# Importing Data

We can create new tables and fields in Airtable to build a base from scratch. But chances are you want to work with some existing data. When you import data that was effectively locked away in an Excel file or an old database system, the collaborative features of Airtable can shine.

For instance, we can import data from different sources and compare them in the same table. Or we can import data and clean it up for our own analysis. Finally, and perhaps most of all, we benefit from the ability to import outside data and make it available to our collaborators in Airtable, which gives them the ability to customize how they view it.

We'll look at ways anyone on your team can learn to access data from static files or dynamic sources. For example, if you have data locked away in spreadsheet files, Airtable has straightforward ways to bring that data into your base. Airtable also has several built-in integrations with third-party tools, like Box or Jira, and you can have an ongoing synchronization from those tools to your base using Airtable's Sync capability.

Lastly, Airtable provides users with a useful built-in form builder. Forms enable an easy way to solicit data from customers or other stakeholders. The Form view functionality doesn't have every bell and whistle, but it is convenient since the forms you build and manage are tied to your base without any extra integrations. But first, let's start by understanding how to import data from spreadsheets and CSV (comma-separated values) files, which is a generic tabular spreadsheet format.

## Importing CSV Files and Spreadsheets

Whether you need to analyze data that's been locked away in a spreadsheet for years or you've exported fresh data from another web app as a CSV file, you can bring it into Airtable with a one-time import.

## Importing Tabular Data from CSV Files

The CSV format has become a common data format on the web, and most web applications allow exporting data in a CSV file. When you import a CSV from your local machine by clicking "Add or import" next to the rightmost table, Airtable will attempt to guess the field type of columns in your CSV. This can be a timesaver, but you can also override the field type suggestions in the importer dialog. (Or, of course, you can change the field type after the data has been imported via the field customization menu.) As seen in Figure 5-1, Airtable marked our "email" column as a long text field, but we changed that to an email field type.

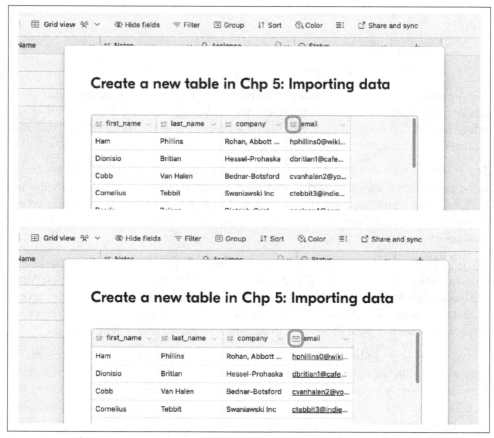

*Figure 5-1. The icon next to the field name Email shows the field type from long text (first image) changed to email (in the second image).*

# Importing Google Sheets and Excel Data

You can import spreadsheets into Airtable via several methods. Even though a collaborative Google Sheets document is designed for real-time collaboration and change, bringing in data from a Sheets doc using Airtable's import is the same: a one-time snapshot of your rows and columns.

Airtable uses the same rules for importing data from both Google Sheets and Excel files. Since that means we'll have the same considerations for data prep between the two formats, we'll use the term "spreadsheet" to refer to rules applicable to both Google Sheets and Microsoft Excel files throughout the rest of this chapter.

 Remember that when importing data from a spreadsheet work sheet, we only grab a static snapshot of the data. So if we add a row or change a cell value in the spreadsheet after the import, we'd have to import the file again to reflect that change in Airtable.

Airtable attempts to understand the types of data in each column being imported from a spreadsheet. In later sections, we'll walk through the rules Airtable uses to parse spreadsheet data, so you'll know what to expect and whether to clean/standardize your spreadsheet data before importing it.

 After importing a spreadsheet (or CSV), you can change the field type from what you first chose, or what Airtable assigned on import. Importing a column as a text field type will always echo the original value of cell data in a spreadsheet column. So you always have the flexibility to change a field from a text field to a Date or Duration field, for example.

Let's look at an example use case for importing a spreadsheet. We'll need to start planning for the next tour when we will perform in many more cities. Luckily, our record label compiled a list of music festivals happening in the next year and sent it to us as an Excel file.

Let's import this Excel file into our Airtable tour tracker base. We can click "Add or import" to the right of our base's rightmost table and then choose to "QUICK IMPORT" our Excel file, as shown in Figure 5-2.

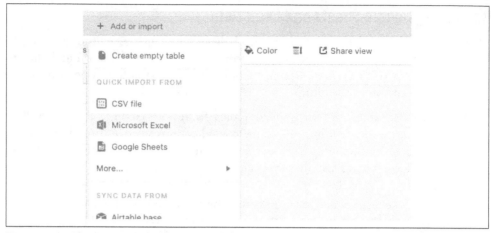

*Figure 5-2. Choosing to import an Excel file into a new table of our base.*

Airtable opens a dialog to allow us to directly upload the file from our local machine, from a URL, or by integrating with a cloud service like Dropbox or Google Drive. After we click the Upload button, we see a prompt to import the data into either an existing table or a new table. We're going to make a new table for this data. As shown in Figure 5-3, Airtable has labeled the festival name, city, and state as Long text fields. Our "genres" field is a Multiple select field. Airtable recognizes the date of each festival and imports that data as a Date field.

## Create a new table in Tour tracker

| festival | city | state | date | genres | radius cla... |
|----------|------|-------|------|--------|---------------|
| Harmony Festival | Orlando | FL | 9/19/2023 | rock  folk  me | 550 |
| Hypebeast Mus... | Orlando | FL | 5/12/2023 | electronic | 400 |
| Music of the Sp... | Memphis | TN | 7/15/2023 | electronic  hip-l | 70 |
| Rock the Leaves | Shawnee Mission | KS | 9/22/2023 | metal | 60 |
| The Oasis Musi... | Clearwater | FL | 4/21/2023 | folk  rock | 150 |

*Figure 5-3. Importing an Excel file with different field types.*

The last field in the worksheet is "radius clause." This obscure contract provision stipulates how far away (how many miles) an artist must perform from that venue if they're planning on taking other gigs in the same area. The radius clause data is a column of integers, so it makes sense that Airtable suggested it as a number field. However, we might consider making this a Single select field, which would allow us to have a clear, color-coded visual representation of the festivals when we group and filter by the value of the radius clause for each record.

Now that our data is in Airtable, we can sort by the date column in ascending order, as we can see in Figure 5-4.

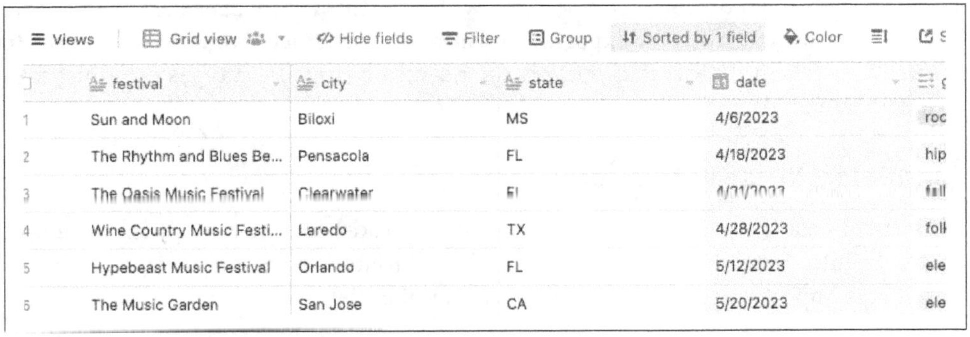

| | festival | city | state | date | |
|---|---|---|---|---|---|
| 1 | Sun and Moon | Biloxi | MS | 4/6/2023 | roc |
| 2 | The Rhythm and Blues Be... | Pensacola | FL | 4/18/2023 | hip |
| 3 | The Oasis Music Festival | Clearwater | FL | 4/21/2023 | fall |
| 4 | Wine Country Music Festi... | Laredo | TX | 4/28/2023 | foll |
| 5 | Hypebeast Music Festival | Orlando | FL | 5/12/2023 | ele |
| 6 | The Music Garden | San Jose | CA | 5/20/2023 | ele |

*Figure 5-4. Sorting imported records by date.*

We might turn the "State" field into a Single select field type to easily see each state when we group by state to see if any festivals are happening around the same time in the same state, as shown in Figure 5-5.

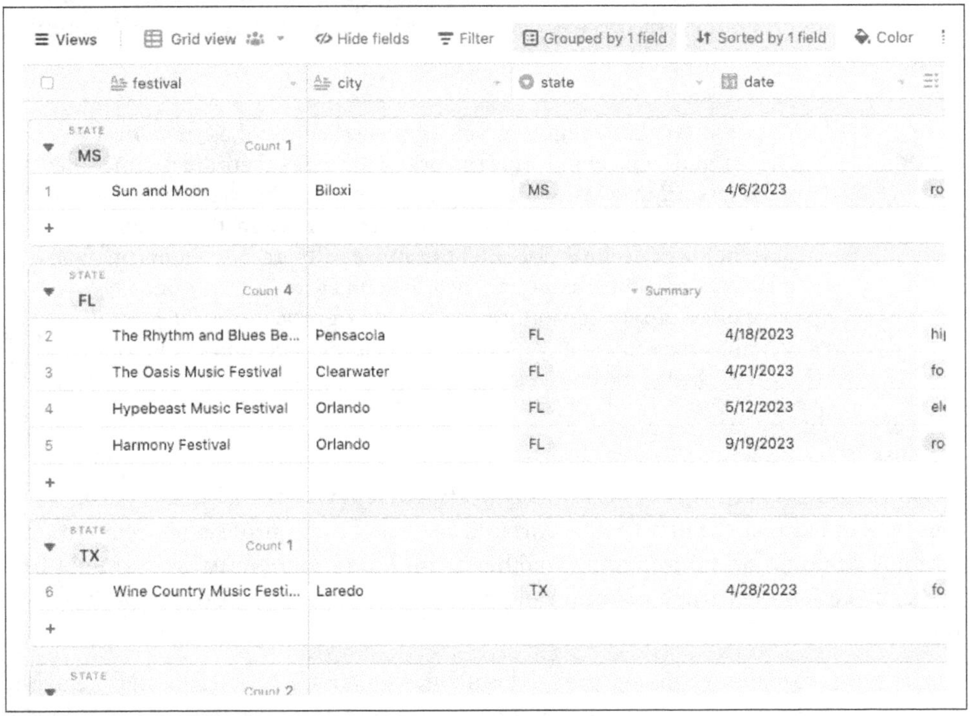

| | festival | city | state | date | |
|---|---|---|---|---|---|
| **STATE MS** | | | Count 1 | | |
| 1 | Sun and Moon | Biloxi | MS | 4/6/2023 | ro |
| + | | | | | |
| **STATE FL** | | | Count 4 | Summary | |
| 2 | The Rhythm and Blues Be... | Pensacola | FL | 4/18/2023 | hi |
| 3 | The Oasis Music Festival | Clearwater | FL | 4/21/2023 | fo |
| 4 | Hypebeast Music Festival | Orlando | FL | 5/12/2023 | el |
| 5 | Harmony Festival | Orlando | FL | 9/19/2023 | ro |
| + | | | | | |
| **STATE TX** | | | Count 1 | | |
| 6 | Wine Country Music Festi... | Laredo | TX | 4/28/2023 | fo |
| + | | | | | |
| **STATE** | | | Count 2 | | |

*Figure 5-5. Modifying a field type to enable grouping.*

# Importing Different Types of Data

Here's a breakdown of how Airtable deals with data from spreadsheets. Then, as you begin prepping your data for export, you can reverse-engineer some of these rules to ensure an efficient import that reduces the need to change field types or adjust broken data later.

## Numbers, Currency, and Dates

Numerical data is the main attraction in most spreadsheets, so it's critical to import this data into Airtable accurately. Let's look at Airtable's rules for when and how it designates imported spreadsheet columns as number fields.

### Numbers

For Airtable to classify a column of numbers as a number field, that column can't have a single cell containing other types of data (for example, a word or string of characters). Mixed data types aren't allowed in most relational databases. The same is true for Airtable, which has a simple rule for classifying spreadsheet columns. If all cells in a column contain numerical data, then Airtable will suggest using a number field.

 Suppose another column in your spreadsheet only has numerical values, and some of the values are integers while others are decimal numbers. In that case, Airtable will create a number field with the number of decimal places for whichever number in that column has the most decimal places. For example, if there's a column primarily made up of one- and two-digit integers but also one cell containing a number to three decimals of precision, Airtable will set that number field to three decimals of precision. (You can always change the precision later.)

### Currency

Of all the numbers in the world's spreadsheets, currency is probably the most prevalent type of number. Similar to how Airtable decides if a column is a number column, Airtable has rules when evaluating whether a column in your spreadsheet might be a currency column. Again, a column can't have mixed data types; otherwise, it will be regarded as a text field.

If a column contains numbers prefixed with the dollar sign, Airtable may read the column as a currency field. It's also important to note that Airtable only recognizes the dollar symbol when importing a column of currency data. If you use a currency other than US dollars, such as the euro, yen, or Mexican peso, that will be formatted as a text field.

If Airtable imports your data as dollars because you have a dollar symbol in front of the numbers, you can change the currency symbol to euros, yen, or anything else later. If you're dealing with currencies other than the dollar, the quickest workaround is to import these columns as a text field, which Airtable will probably do as a default, then change the field type to a currency field. And finally, you can change the currency symbol to whatever the currency symbol is for that column within the field customization menu, as can be seen in Figure 5-6.

*Figure 5-6. Changing currency symbol from $ to another currency.*

## Dates

Dates are another type of formatted data that's common in the average spreadsheet. Airtable is flexible with parsing many different ways a date might appear in a spreadsheet. (For example, whether a date is formatted with the year at the beginning or the end, Airtable can classify that column as a Date field.)

The rule for numerical and currency columns—that different types of data in a column will default to making that column a text field—also holds true for spreadsheet columns of dates. If even one of the cells in that column has a stray type of data, it won't be picked up by Airtable as a date, and Airtable will import it as a text field.

The Date field type in Airtable can hold the day, month, year, and time. Displaying the time is optional, but it's important to know this is the only way to capture time data in Airtable. The Duration field looks similar to time measurement, but that field is a way of capturing an *amount* of time, not a place in time.

If we have a spreadsheet column listing when each episode of *The Simpsons* first aired, Duration is not a proper way to use the Airtable Date field. The best solution here would be to put that data as a string in a text field.

## Outliers When Importing Spreadsheet Data

As we've seen, Airtable has well-defined rules about assigning field types to imported spreadsheet data. There are some additional common kinds of data Airtable can parse into distinct field types that may be classified on import. For example, Airtable can column data as being Boolean, either true or false, which it can convert to a checkbox field type.

### Checkbox

Depending on the flexibility of the platform you're using to export your data or your ability to manipulate it before importing it, Airtable can convert a spreadsheet column into a checkbox field. If you have a column in your spreadsheet with a pair of Boolean values that aren't on Airtable's list, you might consider converting those so Airtable will recognize and immediately import that column as a checkbox field. Here's a list of exactly what pairs of characters Airtable will recognize as these Boolean, true-or-false data types:

- checked/unchecked
- x
- yes/no
- y/n
- 1 checked out of 1/0 checked out of 1
- [x]/[ ]
- ☑

- ☑
- ✓
- ✔
- enabled/disabled
- on/off
- done

Notice that simple 1 or 0 is not in the list.

### Multiple select field

If we have a column that's holding one or more distinct values, separated by commas, Airtable can read that data as a Multiple select field. It is easier to import that type of column as a Multiple select field from the start since it can be cumbersome to convert a text column to a Multiple select field inside of Airtable without getting messy.

You'll need a column in your spreadsheet with values inside of it, separated by commas. Beyond the commas, a spreadsheet column must follow a handful of rules for Airtable to recognize it as a Multiple select field. The rules can seem tedious at first, but they are logical and not hard to understand.

First, you can't have the same value twice within a single cell. Second, the comma is the only punctuation marks allowed in a column that will be converted to a Multiple select field in Airtable; no periods, quotation marks, or any other punctuation are allowed. Each item can have a maximum of 20 characters, including whitespace if the phrase has more than one word. If there are two commas in a row, which is an empty value, Airtable will kick this data out and turn the column into a text field. Lastly, if any of the items separated by commas within a cell are only comprised of numbers, Airtable will also default to a text field and not create a Multiple select field for that column.

## Beware of spreadsheet formulas

Here's a final rule to be aware of as you're importing data from an Excel or Google Sheets file into Airtable. For any columns with cell values calculated by a formula, Airtable will only import the calculated data, not any data about the spreadsheet formulas. (As you'll see in Chapter 8, and not surprisingly, the syntax of Airtable formulas and spreadsheet formulas is different.)

So Airtable will only import the calculated values for any cell in a spreadsheet. This naturally raises a larger question about what kinds of data from spreadsheets make sense to move into Airtable. One way to frame this issue is to think about spreadsheets being your purpose-built tool for more complex financial calculations and Airtable as your tool to organize different things linked by relationships.

# Sync

A one-time import of a spreadsheet brings data into our base. But every time data from that source changes, we'll have to go through the steps to import that data again. And, of course, that's a manual process that requires we monitor the changes and import them ourselves.

Airtable Sync lets us keep data updated from both other Airtable bases and third-party applications. Sync is a one-way update, whether the source is another Airtable base or a third-party application with a Sync integration, such as GitHub or Google Calendar. The terms used with Sync are "sources" and "destinations." We consume data in the destination base, but we can't change it there.

What you can do with Sync is very dependent on your pricing plan. (As a reminder, a pricing plan applies to a workspace and whatever bases and users are in that workspace.)

There's no Sync functionality on the Free plan. The Team plan allows for 10 synced tables per base via the "standard" sync integrations, including Google Drive, Box, Miro, and GitHub.

As you move up to the Business plan, you gain two-way sync, multisource sync, and the ability to sync with "premium" third-party apps like Jira Cloud, Salesforce, Tableau, and Google Calendar.

Let's start by syncing from one Airtable view to another table. The starting point for syncing data from an Airtable view is to activate sharing. To create that Airtable source, we need to click the "Share view" button along the same row as grouping, filtering, and other controls. Once we click "Share view" and "Create a shareable grid view link," we have five options. This automatically generates a URL for that view and Airtable defaults to toggling on "Allow viewers to copy data out of this view," as seen in Figure 5-7.

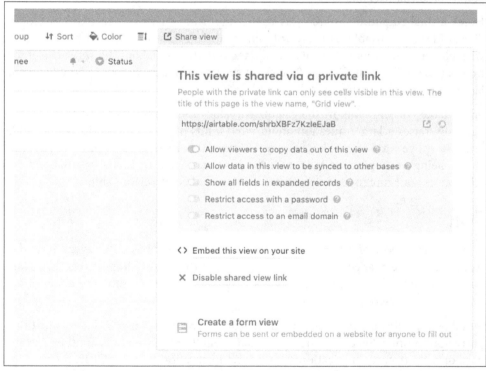

*Figure 5-7. Creating a URL to share data from a view.*

The next option is "Allow data in this view to be synced to other bases." Toggling this option on is the first step to authorizing a sync sourced from this view.

 If clicking a couple of buttons and generating a URL that potentially exposes your data to anyone on the web gives you heartburn, you're not alone. We'll return to the other three options in this menu, which provide ways to control who can access your data directly from that view's autogenerated URL (or Airtable Sync).

## Syncing an Airtable View

Now that we've allowed data in our source view to be synced to other bases, we can automatically draw that data into another table in our account. When we click "Add or import" next to the rightmost table in our base, as seen in Figure 5-8, this opens a menu with options to import or sync data into that table.

*Figure 5-8. Syncing data from another Airtable view.*

The first sync option is Airtable. There are two options for syncing from an Airtable view, as seen in Figure 5-9. We can specify the base, the table, and the view, which applies to any shared views across our workspaces in our account. (Although we can choose any base and table in our account, we can't sync the view unless we specifically authorize it via "Share view" as we just did.) The other option is to paste in an Airtable URL created with "Share view."

*Figure 5-9. Option to select a base in our account with a shared view or enter a URL of a shared view from any workspace.*

Let's sync from the view we just enabled for sharing by selecting the base, the table, and the view. We move to the next dialog by clicking "Next" and have the option of which fields to sync. The default is to sync all the fields (and future fields) from the source, which in this case is our Airtable shared view. The benefit here is that any additional fields created that are visible in that view will automatically sync to this destination table we're setting up. However, if we only want a handful of fields and are comfortable that we may miss out on newly created fields, we can choose to specify which fields to sync.

After deciding whether to import some or all fields, the final dialog gives us a couple more important options. The first is to choose whether we want to automatically sync changes from the source view regularly, as seen in Figure 5-10.

For instance, let's assume you want to control when new records and possibly fields from the source view are synced. In that case, you could choose to only manually sync changes. The other important decision to make is whether you want to have records deleted from the source also be deleted from this destination view. The default is that records deleted from the source view are also deleted from your destination. Again, there may be a reason to switch from the default to leaving orphaned records in your destination view.

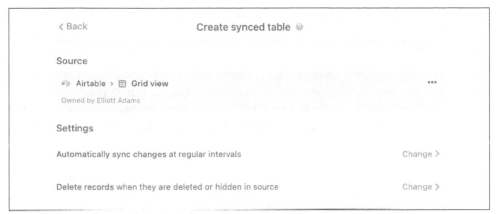

*Figure 5-10. Option to automatically sync or manually sync records.*

Finally, click the "Create table" button, and you should see all of the data from our source. The name of this synced table will be the name of the view that is synced from the origin. (You can always change the name of the destination table after the sync is created.)

The way to identify the synced fields is by the small lightning bolt icons that are next to each field's name, as seen in Figure 5-11.

| | A↓ Episode | ◎↓ Season | A↓ Episode (of season) | ⏛↓ Airdate |
|---|---|---|---|---|
| 1 | Simpsons Roasting on an ... | | 1 | 12/17/1989 |
| 2 | Bart the Genius | | 2 | 1/14/1990 |
| 3 | Homer's Odyssey | | 3 | 1/21/1990 |
| 4 | There's No Disgrace Like ... | | 4 | 1/28/1990 |
| 5 | Bart the General | | 5 | 2/4/1990 |

*Figure 5-11. Synced tables and fields identified by the small lightning bolt icon.*

## Trade-offs when syncing

Earlier in this chapter, when importing spreadsheets, some columns were cleanly translated to field types in Airtable, and some edge cases weren't quite as neat. Similarly, there are some trade-offs when syncing an Airtable view to another table.

The fields in a source view that are synced will usually sync to the destination, as you might expect. A text field in the source is also a text field in the destination, and a Single select field in the source is the same in the destination, for example. However, you may recall from importing a spreadsheet that it was only possible to bring in the values calculated from a spreadsheet formula. It was not possible to reference the formula that calculated the values in the same way. Computed fields, such as Airtable formulas, only sync the values, not the formula that created the values in that field.

Other fields are explicitly linked to data in the context of a larger base. For example, when we're syncing a view containing a User field, the context for those collaborators is at the base level, not the table level. So Airtable can sync the data, but the collaborator names that show up in the destination table are text. (The same is true for linked records.)

If the source view uses a filter to exclude records, that will be reflected in the destination. And if the source view hides or reveals fields over time, the destination view will reflect that, too. However, the way records are sorted in the original Source table can differ from the destination table. You can sort and group them however you want once the sync has happened.

### Syncing from another source

Now, let's create a new sync with a source outside of Airtable. We could sync from Jira, GitHub, Zendesk, or others, but we're going to sync from a folder in Google Drive. The folder has a contract for each show performed during the summer tour in our initial table of this base. By adding a synced table with links to each contract, we can quickly open any contract and refer to the terms as we begin negotiating for the tour we're planning.

To start, we again click "Add or import" and then choose to sync data from Google Drive. Next, Airtable will ask us to either use a Google Drive account we've already connected to or connect a new drive account, as shown in Figure 5-12. We then choose the root folder for the data we want to sync to this new table. Finally, in this dialog, we have an option to sync our folders. The folder we are syncing has contract documents; but if we opted to sync folders, we could see similar metadata about folders that might be within the root folder we've chosen.

*Figure 5-12. Choosing an account for a third-party sync.*

Just as when we synced an Airtable view to this base, we can choose to sync either all of the fields or just specific fields. We will sync all the fields, but we also want to ensure we choose the right piece of data to store in our primary field. By clicking "Advanced," as shown in Figure 5-13, we can opt to make the file name the primary field instead of the default. (In Airtable, the default is to make the file path the primary field.) It seems more intuitive to refer to the file's name, so we'll go with that choice.

< Back                Select fields to sync  ❷

Select fields to sync

● All fields in the source and fields added in the future

○ Specific fields in the source...

▾ ADVANCED

Which field should be used as the primary field?   A Name                    ▾

                                                   Find an option

                                                   A File Path

                                                   A Name

                                                   📅 Created

*Figure 5-13. Choosing a field to be the primary field in a synced table.*

We again have the choice to automatically sync records when they are changed, which we will. Plus, we can choose whether to delete records when they are deleted in the source. In this case, we'll opt to "Leave records in this table" to ensure we at least have a list of all the contracts from the first tour.

Then we click the "Create table" button to generate our new synced table with a record for each Google Drive file in our contracts folder. Airtable has used the folder's name, "Summer tour docs," as the table's name and placed a small "Drive" icon next to that name, as shown in Figure 5-14. (If your connection to a third-party source is lost, a hazard sign will be next to the table name to warn you to reconnect the sync.)

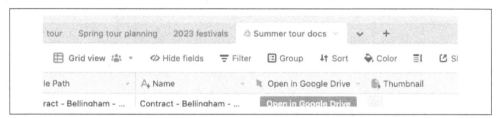

*Figure 5-14. Google Drive icon next to the name of the synced table of Google Drive data.*

This initial Grid view has some fields we may not need. However, a handful of fields are unique when syncing from Google Drive, and we should stay in this view. Of course, we have the primary field we designated as the file's name.

We won't hide the Button field in this view that Airtable created to open the document directly in Google. A document thumbnail might be helpful, so we'll leave that for tracking. We also want to show a few metadata fields from Google Drive, as shown in Figure 5-15, including "Last viewed by me," "Last modified," and "Last modified by." These fields can help us track when our teammates make notes or changes to the contracts.

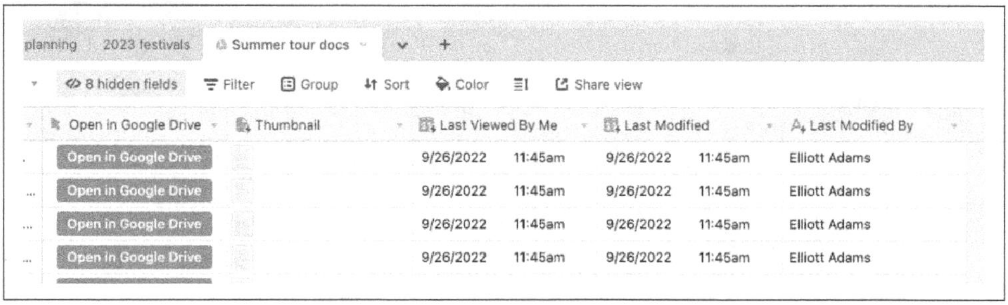

*Figure 5-15. Hiding unnecessary metadata fields for the records in a synced table.*

With any third-party sync, the source will have fields unique to that application. You likely don't need to access all fields from the application you're syncing, but unneeded fields can be hidden in a view, like when you've created a table from scratch.

# Multisource Sync

Your team, and perhaps your larger organization, will inevitably have different Airtable bases for different parts of your work. You might have one team working on scoping new projects and another that's dedicated to managing projects, perhaps syncing a single view from one team's base to another. As we just saw, syncing a single view to a destination can give a window into data living in a different base. However, a multisource sync within the same table allows us to combine data from up to three sources, including Airtable or third-party applications.

## Setting up multisource sync

The first step to building a multisource sync table is to build a single-source sync. As we saw previously, we can choose from Airtable or any number of other app integrations to pull fields into our synced table. Now that we have this synced table, we repeat a similar workflow to add additional data sources.

## Manage fields in multisource syncing

When using Airtable Sync with just one source, we can choose the fields we want to sync into our new synced table. As we add another source to that same table, we have more options, and things can get more complex. When syncing more than one source, we have a critical decision for each field in every source. After the first source, we must decide whether to use an existing field from that original primary source or create a new one for each field in every additional source.

There is a critical decision for every field in every new source we add to a synced table: we first need to decide if we want to sync it. (This is a decision that must be made even when syncing just one source.) Then there's a second decision with two paths.

First, we can merge a new field with an existing one in the synced table. This option should happen when two or more sources have a field representing the same data.

Second, we could create a new field for any of the fields from this new source. These fields might offer critical attributes about records from the new synced source. But in this new field, only records from this particular source will have a value unless we add yet another source and potentially merge one of its fields with this new field we've just created.

Combining fields from different sources and creating new fields both have benefits. If we have a table of synced data that includes a Date field, we might like to sync another table with a Date field representing the same type of deadline. We might want the data from the records in those two tables to share that same field. On the other hand, there are plenty of cases where multiple sources synced to one table have data fields that wouldn't make sense to be put together, and each should be in its own field.

## Manage and enhance multisource synced tables

Airtable automatically creates a Sync Source field after syncing a new source to an existing table. This field is looks like a Single select field, but it's a special field type of its own that's not editable. Airtable automatically adds a designated source for each record, as seen in Figure 5-16.

The field could contain the name of a view if the information is coming from an Airtable base or the project is from a third-party source. For example, if we import a list of files from a Google Drive folder as a Sync Source, Airtable will create a new value in that Sync Source field named after the folder from which we're listing the files.

It's important to remember that in addition to these synced fields from sources, we can still do most of the things we might normally do in a table. For example, we can create different views to organize and filter records and create new fields. These newly created fields in a destination table can hold a value for every record in a table, regardless of its source.

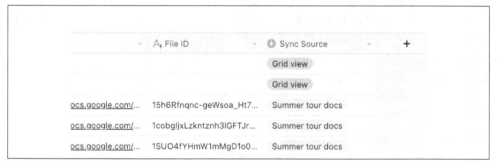

*Figure 5-16. A Sync Source field created by a multisource sync.*

While you might expect this field to be essentially locked since the value is unchanging, be cautious about accidentally breaking this field. You can't change values in a Sync Source field, but you can change the field type, turn the data into text, or erase it completely.

Syncing from a single source or multiple sources of data unlocks an Easter egg of an option for the Button field. When creating a button, as seen in Figure 5-17, you'll see a new option, "Open source record." If you're syncing data from another base, this option will open a new tab and take you to that record in the base, where you can view the record in the expanded view. If you're syncing from another source, such as GitHub or Google Drive, clicking the button should open a new tab and take you directly to that document or part of the application reference in the record.

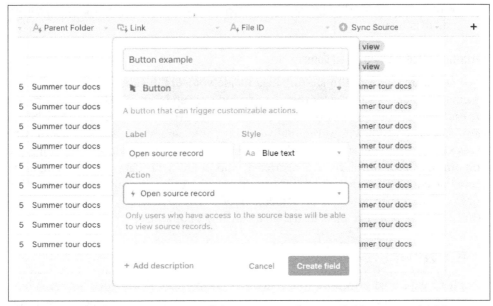

*Figure 5-17. The "Open source record" button example is available in synced tables.*

## Security When Syncing

Airtable makes it easy to take a view in your base and quickly display it publicly, allowing anyone to see the data for some use cases. That option can be a blessing, but it's understandably terrifying for most organizations in many other ways. Let's discuss the different options to rein in the risk of exposing data unintentionally.

If you click the "Share view" button in the controls section, the first of five toggles is activated, "Allow viewers to copy data out of this view." Once this option is activated, we have a unique URL that can be visited to view the data in that shared view. We can also use this URL to sync this view to another table, as long as the second toggle is turned on: "Allow data in this view to be synced to other bases."

If someone opens that URL and the third toggle, "Show all fields and expanded records," is not turned on, they are limited by what is visible in the shared view. However, if the toggle is switched on, anyone can pull up that URL and access all of the fields, not just the ones visible in the view. The final two toggles in this menu are the most powerful for security.

### Securing shared data with a password

Switching on the fourth toggle in the Share view, "Restrict access with the password," puts one layer of authorization between the world and your data. Adding the password to a view after it's already been synced to another table will break the sync. Furthermore, you'll need to go back and enter the password to grant permission for that sync to continue.

### Securing shared data via email domain

If you're more interested in sharing data inside your organization, restricting access by email domain is much smoother than trying to keep track of a different password for each shared view in your bases. The URL we created when we first clicked "Share view" is still accessible. However, that view-only, autogenerated page can now only be accessed by users who are logged into Airtable with an email address matching the domain specified. Similarly, we restricted who could sync data from that table to users logged in under that email domain. It's worth noting, however, that this option doesn't restrict who else can be a member of a base that's the destination for this synced data, even if sharing is restricted by an email domain.

## Form View

Chapter 2 explained how a Button field differs from other fields since it doesn't hold data. The Form view is similarly unique among views. Instead of a unique visual way to organize and understand your data, it's a conduit to get structured data into your base through a simple web form.

Many tried-and-true form solutions, such as Jotform and Typeform, have dedicated functionality to send data to Airtable. Still, the obvious advantage of the Form view is that it's already included in the platform and doesn't need to be connected to a third-party form service. While the Form view is relatively spartan and doesn't have every bell and whistle of a dedicated form builder platform like Jotform, it does have many of the basics you need.

Whether you're gathering customer feedback, taking a survey, registering participants for an event, or doing anything else that needs to gather data from outside parties, Airtable's Form view covers the basics. It has the option to attach files, it's mobile-friendly, and the fields in your table are already immediately at your disposal in your form. We can learn about these features by walking through how we set up a form in Airtable.

## Setting Up a Form

Let's return to our tour tracker base to create our first form. In the "Spring tour planning" table, we've begun compiling a list of tasks we need to complete as we prep for our larger tour. Between the band members and management, we have many things to consider while prepping, so let's create a form where anyone can add a new task to be completed.

Since "Form" is a view, we can open the sidebar we used in Chapter 4 to create a view and click Form view. Airtable creates the form and defaults to including all of our fields. As shown in Figure 5-18, you can either drag fields in the sidebar there to hide them or create new fields in your table directly in that sidebar.

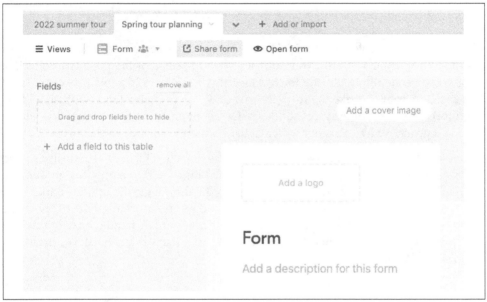

*Figure 5-18. Setting up a form.*

Now, let's start to customize our form. We can change the title from the generic "Form" and add a description below. As we can see in Figure 5-19, we've changed the form's title, added a description, and added a background image. We might add a logo to brand our form if we plan to use it for people outside our organization.

*Figure 5-19. Changing the background image and title of a form.*

Now that we've completed the initial form setup, we can begin to customize the fields visible to our team. Typically, you don't want to expose all of the potential fields in a table to someone filling out the form, especially if the form is publicly accessible. In our case, we want to make the form as brief and easy to understand as possible. Furthermore, there are some aspects of the tasks we are planning for that we'll decide on later as a group. So let's consider which fields we want to include in the form.

Airtable titles each question as the field name by default. This isn't as intuitive to end users as it could be. So, for the first field called "Tasks," let's rename this question to "What's a task we need to add to our list?" We can also toggle the option to make the question required, as shown in Figure 5-20. If we wanted to change the order of the questions, we could also use the grab handle in the upper left-hand corner of this dialog box. (For all required questions in a form, we'll see a red asterisk on the right-hand side of the question.)

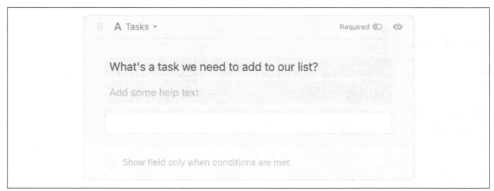

*Figure 5-20. Changing a field title in a form to a question.*

Airtable puts all the input fields into our form by default. Let's trim those down. The next field is "Task group," and whoever fills out the form from our team probably has a good sense of what kind of task they're proposing. Let's keep this one and make it a required question.

Although the person who fills out our form may not be the best judge of this task's importance, let's leave in the "Importance" field for now. This is a Single select field, as shown in Figure 5-21, and we can customize how this question is presented. It can be shown as either a drop-down menu or a list of options with a radio button. Additionally, we could choose to limit a user's options in this Single select field.

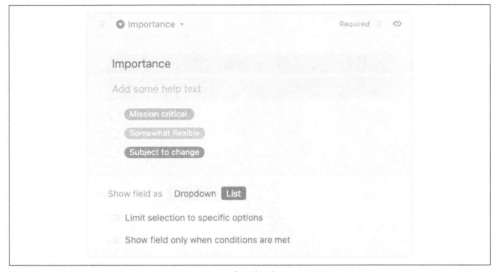

*Figure 5-21. Presenting options as a set of radio buttons.*

Our "Status" field won't be helpful here since these new tasks haven't been started yet, so let's remove it. And while we gave the form's users the option to estimate how important a task is, we will want to decide as a group exactly when we start a task and when our deadline is. Let's also remove those two fields. It would be helpful for the user of this form to estimate how long a task might take, so let's leave in the "Hours to complete" field.

Now we have the basics of our form completed! As shown in Figure 5-22, we've whittled our form down to just four questions. We've also moved unnecessary fields to the left-hand sidebar, which removes them from our form.

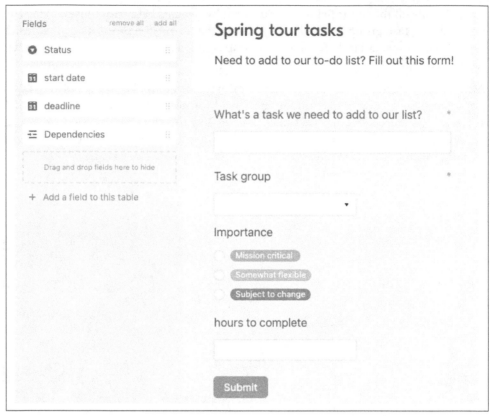

*Figure 5-22. Unnecessary fields moved out of the survey form to the left-hand side.*

Below the Submit button in the form builder in our table, there are several options for what happens after the form is submitted. We can show the Airtable logo afterward, and we can choose whether or not Airtable will send an email to our Airtable account email address each time the form is submitted. You can take two steps to dictate what the user sees after submitting the form. The first option is to toggle "Redirect to URL after the form is submitted," which can send the user to your website or a landing page you created especially for this form.

If you don't toggle the option to redirect to another site after the form is submitted, Airtable offers several options, as shown in Figure 5-23. You can customize the message, too. We've changed our message to "Thanks for sharing this task for our tour!" We can also add a button that the user can click to submit another response, and we can toggle the option for Airtable to present a new blank form if the user stays on the page for more than five seconds. Let's toggle on both of these options.

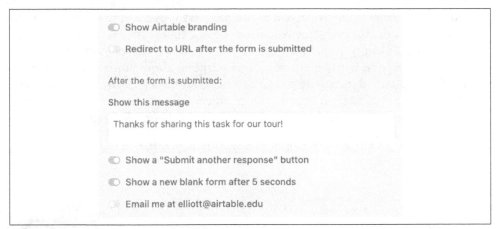

*Figure 5-23. Adding a completion message and option to offer another form.*

Now that we've set up our first form, let's put in some controls on who can access it.

## Managing Form Access

Forms are the most accessible way for other people to add information to your base, but this can also make them vulnerable to abuse. Airtable has methods to control who can access your forms. The "Share form" button in the taskbar, as seen in Figure 5-24, offers three options to toggle on or off. We can restrict the form's password, allow people only with a certain email domain to access it, or turn the form off altogether.

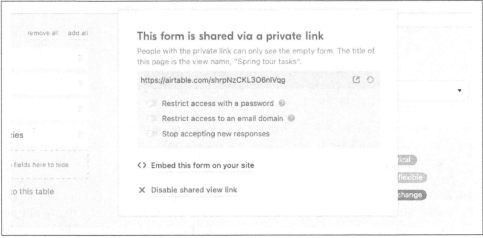

*Figure 5-24. Restricting form access with the "Share" dialog.*

The most secure way to control access to our form is to restrict it to users with a certain email domain. However, this requires everyone filling out the form to have an Airtable account to authenticate their email. This can be a great solution for organizations where everyone is using Airtable. The purpose of our form is to let anyone involved in the tour contribute to the task list without having to already be an Airtable user. So instead of restricting access by email domain, let's put a simple password on the form. As shown in Figure 5-25, we simply toggle on "Restrict access with a password" and enter a string of characters.

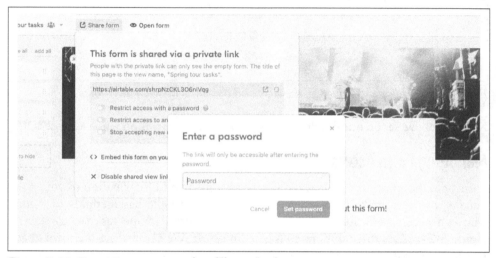

*Figure 5-25. Requiring a password to fill out the form.*

Our third toggle option allows us to pause accepting new submissions. We can simply turn this toggle off if we change our minds later.

Now that we have created a form and explored options to secure it, let's dive into more advanced options for our forms.

## Conditional Form Fields

Airtable forms can show or hide form fields based on a user's answers in a previous field. These conditional fields are hidden from users unless their answer to the previous question triggers the conditional field to be visible. We can set up a logic to trigger these conditional form fields using filtering, which we covered in Chapter 4. Let's look at an example of how we can implement a conditional form field in our "Spring tour tasks" form. Of the fields in this form, we care less about the user filling out the "Hours to complete" field, unless the task is marked as "Mission critical." So let's make the "Hours to complete" field conditional, based on what the user marks under the "Importance" field.

In our form builder, we can click the field we want to make conditional, which brings up a very familiar dialog: the condition groups of filtering from views in Chapter 4. After we toggle on "Show field only when conditions are met," we will set the field to "Importance," choose the operator "Is," and choose for the value the Single select option "Mission critical," as seen in Figure 5-26.

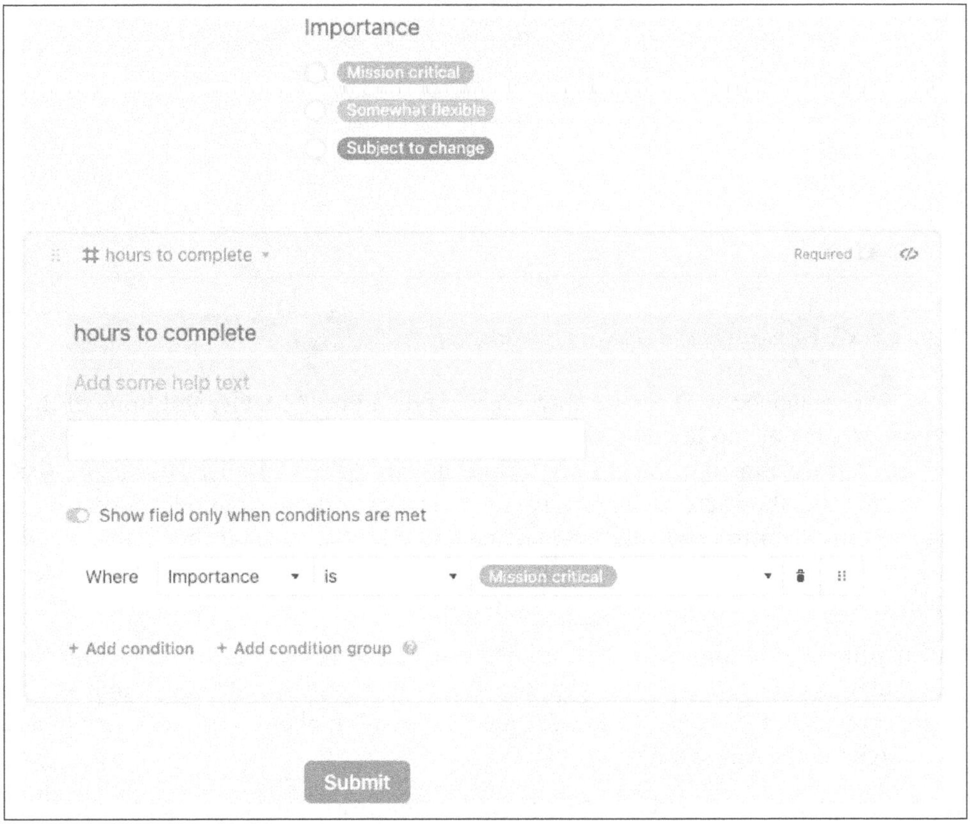

*Figure 5-26. Making a form field conditional on the previous response in the form.*

We can open our form to try this out. Under the Importance field, if we choose "Somewhat flexible," then importance is the last question on the form. However, if we select "Mission critical," the "Hours to complete" form appears. (Note: Because we have made this conditional form field reliant on the Importance field, Airtable now presents the option for the user to "Clear selection," as we can see in Figure 5-27.)

Conditional form fields have the same complexity as filtering in views, so we can add multiple conditions, nested conditions, and condition groups.

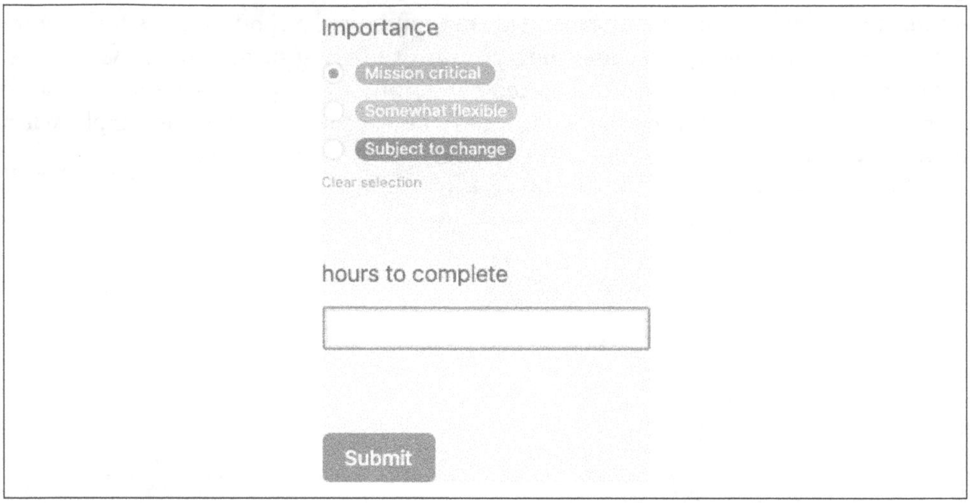

*Figure 5-27. Form users can clear a previous response.*

Now we're equipped with several ways to bring data into Airtable, and none of these require writing or modifying code. Whether you are interested in the no-code capabilities of the platform or have a nontechnical teammate who might use them, tools like forms, and the ability to import live or static data without code, allow everyone in your organization to create and connect data in Airtable. Later in this book, we will look at other no-code solutions, such as the Automations component of Airtable in Chapter 11.

But if you are a developer or at least have some basic knowledge of JavaScript, then this unlocks even more power with the ability to create Airtable apps and scripts inside your bases. Chapter 13 is dedicated to learning about apps and scripts and working with the Airtable API.

In this chapter, we explored how to import data into Airtable from spreadsheets, CSV files, and other sources. We learned how to handle different field types when importing data and how to leverage the power of Airtable Sync to keep our data up to date. We also delved into the Form view, which allows us to collect data from external sources easily.

Now that we have a solid foundation in importing data, the next chapter will dive into the various views available in Airtable. In the next chapter, we will go beyond the Grid view from Chapter 4 to explore the other views available in Airtable, such as Gallery, Kanban, List, Calendar, and Gantt. These views offer different ways to visualize and interact with your data.

# CHAPTER 6

# View Types

Views are like different lenses through which we can visualize our data in unique ways, allowing us to gain insights and make informed decisions. In Chapter 4, we learned that views are an essential piece of what makes Airtable such an effective collaboration platform. Compared to a basic spreadsheet with just a single snapshot of the data, Airtable provides us with multiple views that give us (and our team) a more dynamic and versatile way of understanding our data.

In Chapter 4, we focused on the Grid view, which is the default view when creating a new Airtable base. We learned that the Grid view is where we lay the groundwork for configuring our base, setting up and customizing fields, and entering data. We also explored the different configuration options available in the Grid view, such as filtering, sorting, hiding fields, changing row height, and utilizing the summary bar.

Building upon our experience with the Grid view, we'll now delve into the other Airtable view types. We will explore the List view, which offers a simplified and efficient way of working with data in a spreadsheet-like format. The Calendar view allows us to visualize our data over time, while the Gallery and Kanban views will provide more visual representations of our records. Additionally, we will dive into the Timeline view, which allows us to plan and track projects with ease, and the Gantt view, which provides a comprehensive visual timeline for project management.

By understanding the principles and functionalities of each view, we will be able to harness views as a powerful tool for organizing, analyzing, and collaborating on our data.

# Visually Organizing with Cards: Gallery and Kanban Views

If you are working on a project in Airtable with records that include images in an attachment field, the Gallery and Kanban views are excellent ways to highlight those images within your workflow.

## Gallery View

The Gallery view puts records on a card with an image from one of your fields. You can still apply filters on the records within the view, as well as sort and color records. In the Grid view, hiding or displaying fields is under the Hide fields menu, which is called "Customize cards" in the Gallery view.

As you can see in Figure 6-1, the Customize cards menu has one difference from other Airtable menus. Specifically, we can choose any Attachment field in our base to be on the top of each card. If we choose the Crop option, Airtable will fill the space at the top of the card with the image. But if we choose the Fit option, it will show the entire image. If you choose the Fit option, you will probably have some whitespace on either the sides or the top and bottom.

*Figure 6-1. Containing the entire attachment image in the gallery view with the Fit option.*

Let's walk through creating a new Gallery view. In our "2022 Summer tour" table, we can open the Views sidebar and click the + sign next to "Gallery" under the "Create..." set of options at the bottom of the sidebar. Let's change the name of our new view from the default name of "Gallery" to "Venue images" and create the view.

While we're in this new view, we can customize which fields we want to see. Since we already have the city and date in the card's title itself, which is the name of our record, let's remove the City and Date fields. Since our record name is too long to fit on a card, let's choose to show the venue name below the image. Let's also choose to toggle on the Capacity field.

If we want to see Gallery cards of performances not in California, we simply set up a filter, as shown in Figure 6-2, which has the field "State" and the operator "Is none of." For the value, we can choose to exclude California. The cards were already sorted by date in the Grid view, and they show up here that same way. Instead, let's sort them by their capacity. Once we click "Sort" in the toolbar, we choose "Capacity," and sort from high to low by clicking the "9-1" button.

*Figure 6-2. Using a filter to limit what records are shown in the Gallery view.*

## Kanban View

Kanban-type systems are helpful to obtain a visual idea of the progress of any project you might be tracking. The columns in a Kanban are used in all kinds of engineering projects, including software development, to track the stages of an issue or enhancement. Airtable's Kanban view clusters records into columns based on each record's value in a Single select field or a User field. (So if you don't have a Single select field or collaborator field in the table where you're creating a Kanban view, Airtable will prompt you to create one.)

One key advantage of using the Kanban view is that dragging a record from one stack to another changes the value of the Single select field you've chosen, as shown in Figure 6-3.

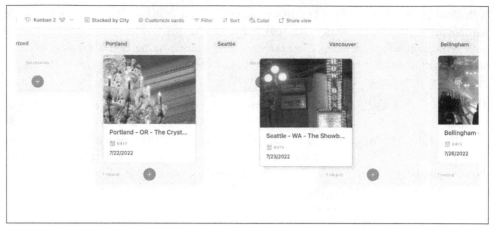

*Figure 6-3. Records in the Kanban view can be dragged horizontally to change the Single select field value that organizes the Kanban.*

Let's create a new Kanban view and title it "Contract tracking."

After creating the view, Airtable presents a choice of fields for grouping records in this Kanban view. Since this will be our place to reference the status of the contracts for the tour, we'll use the "Contract status" Single select field. Next, Airtable creates a column for each option in the Single select field, ordered by how they appear in the field customization menu (as we saw earlier, when we sorted the *Simpsons* seasons that are in a Single select field).

Any records in the view that don't have a value for the field you're grouping by will automatically go into the "Uncategorized" column. It may not be helpful to see these cards, and you can click the arrows in the bottom right corner of a column to collapse it.

If you scroll to the right edge of the view, you'll see a final column titled "New stack." Clicking this button creates a new column, and a new option for the field, which you can drag records to in a Kanban view. Keep in mind that this creates either a new option in a Single select field or a new collaborator, depending on which of those two field types you are using to organize the Kanban view.

Let's wrap this up by choosing a customization for the view. We can filter the records, sort them, color them, and customize the fields. For this Kanban view, which is tracking the status of each performance contract, it can display an image. But instead, as shown in Figure 6-4, let's just add the venue phone number to each card in the view to have those numbers handy, as we might need to call the venue. Now anyone who is a collaborator in this base can pull up this Contract tracking view to see the status of each contract, although they can't modify the view because it's set as a Personal view.

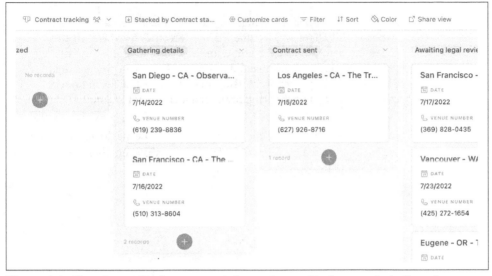

*Figure 6-4. Choosing to display contact information on Kanban cards, in lieu of an image.*

# Visually Organizing Using Dates: Calendar, Timeline, and Gantt Views

Working with information about dates and times when creating software can be challenging. Calculations often involve intricate logic and considerations such as leap years, daylight saving time adjustments, and different calendar systems. It's easy to introduce errors and miscalculations.

The three views that are based on dates (Calendar, Timeline, and Gantt) are examples of how Airtable makes creating and customizing accessible to nondevelopers by abstracting away the underlying complexity. (Later, we'll look at how to format and modify dates in your records by writing code.)

## Calendar View

Like any software that handles the complexities of dates and times, Airtable's Calendar view has a lot of power. Let's create a new Calendar view that plots the shows on our summer tour and title it "Shows."

Similar to the Kanban view, once we create the view, Airtable prompts us to specify a field that will be the basis of the view. For the Kanban view, we could sort only by a single field, either a Single select field or a Collaborator field. For a Calendar view, we must have at least one date field, but we can also use more than one field to build out a more complex view.

 As a reminder, when we change the value of a record in any view in Airtable, this changes the value for the record everywhere. In the Calendar view, we have the ability to drag records around the calendar, and this changes that value for the Date field we're using. (This applies only when we're using an editable Date field and not a calculated date value that's the result of a formula, for example.)

Our summer tour table only has the Date field to specify the performance dates, so we'll use that. In Figure 6-5, we can see that Airtable has placed these records with their respective dates using the name of the record.

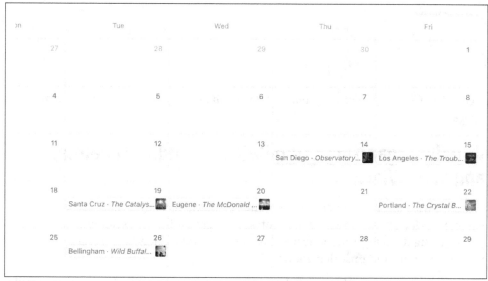

*Figure 6-5. Choosing a field to map records onto the Calendar view.*

If we click a record, such as "Bellingham - WA - Wild Buffalo House," we see a small pop-up with the name of the record and the date, as shown in Figure 6-6. Similar to "Hide fields" and "Customize cards," the Calendar view can hide and show fields using an option called "Customize labels." When we click on a record in the Calendar view, the fields that appear in the pop-up are hidden and shown via the "Customize labels" button.

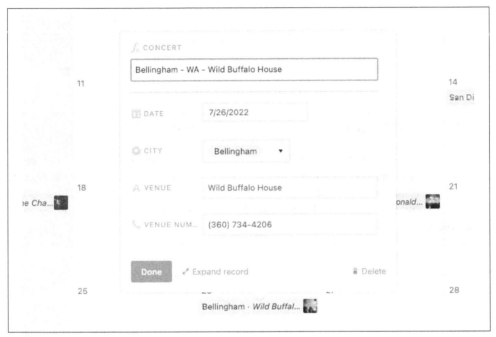

*Figure 6-6. Viewing the details of a record in the Calendar view.*

Let's customize this view. Instead of using the concatenated record name, let's instead just use the city, venue, and the venue's phone number. The Calendar view allows some simple text formatting, as well. As shown in Figure 6-7, we can put that phone number in bold and apply the name of our lodging for the night. (It's easiest to see this formatting in the three-day and one-day views.) We can also add an image to each calendar event, so we will toggle on the picture of the venue we used in the Gallery view.

*Figure 6-7. Customizing the display of text in the calendar.*

If we click the "See records" icon in the upper right corner of the Calendar view, it expands a list of records, as shown in Figure 6-8. We can filter by (1) records that do have an entry in the Date field we're sorting by, (2) records without a date, or (3) all the records in the view. As with our other fields, we can apply filters to remove some or all records from what's visible in this view.

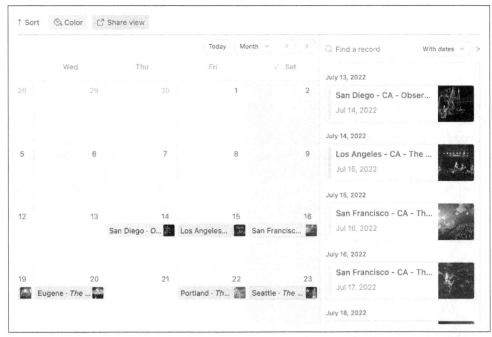

*Figure 6-8. Opening a list of records in the Calendar view and sorting by those "With dates."*

In addition to also being able to sort records in the Calendar view, we can use the Color option, which gives us two paths. We can apply the same color of the text bubble options in a Single select field for each record, or we can designate "Conditions" to determine how our records are colored. Setting up these conditions is an identical structure to filters: each has a field, an operator, and a value. Just like filters, we can add multiple conditions and even condition groups that determine the colors that apply to the records in the view.

Let's color our records on this calendar using the colors of the options in the City field. As shown in Figure 6-9, we have a unique color for all of the records, except for our two records where the performances occur in San Francisco.

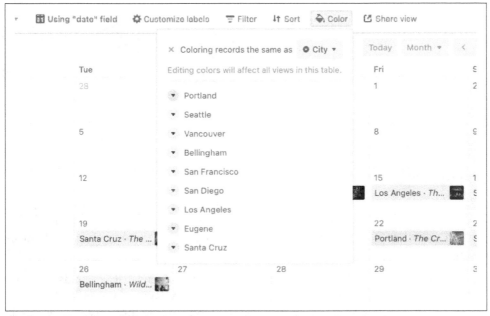

*Figure 6-9. Coloring records based on a Single select field in the calendar.*

Airtable makes it easy to share a Calendar view and in another calendar format. Once you create a Calendar view and apply any desired filtering or sorting to it, you can use "Share view" to sync it to an external calendar. (The options for sharing views are discussed in the latter half of Chapter 4.)

After opening the Share view dialog, click "Sync to an external calendar," as seen in Figure 6-10, and Airtable creates a custom link that can be pasted into an application such as Google Calendar.

The Calendar view has much more complexity than initially meets the eye. For example, we can add ending dates to records so that they span multiple days. The Calendar view also has many easy user interface controls, such as dragging records across the calendar to change the date value for that record.

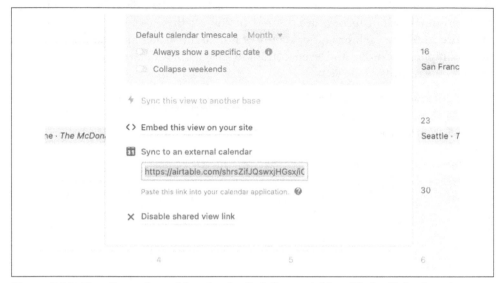

*Figure 6-10. Creating a shareable calendar link from a table with the Calendar view.*

## Timeline View

Let's add a new table that will track the major milestones for next year's spring tour. We can use it to create an example of the Timeline view. Just like the Calendar view, we can move items in the timeline view, which changes the underlying Date field we are referencing.

In the new "Spring tour planning" table, we have several Single select fields and Date fields, as seen in Figure 6-11. The primary field is the name of the task. We have a "Task group" Single select field, which specifies which of the three task buckets each milestone fits into. The "Importance" Single select field buckets each milestone into whether it is "Mission critical," "Somewhat flexible," or "Subject to change."

| | Task group | Importance | Status | start date | deadline |
|---|---|---|---|---|---|
| 5 target cit... | Booking | Mission critical | Done | 2022-09-14 | 2022-10-04 |
| rch design... | Merchandise/Posters | Somewhat flexible | In progress | 2022-09-13 | 2022-10-17 |
| | Booking | Mission critical | In progress | 2022-09-13 | 2022-10-17 |
| 'ailable dates | Booking | Mission critical | Todo | 2022-10-18 | 2022-11-08 |
| ɪn contracts | Booking | Mission critical | Todo | 2022-11-09 | 2022-11-30 |

*Figure 6-11. Tables with Date fields and Single select fields are ideal for using the Timeline view.*

The last two fields, "start date" and "deadline," are for our estimated time to begin and, hopefully, when we have each task completed. We are also using the default "Status" Single select field that Airtable puts in by default when you create a new table. Its options are "Done," "In progress," and "To do."

To create our first view of the tour, let's make a collaborative Timeline view and call it "Milestone timeline." Just like the Calendar view, Airtable prompts us to choose a Date field, so we will use our "Start date." And since this table has an end date for records, we can use our Deadline Date field to see how long we've allotted for each milestone in the timeline.

 If we drag records around on the timeline view, this changes the value of the underlying date fields. As always, changing a field value for a record in any view changes it everywhere!

In the next dialog box, Airtable asks if we want to group our records, like the grouping from the Grid view. However, as a reminder, if the field we plan to group by is all unique values, this grouping may not be useful. Since we will usually use a Single select field to categorize more than one record into a given category, we'll use our Importance field to group these records in the timeline, as seen in Figure 6-12.

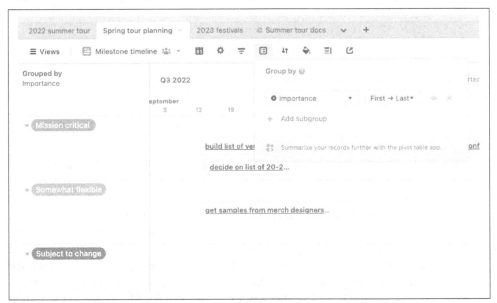

*Figure 6-12. Grouping records in the Timeline view into swimlanes via a Single select field.*

We still have our critical "Status" field that we want to make sure we can visually reference in our timeline. "Color" is ideal for providing a visual reference of where a task is in our process. Since completed tasks marked as "Done" are represented by a green option in the Single select field, activating it colors any records that have been marked as Done in green. Those tasks that are "In progress" show up on the timeline in yellow. Those still in the "To do" stage appear in the timeline as red.

Let's switch things around to see another option of how we could visualize our milestones. Let's group them by status and color them by importance. In Figure 6-13, we see columns for "To do," "In progress," and "Done." We can see that our orange, or "Mission critical," milestones are next to the blue "Somewhat flexible" milestones along the timeline. You can configure these options in several ways. Let's visualize the color of each milestone by its status to give us a sense of how we are doing overall relative to where we are today.

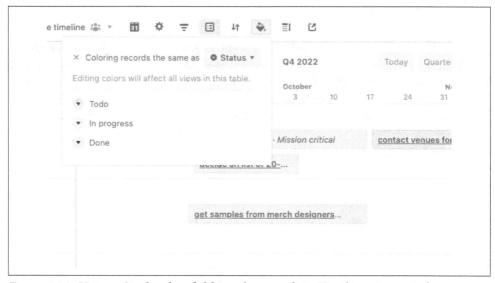

*Figure 6-13. Using a Single select field to color records in Timeline view swimlanes.*

The Calendar view offers different timescale options to look at events over a month, a week, or a day. The Timeline view is even more flexible. In the upper right corner, we can see options that span from "Day" through a "5 year" window. The Timeline view has a unique control, titled "date settings," which gives options such as displaying only work days and setting the timescale that a collaborator sees when they open the view during the same range of options from earlier (between a day and a year, but not up to 5 years). The Timeline view also has a similar right-hand sidebar as the Calendar view, which, when "See records" is clicked, pops out a list of records in the view.

You can quickly edit records in the Timeline view by double-clicking the record and clicking "Expand record" to see if you can edit any fields for that record.

To help us understand if our deadlines are reasonable, we will add an estimate of the number of hours each task might take to our new table. To measure the time we estimate it will take to complete, we could use a Duration field. However, in this case, we are using imprecise estimates. So instead we will use integers in a new Number field that tracks the number of hours we estimate for a task.

This summary bar in the Timeline view has a unique setup. In the Grid view, we can calculate a value using a summary function for each field, which appears as a column. In the Timeline view, the summary bar is still located at the bottom of our browser window. But instead of calculating a field, it's calculating a value for each unit of the (horizontal) timescale. So, for example, if we set the timescale to quarters of a year, then we only see a value calculated for each month because that's the unit of time displayed in the quarter timescale. Or as another example, if we are looking at the timeline over the two-week timescale, then the unit is days, and the bottom of the browser has a series of calculations corresponding to each day, as shown in Figure 6-14.

Under "Customize labels," we can toggle on the new "Hours to complete" field. Clicking on the summary bar allows us to choose what function we want and which field we want to calculate; we can even set a customized function name. The two-week timescale doesn't have a lot of space, as shown in Figure 6-14, so we'll choose to label it something short: "Hours." Although it's hidden, the menu has an option to color the different results in the summary bar. We can color based on mathematical operators, such as greater than or lesser than, and set up values for coloring different records.

Furthermore, we can set a simple pair of conditions to the records if the summary value is more than 40 hours or less than 40 hours. In this case, we used the Sum function to tally the hours we estimate it will take to complete the tasks at any given time. The more we zoom out, the more the summary function will measure a larger time unit. For example, Airtable denotes days in the two-week view; but in the quarter timescale, it measures months.

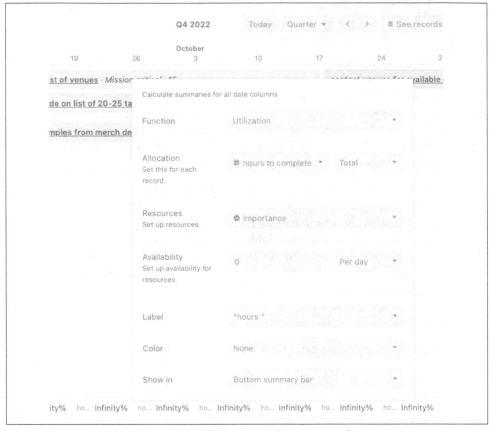

*Figure 6-14. Creating a label for a calculation in the summary bar.*

## Gantt View

At first glance, a Gantt chart looks similar to the Timeline view. However, the Gantt view is specifically intended to track a schedule of tasks or activities along with the order they're supposed to occur in and whatever dependencies may exist between tasks (represented by the linked records we looked at in Chapter 3). Let's use the same "Spring tour planning" table in our tour base to see the unique features of the Gantt view using our list of tasks in that table.

We'll create a new Gantt view and title it "Schedule of tasks." Airtable prompts us to choose a "Start date" field and an "End date" field. In this case, Airtable has taken a guess, and guessed correctly, so we'll use our Start date and Deadline fields.

Airtable then asks us to choose a "Dependencies" field, which must be a Linked record field. For now, we can create a Dependencies field for a Gantt chart to begin to understand the utility and advantages of using a Linked record field.

Since we don't already have a Linked record field, we can use as the suggested Dependencies Linked record field, let's choose the "Create a new linked record field" option. Now that we have a Dependencies field, we can choose for these dependencies to be either "Predecessors" or "Successors." For this example, let's stick with the default of Predecessors and keep "Highlight critical path" toggled on.

In the final step, Airtable asks if we would like to enable milestones, which, as we saw in the Timeline view, creates a diamond in the view if the record only has a start date. So let's enable "Use milestones." Once we do, Airtable will present us with a new option to "Convert existing one-day records to milestones." Let's also toggle that on.

Looking at our data using the "year" time span, we're able to see the events that occur from September through January (our range of dates spans a bit more than a quarter of a year). To help us visually comprehend the differences in our records, let's use some of the tools we were just using in the Timeline view. For example, under "Color," let's choose to color our records using the "Importance" Single select field. And let's group our records using the "Task group" Single select field.

Many of our tasks occurring in the first couple of months are related to booking; we can see these tasks better if we zoom in using the quarter time span. For example, we need to draw a list of concert venues, and we also should decide on a list of cities where we hope to book performances. Both of these tasks must be completed before we reach out to venues to inquire about potential performance dates.

In this case, we can use the "Dependency" feature. Hovering over our "build list of venues" record, we see a small icon in the lower right-hand side of the bar, which we can drag to the "contact venues for available dates" record. We can do the same by hovering over "decide on list of 20-25 target cities" and dragging that to the "contact venues…" record, as seen in Figure 6-15. We now have two items in our view that are predecessors to another item. This directionality is shown by the arrow pointing into the future.

*Figure 6-15. Two lines converge on the "contact venues for available dates" record.*

Now, let's go a step further. Let's hover over the "contact venues…" task and pull a line down to the "confirm dates and sign contracts" task. The arrow is there, but the line is dotted red. This dotted line represents an invalid dependency. In this case, it is invalid because the deadline for "contact venues" is after the start date for the "confirm dates" task. We can fix this invalid dependency by either changing the first task's end date or changing its successor's start date. In Figure 6-16, we zoom into the month time span to have more granularity and simply drag the "confirm dates" record until it begins just after its predecessor, "contact venues for available dates."

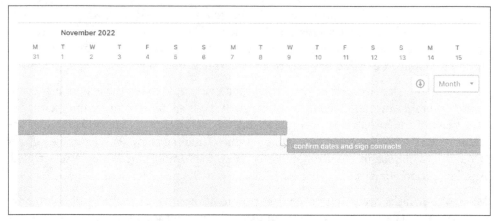

*Figure 6-16. Getting a closer look at a dependency between records in the Gantt view.*

To understand how linked records work and how they are the logic behind the predecessors and successors of dependencies in the Gantt view, let's create a new Grid view and call it "Dependency inspection."

We now have a chance to create a view that allows us to cut out unnecessary information and just reference what we want to see for this particular purpose. In "Hide fields," we can toggle off "Status start date," "Deadline," and "Hours to complete." Let's also add a simple filter that defines the condition where our Dependencies field "Is not empty." Now, as shown in Figure 6-17, we see that the two tasks with dependencies are "contact venues for available dates" and "confirm dates and sign contracts."

*Figure 6-17. Assessing which records have internal links from our Gantt view.*

The first task we see, "contact venues," has two dependencies. Those dependencies are the two tasks to the left of this record in the timeline, where we drew arrows earlier. As we can see in the Dependencies column that Airtable created for us, there are two different dependencies, the "build list of venues" and "decide on list of 20-25 target cities" fields. If you look at the next task in this view, we see something similar. The predecessor for "confirm dates and sign contracts" is "contact venues for available dates," which we also drew an arrow from earlier. So we can see that the first record, "contact venues," has two dependencies that are predecessors in this case. The second record we see listed has one dependency, "contact venues for available dates," which is a predecessor.

We usually encounter linked records that connect one record with another when those records are in different tables. A linked record referencing another record in the same table is unique and most often happens with the Gantt view. Still, we can use this case to understand that the Linked record field is a field that associates one or more other records with that record.

A similarity with the Timeline and Gantt views is events that don't have an end date are considered "Milestones" and show up on the view as a diamond instead of a rectangle spanning some amount of time.

There are also small differences in how the Gantt view operates compared to the Calendar and Timeline views. Unlike other views we've looked at, the Gantt view does not have an option to Hide fields or customize which field is visible. If we double-click directly on a record, we first have a sidebar on the left, which we can see in Figure 6-18. This sidebar gives us access to the name of the record, its start and end dates, the number of days for the length of the record, and a list of its predecessors and successors. We can edit any of these fields through this dialog, including the ability to add predecessors and successors. Clicking on the record again brings up a pop-up dialog with access to every field and an activity list.

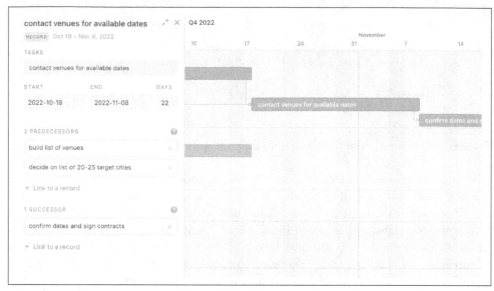

*Figure 6-18. Inspecting a record in the Gantt view to see its predecessors and successors.*

# List View

List view in Airtable is a powerful tool for creating and managing hierarchical data, such as tasks and subtasks. Unlike Grid view, List view allows you to view records from multiple tables, making it ideal for context-heavy projects. For example, if you have a product launch to manage, you can pull in the launch Date field from one table and the status and assignee fields from another.

The hierarchy in a List view comes from linked record relationships. To set up a List view in a base, you first need to decide which table will contain your lowest level of records. In that table, you can create a new List view and configure it according to your needs. In List view, sections represent parent records, and records within those sections are displayed as child records, as shown in Figure 6-19.

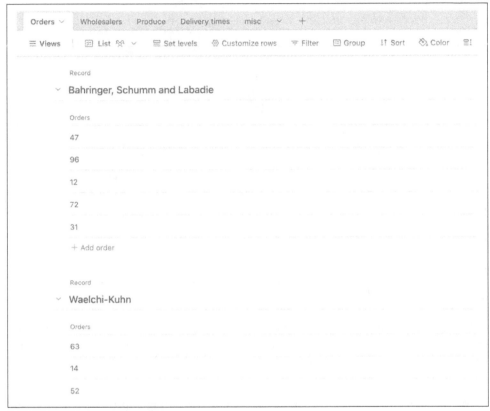

*Figure 6-19. Parent and child records in the List view.*

List view has options to show or hide empty sections, as shown in Figure 6-20. Like the Grid view, you can adjust the row height for each level, giving you control over how much screen real estate is allocated to each element.

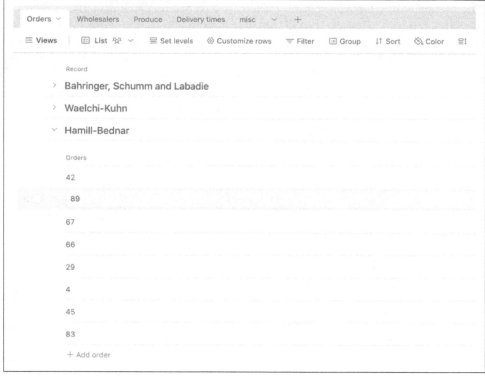

*Figure 6-20. Hiding child records in the List view.*

Interacting with List view is straightforward. You can easily create new records at different levels, move or link records to establish connections between levels, edit existing records by clicking into fields, expand records for a more detailed view, and delete records as needed.

Overall, List view allows for a comprehensive understanding of project structures and relationships between tables, making it easier to stay organized and track progress.

In this chapter, we explored different view types in Airtable, including the List, Calendar, Gallery, Kanban, Timeline, and Gantt views. We learned how each view can provide a unique perspective and enhance our ability to organize and analyze data. We also discussed how to create, customize, and organize views in our bases, exploring the options of collaborative, personal, and locked views.

In the next chapter, we will dive into Airtable Extensions, which open up a world of possibilities in the Data section of Automations. Extensions allow you to integrate Airtable with other tools and systems, streamline workflows, and automate repetitive tasks. From integrating with popular apps to automating data imports and exports, Extensions expand the functionality of your Airtable bases and help optimize your workflow.

# CHAPTER 7

# Creating the Fall Tour Tracker Base

In this chapter, we'll look at a practical application of Linked records by creating a "Fall Tour Tracker" base. This chapter builds on the foundational knowledge we gained from Chapter 3, and we'll explore how Linked records can help us efficiently manage our upcoming tour.

We'll learn about creating relationships between tables we create—Cities, Venues, Lodging, Shows, and Regions—and see how these connections enable us to easily understand the intricacies of the tour. This base will serve as the foundation for future chapters as we explore more advanced functionality in Airtable.

Our fall tour will include many more stops than our summer tour, and we want to make our tour tracker a more efficient database by leveraging the Linked records feature in Airtable. Our first table in this new base is called Cities.

Let's start by importing a CSV of the cities where we plan to have a concert on this tour. As seen in Figure 7-1, we've created a simple formula to combine the City and State fields in our City, State primary field:

```
City&", "&State
```

*Figure 7-1. Importing a list of cities for the fall tour and creating a simple primary field name that combines the two imported fields.*

Next, let's import a list of venues built by a team member in another Airtable base by using the "Synced table" feature, as seen in Figure 7-2. We now have a Venues table in our base where we can see fields, including the name of the venue, its website, the city, address, capacity, and more.

*Figure 7-2. Syncing a table of Venues from another base.*

Our intern researched hotel options for the cities we plan to visit on the fall tour. We will also import that information as a Sync table to our new Fall Tour Tracker base, as seen in Figure 7-3.

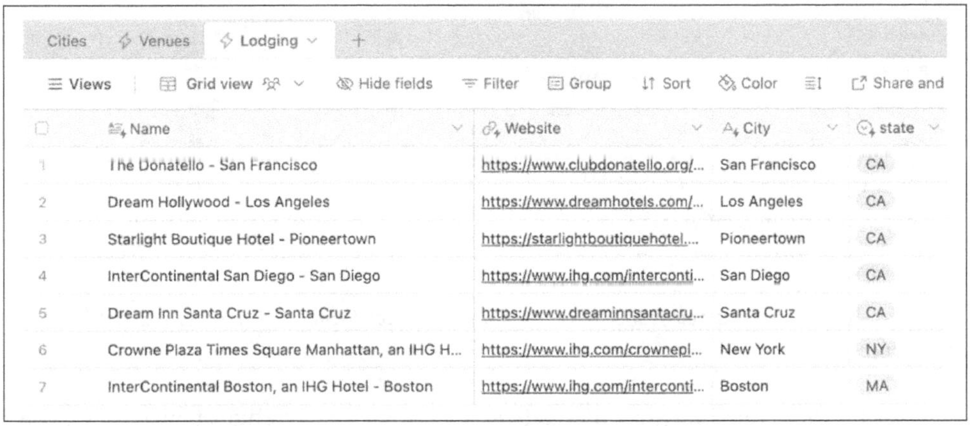

*Figure 7-3. Syncing hotel options for the fall tour from another base.*

# Creating Relationships Between Tables

Starting with our first three tables (Cities, Venues, and Lodging), we can use linked records to define how these entities relate to each other generally and which specific entities in a given table relate to entities in another table.

First, we're going to make a relationship between Lodging and Cities where each city is linked to just one hotel. This is because of particular business logic: there's just one hotel in each city that the band's booking agent and the band's tour manager have agreed upon after considering price and amenities. (In another scenario, we might have more than one hotel in our Lodging table that could be in the same city.)

We'll only stay at one hotel per city, and we'll only play one venue in each city on this tour. Therefore, the Cities and Venues tables also have a one-to-one relationship, as shown in Figure 7-4.

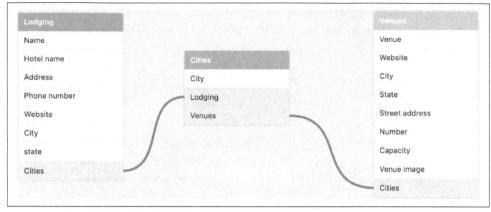

*Figure 7-4. One-to-one relationships between the Cities table and the Venues and Lodging tables.*

Let's set up these relationships, first between the Cities and Venues tables. Then, we'll create a linked records relationship between the Cities and Lodging tables.

## Connecting Cities to Lodging

The first step to create a linked record field is choosing "Link to another record." Let's start by choosing the Lodging table to connect to our table of Cities, as shown in Figure 7-5.

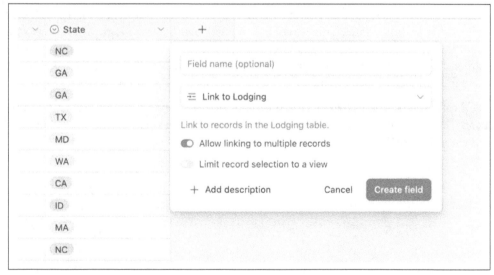

*Figure 7-5. Creating a linked record field.*

Now that we have created the field, as seen in Figure 7-6, we can click inside the cell and see a list of records from the Lodging table.

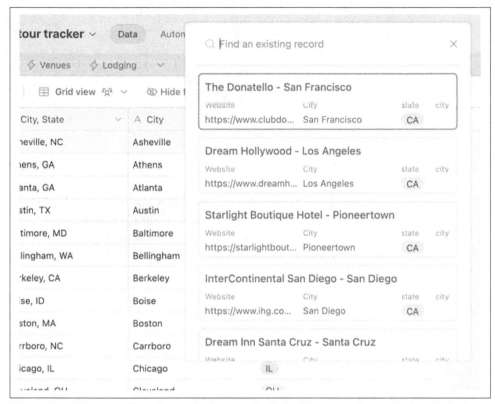

*Figure 7-6. Viewing a list of records that can be linked from another table in a linked record field.*

Clicking one of these records creates a relationship that links a record in the Lodging table to a record in the Cities table. Later, we will use a Lookup field to leverage this relationship to pull data from the Lodging records into the Cities table based on what records are linked between the two tables.

Before we move on to creating relationships between Cities and Venues, let's take a look at our Cities and Lodging relationship. We can see the linked record in the Lodging field of our Cities table, as shown in Figure 7-7.

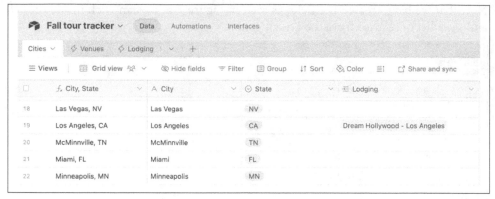

Figure 7-7. A linked record field showing the two records connected between two tables.

As seen in Figure 7-8, Airtable automatically created a new Linked record field in the Lodging table, titled Cities. Every time a linked relationship is created in the Cities table, the name of that record will show up in the Lodging table in this new Cities field that is automatically created to reflect the linked record relationship between records in these two tables.

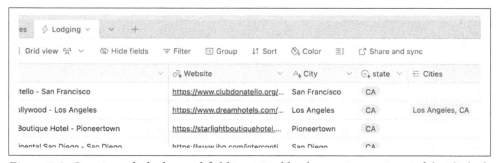

Figure 7-8. Creating a linked record field in one table also creates a mirror of that linked record field in the other table.

If a Linked record field is created in Table A that links to Table B but is later deleted, the Linked record field that used to be in Table B will now turn into a Single line text field. If there were linked record values between the two tables, the field in Table B would still have those values as plain text.

## Connecting Cities to Venues

We previously mentioned that it isn't possible to play more than one venue in a city on this tour, so we have only one venue linking to each city, which creates another one-to-one relationship.

Let's create a new Linked record field in the Cities table for linking to Venues. When we do, we'll associate one venue with each city using a linked record relationship, as seen in Figure 7-9. The venue record is visible in the "Venues" field.

| A City | ⊙ State | ⊞ Venues |
|--------|---------|----------|
| Asheville | NC | The Orange Peel |
| Athens | GA | The 40 Watt |
| Atlanta | GA | Masquerade |
| Austin | TX | Mohawk |
| Baltimore | MD | The Crown |
| Bellingham | WA | Wild Buffalo House |
| Berkeley | CA | Greek Theatre |

*Figure 7-9. Creating a one-to-one relationship between Cities and Venues.*

# Creating the Shows Table

Our first three tables in the new tour tracker were created with existing data. We had a spreadsheet of cities, and we also synced tables with records for Venues and Lodging. The Shows table will have different linked connections to the other tables in the base. This is the table that we will refer to most. Let's build it from scratch.

The first field we can add is for the date of the show, but what else do we need to know about each show? For starters, we need to know the location, where the show is being played, and where we'll stay that night. To do this, we will create relationships between this new Shows table and the Cities table, as shown in Figure 7-10.

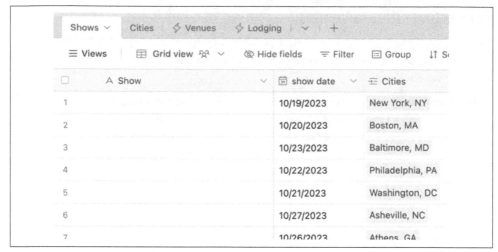

*Figure 7-10. Each row in the Shows table is linked to a city.*

We can choose "Add lookup fields" from the field customization menu to create new Lookup fields for the "Venues" and "Lodging" fields from the Cities table, as shown in Figure 7-11.

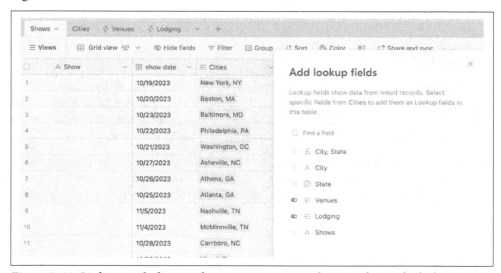

*Figure 7-11. Linking each date on the upcoming tour with a city, from which the venue and lodging are looked up.*

These two Lookup fields are looking up fields that happen to be linked records from the Cities table. This might seem a little confusing. In Figure 7-12, we can see that the fields for Venues and Lodging look the same as the city's linked record, but we can distinguish them as Lookup fields because there is a small magnifying glass next to the field name. Airtable has titled these Lookup fields "Venues (from Cities)" and "Lodging (from Cities)" because they are being referenced from the Cities table.

| show date | Cities | Venues (from Cities) | Lodging (from Cities) |
|---|---|---|---|
| 10/26/2023 | Athens, GA | The 40 Watt | Hampton Inn Athens - Athe |
| 10/25/2023 | Atlanta, GA | Masquerade | The Westin Peachtree Plaz |
| 11/5/2023 | Nashville, TN | The Basement East | Loews Vanderbilt Hotel - N |
| 11/4/2023 | McMinnville, TN | Cumberland Caverns | Americas Best Value Inn M |
| 10/28/2023 | Carrboro, NC | Cat's Cradle | Hampton Inn & Suites Cha |

*Figure 7-12. Looking up the venue and lodging we have decided upon for each city by referencing two fields from the Cities table via Lookup fields; note the small magnifying glass icon next to the name of the two Lookup fields.*

We've linked each show to a city only rather than directly to a venue. This intentional design choice reflects the business logic behind the planning process. When organizing a tour, it is crucial to establish the geographic travel routing after the specific Venues for each city are finalized.

We first determine the appropriate venue for each city, considering factors such as availability, capacity, and suitability for the show. Then the geographic routing for the tour is determined based on the cities that have Venues appropriate for the tour. This example highlights how the structure of a database can be dictated by specific business logic.

One last item for our new Shows table is to add a proper name for each record, since the primary field in Shows is blank right now. Airtable's formula functions allow us to take information from a records field, manipulate it, and then combine it with other field data for a customized label for each record. We will do this for our Shows table in Chapter 8, which will cover Formulas.

# Creating the Regions Table

Grouping the shows where we plan to perform by region of the United States will help our planning in a few ways. First, we can make sure that we're routing the stops on the tour through cities by one region at a time and not bouncing between regions. Second, we can use the Count field with linked records to calculate how many cities on the tour belong in each region. Later, we can use Rollup fields to understand aggregate data about the shows by region, such as how ticket sales are performing by region (we'll use Rollup fields inside the Regions table in later chapters).

 There are trade-offs for each decision made in designing the schema of a database. If we linked Regions to the Cities table, for example, the relationship between a region and city would stay the same. This would be most reflective of the real-world relationship between these two entities, which happens to be unchanging.

We've chosen to link Regions to the Shows table. This relationship could change: if a show on October 18 moves from Chicago to Albany, that linked show record will be linked to the incorrect region. So we'll need to make sure that if a show moves to a new city, we update the region of that show accordingly.

However, our choice to link the Regions table to the Shows table will allow us to aggregate information directly for the Shows table, such as promotion costs. Otherwise, if we linked Regions to Cites, we'd need to pull the data from the Shows table through a Lookup field into the Cities table to later roll it up in the Regions. Each approach has its drawbacks, and we're choosing to double-check that each show is in the correct region instead of creating a lot of extra Lookup fields.

Let's create a new regions table with six options for different areas of the US: Midwest, East Coast, South, West, West Coast, and Southeast. In Figure 7-13, we have those six records, each representing a region, and a linked record field connecting to the Shows table (using a one-to-many relationship of one region to many shows).

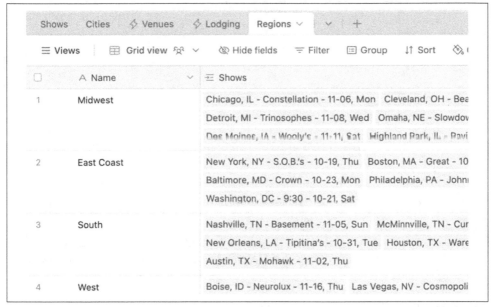

Figure 7-13. Creating a relationship of one region to many shows through linked records between two tables.

Let's add a "Count (Shows)" field in this table to count the number of records in the Cities linked records field, as seen in Figure 7-14.

Figure 7-14. Using a Count (Shows) field to quickly determine the number of linked records for each region in the regions table.

Even if the width of the Shows linked record is narrowed, and we reduce the height of the records in the Grid view, we can still easily consult this Count field to know how many cities are linked to each region, as shown in Figure 7-15.

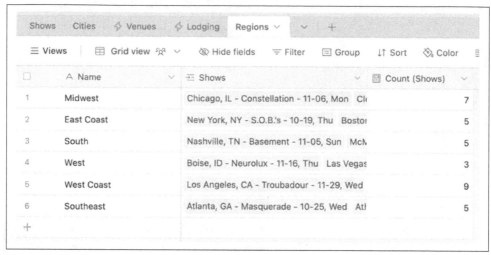

*Figure 7-15. Using a Count (Shows) field to keep track of the number of cities in each region of the tour.*

In Chapter 9, we'll add a Rollup field to this Regions table to aggregate promotional costs from the shows by region.

In this chapter, we focused on creating the Fall Tour Tracker base to efficiently manage our upcoming tour. We used linked records to establish relationships between the Cities, Venues, Lodging, Shows, and Regions tables. The chapter also highlighted the importance of maintaining data integrity and considering specific business logic when designing the structure of a database. In the upcoming chapters, we will delve deeper into the functionality of Airtable, using this tour tracker base for examples of Airtable extensions, formulas, Rollup fields, automations, and more.

# CHAPTER 8

# Formulas

Airtable combines the structured data of a database with the user-friendly ability to easily manipulate data. With Airtable formulas inside a relational database like Airtable, you can also learn different ways to perform mathematical operations, combine and rearrange text, and combine and analyze data from other fields. And all of this can be done in Airtable without understanding programming.

Spreadsheets allow anyone to manipulate and reformat data without understanding programming. Users can incrementally learn different formula types in Excel or Google Sheets and build an arsenal of powerful tools to manipulate and reformat their data. Airtable's "Formula" field is similarly accessible and powerful and lets any user pick up formula functions on an as-needed basis.

Just like a spreadsheet, Airtable can manipulate several types of data. For instance, you can manipulate numerical data. You can also manipulate text, which means you can parse and transform strings of texts into other data types, such as dates, when needed. This level of personalization is getting close to the type of data manipulation one might use when programming, using JavaScript or Python, but through a more gentle introduction for the nondeveloper interested in no-code tools like Airtable.

Formulas can also manipulate date and time data. Date and time data don't look terribly different from strings or numbers, but the many ways a date can be structured make it worthy of having its own category since users can wrangle dates with the same amount of precision as text or numbers.

In this chapter, we will introduce Airtable's "Formula" field with the functions and operators that allow you to perform many different modifications to your data. These functions and operators are the building blocks of formulas in Airtable. We use them in combination with existing fields, text, dates, and numerical data we've entered into a formula. In a formula, we can reference other fields in the table, put in arbitrary numbers or strings, and use Airtable formula functions and operators to manipulate data.

In this chapter, we will explain the formula editor and go through each of the groups of formulas and operators. We'll also show examples of each type of formula or operator. And at the end of the chapter, we will mix and match different kinds of operators and functions to show examples from our tour tracking base of the kinds of complex formulas we can Frankenstein together to build insights about our data.

There are dozens of formula operators and functions, too many to offer an example of each in this chapter. But in Appendix B, at the back of this book, every formula function and operator is listed with a short description and example.

Let's start by understanding the basics of the Formula field type and how it works in the Grid view.

# Basics of the Formula Field

In a spreadsheet, a formula has the power to reach across the entire sheet, grabbing data from any cell and manipulating it as needed. In Airtable, however, formulas are more contained. Each Airtable formula resides in its own field, which can only access and manipulate data for each row in the Grid view (which represents a record).

In a spreadsheet, each cell knows its position in the larger structure of the sheet. It knows where every other cell is in relation to itself, creating a spatial awareness. But in Airtable, the cells of the Grid view don't have that fluid spatial orientation. They are bound to a structure: each "row" in the Grid view is a distinct thing, with attributes organized into fields that are the columns in a Grid view.

So when we input a formula into a Formula field, it can only work with the data in each row (the data for that record). It doesn't care about the spatial placement of the data in other columns or fields. It's all about what's happening within that specific field for each record in the table.

If we start by creating a new Formula field, as seen in Figure 8-1, Airtable will apply any formula we enter into that Formula text box to all the records in the table. And anything we put in the formula box will be echoed into the field. For example, we could simply put the number 17, and Airtable will echo that number into that Formula field for every record.

*Figure 8-1. Entering characters into a Formula field will echo them for all records, since we aren't referencing any record-specific data.*

We can also call the value of another field. Typing the name of another field will display whatever value is in that field for all records in the table. For example, as seen in Figure 8-2, we can type the name of our Status field into the formula box, and the resulting output will be the text of that Single select field value. This example also shows that formatted data, such as a Single select or Multiple select field, will be turned into plain text after it's been used in a formula and after you pull values with a formula.

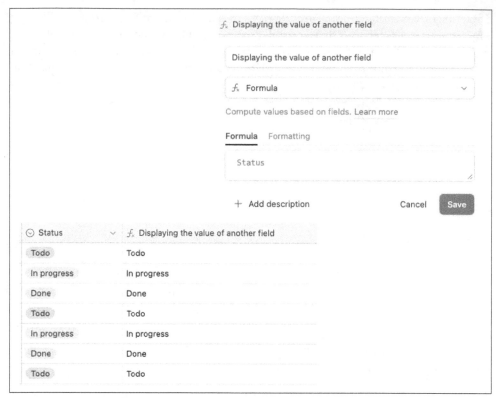

*Figure 8-2. Simply referencing a single-select field in a Formula field to echo each record's value as plain text.*

When referencing a field in a formula, a one-word field can stand on its own—with or without curly brackets surrounding it. However, a field with a multiword name should be encapsulated in curly brackets. The brackets tell Airtable that we are referring to the name of a field. A string of text characters should always be encapsulated with quote marks.

Let's look at the elements that go into a formula.

# Formula Components

While we can echo static data in a Formula field, like a string of text or a number, Airtable formula functions allow us to perform data manipulation—a lightweight form of coding. There are functions and operators to manipulate and transform numbers, text, and dates, and to apply logic, such as if/then statements.

Here are the components that make up a formula.

# Fields

Any field in a table can be referenced in a formula. The data in any field can be pulled into your formula and modified by a function or simply echoed for each record, as in Figure 8-3. When you've linked to a record and brought up data with a Lookup field, those fields can also be referenced in a formula.

| ⌄  ☰ venues | ⌄  ⧉ Website (from venues) | ⌄  ƒ Referencing a lookup field in a formula |
| --- | --- | --- |
| The Orange Peel | https://theorangepeel.net/ | https://theorangepeel.net/ |
| The 40 Watt | http://www.40watt.com/ | http://www.40watt.com/ |
| Masquerade | http://www.masqueradeatlanta.com/ | http://www.masqueradeatlanta.com/ |
| Mohawk | http://www.mohawkaustin.com/ | http://www.mohawkaustin.com/ |
| The Crown | https://thecrownbaltimore.tumblr.com/ | https://thecrownbaltimore.tumblr.com/ |
| Wild Buffalo House | https://wildbuffalo.net/ | https://wildbuffalo.net/ |
| Greek Theatre | https://thegreekberkeley.com/ | https://thegreekberkeley.com/ |

*Figure 8-3. Any field in a table can be referenced in a formula.*

# Operators

Operators in Airtable formulas are simple symbols used to perform calculations or compare values. For example, the plus symbol (+) adds two numbers together, while the minus symbol (–) subtracts one number from another. Additionally, the greater-than symbol (>) and less-than symbol (<) can be used to compare values and return a true or false result.

# Functions

Functions in Airtable formulas are prebuilt logic that can be applied to data in your table. They allow you to perform more complex calculations and manipulations without needing to write custom code. For instance, the COUNT function can be utilized to count the number of records in a linked field, while the CONCATENATE function can be used to combine multiple text strings into a single string.

Operators sit between two values and do not have parentheses. Functions always have parentheses, and values go inside the parentheses.

## Numbers

Numbers in Airtable formulas are numeric values that can be used for calculations. These can include whole numbers (integers) or decimal numbers (floating-point numbers). They can be typed directly into a formula or referenced from another field. For example, you could calculate the sum of two fields containing numbers using the plus operator (+) and those numerical values.

## Text/String Data

Text/string data in Airtable formulas refers to any sequence of characters enclosed within quotation marks. This can include words, sentences, or any other combination of letters and symbols. Text data is often used for labeling or adding context to records. In a formula, you might concatenate two text strings using the CONCATENATE function to create a new combined string.

# The Formula Editor

Figure 8-4 shows the data entity types in a Formula field editor. Each type has a different color. Functions are green, fields are purple, numbers are orange, and text strings and other data are teal. Everything else is black, including important components of formula syntax that we'll look at like parentheses and commas. Operators are also displayed in black text.

As we will see, formulas in the formula editor can highlight when a formula has missing or extra parentheses or periods. It also allows the formula code to span multiple lines and be neatly folded based on how it is intended. Let's look at an example with some common and easy-to-understand formula functions and operators.

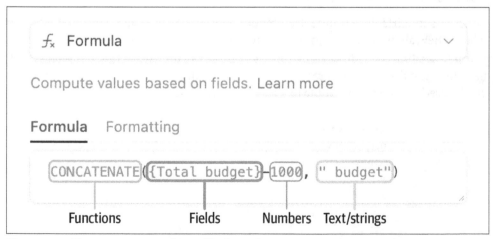

*Figure 8-4. The components of Airtable formulas.*

# Introduction to Operators and Functions

Airtable arranges its functions and operators into seven buckets. The four most commonly used are text, logical, date and time, and numeric. Some categories have fewer functions and operators, including array functions, record functions, and regex functions.

## Text, numerical, and date and time

The functions and operators that pertain to text, commas, numbers, and dates are essentially different ways of formatting existing field content. We can trim part of a phrase from a field. We can round up numbers or find their square root and display dates in many ways. For example, dates can be displayed by month and day only.

## Logic

The first three groups of functions and operators were about formatting and tallying data. However, the logic functions and operators are more about interpreting the data based on conditions.

Functions and operators in the logic bucket move us closer to programming. Using an if/then statement, noted as IF( ) in Airtable, is a powerful starting point. With that function and other logic functions, we can unlock the ability to evaluate multiple field values with conditions we specify.

## Array, record, and regex

A small number of functions and operators have a narrower scope. For example, array and record functions are utilitarian and are useful for wrangling the data in our formulas.

However, Airtable only has three regex functions. Regex, or regular expressions, is a tool used in programming to match and manipulate strings of text based on defined patterns. The Airtable regex functions are doorways to the infinitely configurable world of regular expressions. We will look at how these regex functions can fuel extremely powerful methods of parsing and evaluating data in your Formula field.

There is further discussion of array, record, and regex functions, with examples, in Appendix B.

Let's start by looking at some simple examples using the Formula field.

# Formula Examples

Let's start by looking at an example that uses common formula functions and operators. In the last chapter, we took data from different fields to create a name for each record in the primary field in our new tour tracking base.

## Ampersands (&) and quotation marks (") in formulas

The ampersand operator (&) is used to combine different elements in a formula. It acts as the glue between text strings, fields, and other data types, allowing them to be merged together.

The quotation mark operator (") is used to represent text within a formula. It is particularly helpful when displaying values in Formula fields or when manipulating and formatting text data. Both enable us to concatenate and format data in formulas.

The fields of cities, venues, and show dates are visible in the formula editor in purple. We also see an ampersand symbol, which is crucial to connect text, or any items, in a formula. For other formulas, we might have many individual field values and complicated logic statements strung together in a single Formula field using the ampersand symbol. In this case, we're using it to create a primary field name with rich data from multiple fields and record names that will change dynamically based on the data in those fields. In Figure 8-5, the primary field is reflecting the data in these three fields:

```
Cities&" - "&{Venues (from Cities)}&" - "&{show date}
```

| ƒₓ Show | | 📅 show date ∨ | ⛁ cities ∨ | ⛛ venues (from cit |
|---|---|---|---|---|
| "New York, NY" - S.O.B.'s - 2023-10-19T00:00:00.... | | 10/19/2023 | New York, NY | S.O.B.'s |
| "Boston, MA" - Great Scott - 2023-10-20T00:00:... | | 10/20/2023 | Boston, MA | Great Scott |
| "Baltimore, MD" - The Crown - 2023-10-23T00:0... | | 10/23/2023 | Baltimore, MD | The Crown |
| "Philadelphia, PA" - Johnny Brenda's - 2023-10-2... | | 10/22/2023 | Philadelphia, PA | Johnny Brenda's |
| "Washington, DC" - 9:30 Club - 2023-10-21T00:0... | | 10/21/2023 | Washington, DC | 9:30 Club |

*Figure 8-5. Combining text from several fields to create a unique name in the primary field to identify each record.*

Like the ampersand, quotation marks are another important element in building formulas. You can use quotation marks to represent text without interacting with the rest of the formula. Essentially, we can use quotation marks when we want to display a value into a Formula field, which is what we're doing in our Shows table's primary field.

In Figure 8-5, the "show date" field value is structured MM/DD/YYYY, but in the "Show" primary field, the order is switched around with a bunch of extra zeroes and other characters at the end. That is an ISO 8601–formatted date with GMT time, an internationally recognized way of representing date and time information in a standardized format. If you pull a date into an Airtable formula without specifying how to format it, using `DATETIME_FORMAT()`, Airtable will default to this ISO 8601 format. We'll use `DATETIME_FORMAT()` to improve the look of our primary field later in this chapter.

In this case, we put a space, a dash, and another space between the three fields in this formula. The ampersand is the glue between the Cities field, the spaces, and the dash we have in quotation marks; another ampersand is the glue to the Venues field, and so on.

Let's look at another way we can achieve the same result with the `CONCATENATE()` function.

## CONCATENATE()

When using Airtable formulas, it is important to remember there are usually many ways to get things done. We've just used the simple ampersand quotation mark operator to combine three fields in our primary field. Another way to glue these bits of text together is to use the `CONCATENATE()` formula function. Instead of using operators like an ampersand (&), `CONCATENATE()` simply separates using commas, as in this formula:

```
CONCATENATE(
    Cities,
    ' - ',
    {Venues (from Cities)},
    ' - ',
    {show date}
)
```

As we can see in Figure 8-6, and in the previous formula, using the `CONCATENATE()` function connects the city, venue, and show date for each record with commas between; we've also added a space, a hyphen, and another space between each field.

While we have single quotes wrapping the spaces and the hyphen in this formula, you might recall that the first formula we walked through, in our primary field, used double quotations. Airtable allows both single quotes and double quotes in formulas. When putting some text in quotes, for example, you should begin and end with the same type of quotation mark. However, a single formula can have different quote styles for different bits of text.

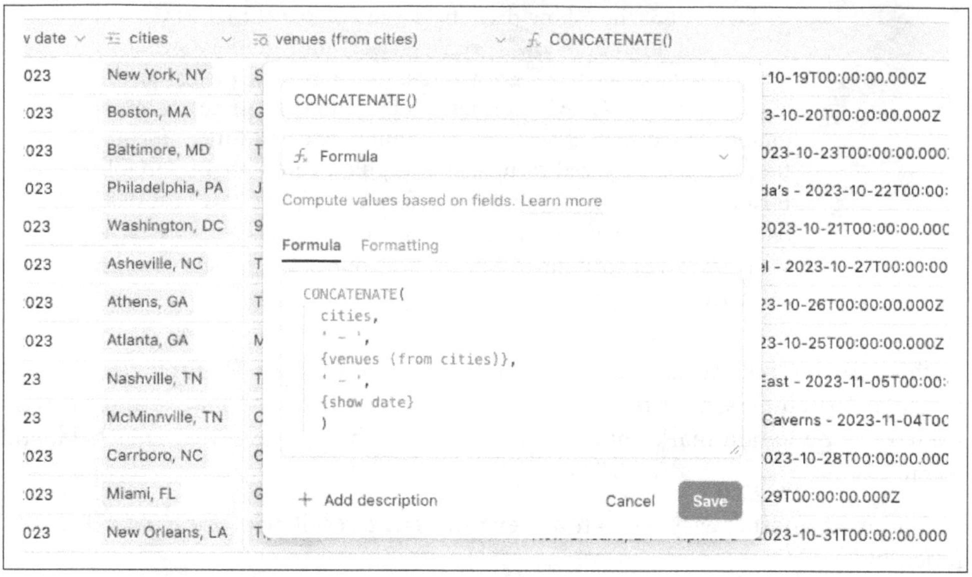

| v date | ⠿ cities | ⠿ venues (from cities) | ⨍ CONCATENATE() |
|---|---|---|---|
| 023 | New York, NY | S | -10-19T00:00:00.000Z |
| :023 | Boston, MA | G | 3-10-20T00:00:00.000Z |
| :023 | Baltimore, MD | T | 023-10-23T00:00:00.000. |
| 023 | Philadelphia, PA | J | da's - 2023-10-22T00:00: |
| 023 | Washington, DC | 9 | 2023-10-21T00:00:00.00C |
| 023 | Asheville, NC | T | el - 2023-10-27T00:00:00 |
| :023 | Athens, GA | T | 23-10-26T00:00:00.000Z |
| 023 | Atlanta, GA | M | 23-10-25T00:00:00.000Z |
| 23 | Nashville, TN | T | East - 2023-11-05T00:00: |
| 23 | McMinnville, TN | C | Caverns - 2023-11-04T0C |
| :023 | Carrboro, NC | C | 023-10-28T00:00:00.00C |
| :023 | Miami, FL | G | 29T00:00:00.000Z |
| 023 | New Orleans, LA | T | 2023-10-31T00:00:00.000 |

CONCATENATE()

ƒ. Formula ⌄

Compute values based on fields. Learn more

**Formula**   Formatting

```
CONCATENATE(
    cities,
    ' - ',
    {venues (from cities)},
    ' - ',
    {show date}
)
```

+ Add description     Cancel   **Save**

*Figure 8-6. Combining three fields together using the* `CONCATENATE()` *function.*

Now that we have explored the building blocks of Airtable formulas and seen an example of how they can reference data from other records, we can delve deeper into applying formula functions and operators to improve our tour base.

# The Grammar of Airtable Formulas

Airtable formulas have a specific grammar that must be followed in order for them to work correctly. Here are some key rules to keep in mind:

- Parameters in a formula need to be separated by commas. For example, if you are using the `CONCATENATE()` function to combine two strings, the two strings would be the parameters, and they must be separated by a comma.

  Correct: `CONCATENATE("Hello", "world")`

  Incorrect: `CONCATENATE("Hello" "world")`

- There should be no trailing comma at the end of a formula.

  Correct: `CONCATENATE("Hello", "world")`

  Incorrect: `CONCATENATE("Hello", "world",)`

- There should be no space between the function name and the opening parenthesis.

  Correct: `CONCATENATE("Hello", "world")`

  Incorrect: `CONCATENATE ("Hello", "world")`

- Other whitespaces, such as spaces within strings or spaces around operators, are generally acceptable and do not affect the functionality of the formula.

Correct: `CONCATENATE("Hello ", "world!")`

Also correct: `CONCATENATE("Hello","world!")`

# Text Functions

As the name suggests, text functions modify text content, which can also be described as strings. In programming, a string is a group of characters that are not defined as a number or something else. In an Airtable formula, a group of characters inside of quotation marks is a text string, even if the string is just a number, for example.

Let's learn about text functions by first improving the display of our primary field for the Show table. At the moment, the city of a show is in quotes. The venue name can be rather long and limits the ability to see the date. Plus, the date itself has an unusual string of zeros that makes it hard to easily understand.

 Many examples of Formula fields in this chapter are shorter formulas that reference other Formula fields. As you become more comfortable with having larger formulas, you can have all the formula logic you might need in a single Formula field instead of spreading the logic and formula across several formulas, as we'll do next in the primary field.

## SUBSTITUTE()

The `SUBSTITUTE()` formula function is helpful for tidying up text. To use it, the pattern is to first list the field, then the text to search for, and finally the replacement text. Let's create a new field called "City without quotes," and let's omit quotation marks. Here's the formula we will use:

```
SUBSTITUTE(Cities,'"','')
```

When the title of a linked record (the value in its primary field) contains one or more commas or quotation marks, the linked record will appear in quotation marks when referenced in a formula.

In our case, quotation marks are around the city in our primary field because it references a linked record with a comma. We have the Cities table linked to our Show table, and the primary field for the Cities table is the name of the city that we're referencing in the formula we looked at earlier. To fix this, we'll use the `SUBSTITUTE()` function to replace the quotation marks. In this case, we're going to replace the commas with nothing at all, as seen in Figure 8-7.

*Figure 8-7. Removing quotation marks from the results of a formula that references a linked record field.*

We are using SUBSTITUTE() to do something pretty simple. We reference the cities field, then look for any instances of double quotation marks, and then replace the double quotation marks with nothing, which is represented by two single quotations with nothing in between.

As mentioned earlier, you can either use single quotes or double quotes in a formula. Since we need to reference removing double quotation marks, we will use single quotes to wrap up the strings we want to substitute using SUBSTITUTE().

## Shortening Venue Names Using SUBSTITUTE(), LEFT(), and FIND()

There's another way we can make our primary field more concise and readable. We can use an Airtable formula to remove extraneous words from the name of the venue. For example, we might not need to read the entire name of Meow Wolf's House of Eternal Return to know we're talking about that venue.

Once we're finished with this formula, we will have just the word "Meow," which should be enough to remind us which venue we're talking about in our primary field. However, we want to make sure we're going to pull a word that will remind us which venue we're talking about. So let's start by getting rid of any venues that have "the" in the title. We can do this by setting up a new "Formula" field and, again, using the SUBSTITUTE() command, as in this formula:

```
SUBSTITUTE(
    {Venues (from Cities)},
    'The ',
```

```
      ' '
)
```

As a reminder, we're bringing in the name of the venue as a Lookup field based on the linked record from the Cities table in the formula. We'll use SUBSTITUTE() to first reference that Lookup field, find any instances of "the," and then we're going to replace any instances of "the" with nothing, as we see in Figure 8-8. The venue named "The Beachland Ballroom & Tavern" now reads just "Beachland Ballroom & Tavern" in that Formula field.

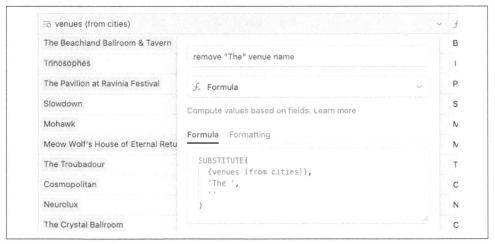

*Figure 8-8. Using SUBSTITUTE() to replace any instances of "The" in the venue names.*

## Using FIND() to Find the First Word

Now that we've removed any instances of "the" from the beginning of venue names, we need to figure out how to extract only the first word of what's remaining. We'll accomplish this by using the FIND() function to identify the first space in the trimmed venue name. In our next formula, knowing where this first space is allows us to remove everything after the space so that only the first word remains.

In our new Formula field, "find first space," we use the FIND() function to search for an empty space, which is the first of three pieces of data in the formula.

First, we specify that we want to find a space that we remember to put quotation marks around. Then we specify the field where we want to find that information, which of course is the field we just created that removed "the" from the venue name. Lastly, we need to specify where in the field to start searching. This action is a powerful aspect of the FIND() function. If, for example, we were using this function on a date that was formatted 09-21-2013, we could start at position six (the 2 in 2013) if we were only concerned with finding something within the year of the values in the date field being referenced by FIND() in the formula.

We want to begin searching from the start of the characters in the field, so we'll use 0:

```
FIND(
    ' ',
    {remove "The" venue name},
    0
)
```

We can see in Figure 8-9 that one-word venue names result in a value of 0. Let's take an example of a venue name with more than one word after stripping out "the". For instance, the Great Scott venue has a 6 in our new "find first space" formula. This number tells us that the first blank space (our search term) the formula function found was in the sixth position. In other words, the word "Great" has five letters and occupies spaces one through five. The sixth position is the space between the words "Great" and "Scott," and that's where the "find first space" formula notes the first space for that record value.

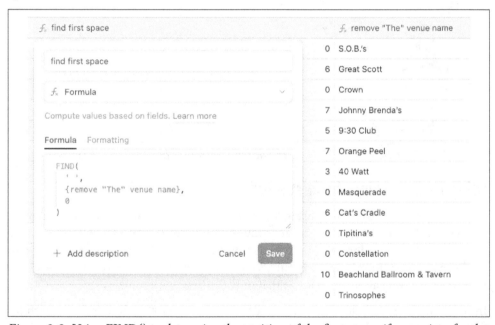

*Figure 8-9. Using FIND() to determine the position of the first space, if one exists, for the record value.*

Now that we know the position for each record after the first word we want to capture, we can use another Airtable formula to remove everything after the first word. The LEFT() function trims off a certain number of characters starting from the beginning of a string. For example, we could do a simpler version of shortening the venue name with the LEFT() function by specifying something like showing the first seven letters of the name. This would simply appear as:

```
LEFT(
    {remove "The" venue name},
    {find first space}-1
)
```

Since we want to leverage our knowledge of the position at the end of each word that we found with the FIND() function, we can try to use LEFT() to reference that position, as shown in Figure 8-10. However, when we look at the results from our new formula in Figure 8-10, we can see that for venue names with more than one word, our formula did a good job of returning the first word only. But for venue names that are only one word, we see a blank because there is no space to find after those one-word venue names for our last formula that used FIND().

*Figure 8-10. Using LEFT() to extract the first word in cases where there is more than one word.*

## Creating conditional logic with IF()

Since using the LEFT() function alone has returned some blank values, this needs a more complex formula. The IF() function is helpful when you need to compare data from different fields in your table. In this case, we need to compare venue names that have just one word with those that have one or more words. Depending on whether a venue name has more than one word, we can decide how to output from the formula.

 The IF() function is one of Airtable's logic functions. We'll examine more logic functions later in this chapter, with additional examples in Appendix B, but the IF() function is probably going to be one of your most used formula functions.

The formula we just used that combined LEFT() and IF() can still be useful. We will create an IF() formula that checks whether the position returned from the FIND() function is less than 1. If it is less than 1, that means that it's only a one-word venue name, and we don't need to find the first space. If we did, Airtable wouldn't find any results and would return a blank because the venue has a one-word name.

In the following formula code, we are setting up a condition that if the first position of the first space found with the FIND() function is less than 1, then we return our first function that just took the word "The" off the beginning of the name. This will catch any one-word venue names:

```
IF(
    {find first space}<1,
    {remove "The" venue name},

    LEFT({remove "The" venue name},
        {find first space}-1)
)
```

The next part of the formula is activated. If the position of the empty space is at a position greater than 0, then it is a space between two words.

If the position of the space is 0, as we found using the FIND() function, then the IF() function will simply return the one-word name of the venue.

However, if the position of the blank space is at position 1 or higher, then the IF()function will use the formula created with FIND() and LEFT() to trim the extra words and return just the first word of the multiword venue name.

As shown in Figure 8-11, we can see this formula and compare how adding the IF() function to help determine whether it's a one-word or multiword venue name fills in the blanks that were in our FIND() function and LEFT() function formulas. We'll look at using the IF() function later in this chapter as well.

There are more text functions at the end of this chapter.

*Figure 8-11. Creating a condition that results in a single-word venue name.*

# Date and Time Functions

Airtable's robust date and time functions can help wrangle complicated data. For the tour we are planning, let's look at a few examples of how we can use these functions to interpret differences in data between records, and how to format the display of how date and time show up in our base.

## Calculating Weeks of the Tour

Airtable's date functions can give context to a date. For example, the WEEKNUM() function takes a date and returns the week of the year that it occurs. Let's use this function to divide up the weeks of our tour.

The first thing we can do is pass our show date field to the WEEKNUM() formula, as shown in Figure 8-12. As we can see, this tells us that our tour begins in the 42nd week of the year. It would be more helpful if we could leverage the WEEKNUM() function to help us group tour dates by which week they fall in. By referencing the function we just created, the formula we just created using WEEKNUM(), we can make a quick calculation to determine the weeks of the tour beginning with the first tour date:

```
WEEKNUM({show date})
```

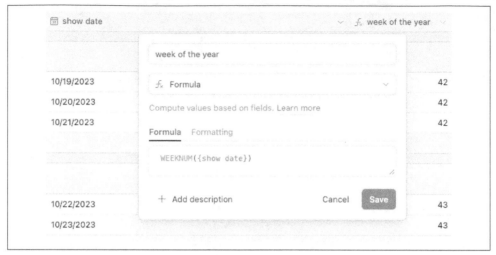

*Figure 8-12. Using the WEEKNUM() function.*

In our new "weeks of the year" Formula field, we simply take the result of the week of the year Formula field and subtract 41, as we can see in this formula:

```
{week of the year}-41
```

 As you become more comfortable with building Airtable formulas, you'll progressively do less referencing of a formula by another formula and more combining everything you need in one Formula field. In this case, for example, we could have simply subtracted the 41 weeks from inside the original "week of the year" Formula field, as shown in the "Week of tour" formula.

Now, let's make the output of this formula more useful. The "Week of tour" formula field has given us a value for every record in the Show table telling us which week of the tour that show falls under rather than which week of the year. If we group records by this "Week of tour" field, we can quickly scan and see how many shows are in each week. As we can see in Figure 8-13, we have three shows in the first week, six in the second, five in the third, and so on.

 The current formulas have limitations for longer tours that span multiple years. A better option is to hardcode the start date and calculate the difference from the current date. Adjustments may be needed for the desired starting day of the week, such as treating Saturday and Sunday as the same "week."

| 📅 show date | *fₓ* week of the year | *fₓ* Week of tour |
|---|---|---|
| 10/19/2023 | 42 | 1 |
| 10/20/2023 | 42 | 1 |
| 10/21/2023 | 42 | 1 |
| 10/22/2023 | 43 | 2 |
| 10/23/2023 | 43 | 2 |
| 10/25/2023 | 43 | 2 |
| 10/26/2023 | 43 | 2 |
| 10/27/2023 | 43 | 2 |
| 10/28/2023 | 43 | 2 |
| 10/29/2023 | 44 | 3 |
| 10/31/2023 | 44 | 3 |

*Figure 8-13. Noting which week of the tour each show falls into.*

## Formatting show dates

In an Airtable Date field, we can choose to easily configure a compacted version of the date that's easy to read. Unfortunately, when you reference that Date field in other fields, including a Formula field, sometimes it's much harder to read because the formatting changes dramatically. This is what happened with the formula we used to create the primary field:

```
"Asheville, NC" - The Orange Peel - 2023-10-27T00:00:00.000Z
```

Similar to how the city we referenced in our primary field has quotation marks around the name, because it's a linked record, the very clean-looking show date field now has a bunch of trailing zeros and the letter Z, which makes it pretty unwieldy. So let's clean it up.

We can first use the DATETIME_FORMAT() function to change how to display the date of the show in our primary field. As mentioned before, these steps to clean up the primary field are something we could combine into a single Formula field. But for the purposes of explaining it here, we're going to make a Formula field specifically for formatting the date that we'll reference in our primary field.

In the next formula, we have the DATETIME_FORMAT() function where we pass a Date field—in this case, our show dates. Then, we must decide how we want to format it after a comma. In our case, we want to have the month and day only. Airtable has a convention of representing elements of a date and time where M is the month and D is the day. Therefore, a date is written as MM-DD:

```
DATETIME_FORMAT({show date},'MM-DD, ddd')
```

Let's also make a reference to which day of the week each show is happening on another Airtable convention for dates. A lowercase "d" is the building block for displaying the day of the week. If we had "dddd", then it would display the full name of the day for this case (e.g., Thursday). Let's instead add "ddd" inside the quotation marks, which will make a three-letter abbreviation of the day of the week (e.g., Mon, Tue). We can now compare our new formatting show date formula with the show date field, as we can see in Figure 8-14.

*Figure 8-14. Formatting the show dates to only display the month, day, and three-letter abbreviation of the day of the week.*

But we still have the original problem of the primary field of the Show table being hard to read. Let's put to use several of the formulas we've made so far to redo the primary field.

## Cleaning up the primary field

Using text functions and date and time functions, we've created more manageable versions of the city for each show, its venue, and the date of the show. Let's combine these three Formula fields into our primary field.

The CONCATENATE() function can easily combine these three elements:

```
CONCATENATE(
    {City without quotes },
    ' - ',
    {using IF() venue name},
    ' - ',
    {Formatting show date}
)
```

As we can see in Figure 8-15, the primary field for our Show table is much cleaner. And again, this action could have been accomplished in a single Formula field instead of using a different formula for each of the three items we wanted to clean up.

| | $f_x$ Show | $f_x$ City without quotes | $f_x$ using IF() venue name | $f_x$ Formatting show date |
|---|---|---|---|---|
| 1 | New York, NY - S.O.B.'s - 10-19, Thu | New York, NY | S.O.B.'s | 10-19, Thu |
| 2 | Boston, MA - Great - 10-20, Fri | Boston, MA | Great | 10-20, Fri |
| 3 | Washington, DC - 9:30 - 10-21, Sat | Washington, DC | 9:30 | 10-21, Sat |
| 4 | Philadelphia, PA - Johnny - 10-22, Sun | Philadelphia, PA | Johnny | 10-22, Sun |
| 5 | Baltimore, MD - Crown - 10-23, Mon | Baltimore, MD | Crown | 10-23, Mon |
| 6 | Atlanta, GA - Masquerade - 10-25, Wed | Atlanta, GA | Masquerade | 10-25, Wed |
| 7 | Athens, GA - 40 - 10-26, Thu | Athens, GA | 40 | 10-26, Thu |
| 8 | Asheville, NC - Orange - 10-27, Fri | Asheville, NC | Orange | 10-27, Fri |

*Figure 8-15. Creating a more readable primary field that concatenates three fields modified by formulas to be simpler.*

### Finding days off in the tour schedule

We have a very busy tour schedule lined up, so it would be helpful to know if there are any days off on the tour. This is a great opportunity to use the DATETIME_DIFF() function, which calculates the difference in whatever units you specify between two dates. Setting this up is going to require a little work before we use DATETIME_DIFF().

First, we need to create a Linked record field that references records in the same Show table that we're working in. This will allow us to compare a given show's date with another show's date. The quick and dirty way to set this up is to select our primary field, copy the values, and then paste those values so they are offset by one record in the Grid view, as we see in Figure 8-16.

> The method of pasting in the list of shows into the linked record field in Figure 8-16 only works because we are taking care to paste them in the same order (offset by one show).

| ☐ | $f_x$ Show | ▾ | ⚏ Previous show | ▾ |
|---|---|---|---|---|
| 1 | New York, NY - S.O.B.'s - 10-19, Thu | | | |
| 2 | Boston, MA - Great - 10-20, Fri | | New York, NY - S.O.B.'s - 10-19, Thu | |
| 3 | Washington, DC - 9:30 - 10-21, Sat | | Boston, MA - Great - 10-20, Fri | |
| 4 | Philadelphia, PA - Johnny - 10-22, Sun | | Washington, DC - 9:30 - 10-21, Sat | |
| 5 | Baltimore, MD - Crown - 10-23, Mon | | Philadelphia, PA - Johnny - 10-22, Sun | |
| 6 | Atlanta, GA - Masquerade - 10-25, Wed | | Baltimore, MD - Crown - 10-23, Mon | |

*Figure 8-16. Referencing records in the same table, offset by one record in the order of shows, to understand how many days there are between each pair of successive shows.*

Each show record, of course, has its own Date field, but we need to have another date to compare it to. We'll create a Lookup field in the Show table for the linked record we just created. So, for example, we've linked the very first show, which is in New York, to the second show in Boston. And when we look up the date of the New York show from the linked record, it brings up the show date of the New York show. We can compare this date with the Boston show using the `DATETIME_DIFF()` function and understand how many days are between the date of the record and the date of the linked record, as shown in Figure 8-17.

*Figure 8-17. Looking up the date value for the linked record of the previous show.*

With the `DATETIME_DIFF()` formula function, we first provide the starting date, then the ending date we're measuring, and lastly the units. For example, the units could be days, weeks, or months. We'll measure days in the following formula:

```
DATETIME_DIFF(
    {show date},
    {show date (from Previous show)},
    'days'
)
```

Now that we've created the "Days between" field for this calculation, it's clear that usually there is only a one-day difference between that record and the date of the next show, as shown in Figure 8-18.

| $f_x$ Show | ▦ show date | ⥮ Previous show | ⤢ show date ... | $f_x$ Days between |
|---|---|---|---|---|
| 1 New York, NY - S.O.B.'s - 10-19, Thu | 10/19/2023 | | | NaN |
| 2 Boston, MA - Great - 10-20, Fri | 10/20/2023 | New York, NY - S.O.B.'s | 10/19/2023 | 1 |
| 3 Washington, DC - 9:30 - 10-21, Sat | 10/21/2023 | Boston, MA - Great - 10 | 10/20/2023 | 1 |
| 4 Philadelphia, PA - Johnny - 10-22, Sun | 10/22/2023 | Washington, DC - 9:30 | 10/21/2023 | 1 |
| 5 Baltimore, MD - Crown - 10-23, Mon | 10/23/2023 | Philadelphia, PA - Johnr | 10/22/2023 | 1 |
| 6 Atlanta, GA - Masquerade - 10-25, Wed | 10/25/2023 | Baltimore, MD - Crown | 10/23/2023 | 2 |
| 7 Athens, GA - 40 - 10-26, Thu | 10/26/2023 | Atlanta, GA - Masquerac | 10/25/2023 | 1 |
| 8 Asheville, NC - Orange - 10-27, Fri | 10/27/2023 | Athens, GA - 40 - 10-26 | 10/26/2023 | 1 |

Figure 8-18. Calculating the difference in the respective dates of successive shows.

It would be nice to have a better way of visually identifying when we have a break on the tour. Using a simple IF()-based formula, we can compare the different results of our "Days between" fields. When we have a break, an emoji displays in our new field with the IF() function, as shown in Figure 8-19.

| ▦ show date | ⥮ Previous show | ⤢ show date ... | $f_x$ Days between | $f_x$ Extra travel day? |
|---|---|---|---|---|
| 10/29/2023 | Carrboro, NC - Cat's - 1 | 10/28/2023 | 1 | |
| 10/31/2023 | Miami, FL - Gramps - 10 | 10/29/2023 | 2 😴 | |
| 11/1/2023 | New Orleans, LA - Tipiti | 10/31/2023 | 1 | |
| 11/2/2023 | Houston, TX - Warehou: | 11/1/2023 | 1 | |
| 11/4/2023 | Austin, TX - Mohawk - 1 | 11/2/2023 | 2 😴 | |
| 11/5/2023 | McMinnville, TN - Cumb | 11/4/2023 | 1 | |

Figure 8-19. Displaying an emoji if there is a difference of more than one between dates of successive shows, which means at least one day in between shows.

The formula to display the emoji is simple. As seen in the following formula, we pass an argument of when the value of our "Days between" field is more than one to return the sleeping emoji.

Normally, in an IF() statement, there's a third element that refers to the value that's returned if the condition specified in the first element of the IF() formula evaluates to false. However, if you leave out the third parameter, the IF() function will default to returning BLANK() if the condition is false. This means that if the condition is false, the result will be an empty value rather than a specific provided value. Leaving out the third parameter can make the formula cleaner and more concise in situations where returning a blank value is the desired outcome. In our "Extra travel day?" formula, we'll skip the third element of this IF() formula:

```
IF(
    {Days between}>1,
    '🌙'
)
```

We're making good progress on using formula functions and operators to make the tour tracker more useful. Using some of the datetime functions, we've grouped the shows by week. We've abbreviated how we display the date in our primary field to make it more legible. And now we have an easy way to identify when we can expect to have at least one night off from the hectic tour schedule.

Next, let's look at numerical functions and how we can leverage those to better understand our tour tracker data.

# Numeric Functions

Airtable has a set of formula functions and operators that are specific for working with numeric data. Many of these functions and operators will be familiar to spreadsheet users because they are similar to common spreadsheet functions that allow you to multiply, divide, add, and subtract.

Let's look at how we can use a numeric formula function, ROUND(), and the operator * to estimate our ticket sales for each stop on the tour.

## Calculating Ticket Revenue Estimates

In the Cities table, we have linked to the venue we will be performing in for each city. Using a Lookup field, we can reference the capacity of the venue for that city, as shown in Figure 8-20.

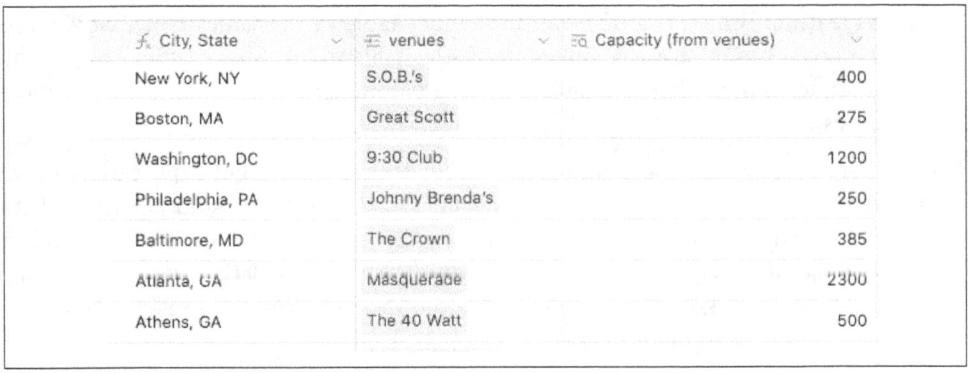
City, State
venues
Capacity (from venues)
New York, NY
S.O.B.'s
400
Boston, MA
Great Scott
275
Washington, DC
9:30 Club
1200
Philadelphia, PA
Johnny Brenda's
250
Baltimore, MD
The Crown
385
Atlanta, GA
Masquerade
2300
Athens, GA
The 40 Watt
500

*Figure 8-20. In the Cities table, we can see the capacity of each venue where we'll perform via a linked record and a Lookup field.*

We can bring this data into our Show table by creating a lookup field from the linked record from the Cities table, as shown in Figure 8-21. While the Lookup field comes from the Cities table, that data originates in the Venues table.

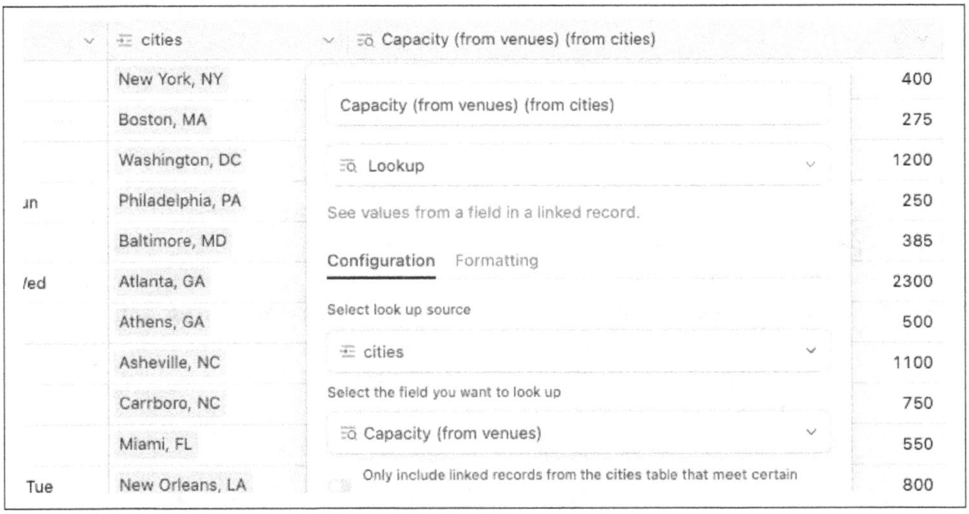
cities
Capacity (from venues) (from cities)
New York, NY
Boston, MA
Washington, DC
Philadelphia, PA
Baltimore, MD
Atlanta, GA
Athens, GA
Asheville, NC
Carrboro, NC
Miami, FL
New Orleans, LA
Tue
Capacity (from venues) (from cities)
Lookup
See values from a field in a linked record.
Configuration
Formatting
Select look up source
cities
Select the field you want to look up
Capacity (from venues)
Only include linked records from the cities table that meet certain
400
275
1200
250
385
2300
500
1100
750
550
800

*Figure 8-21. Bringing the capacity for each show into the Show table from the Cities table, which references it from the Venues table.*

When designing the structure of the Fall Tour Tracker, an intentional decision was made to link each show to a city rather than a specific venue. This was motivated by the tour planning process, which entails working out the travel logistics and routing before finalizing the venues.

We first created a linked record from the Venues table to the Cities table. Now we're creating a Lookup field as we've linked the Cities table to our Show table. This is why the Lookup field's name has two tables listed in parentheses: "Capacity (from Venues) (from Cities)."

To make some estimates about how much ticket revenue we might expect to earn, we first need to know how much revenue we'll get from each ticket sold per show. Let's create two new fields. We'll call the first column "headlining?," which is a Single select field, with the options "headliner" and "opening act." Next, let's create a Currency field titled "rev per ticket." In this field, we'll store the net revenue from each ticket for a given show, as seen in Figure 8-22.

| | *fx* Show | ☰ Capacity (f... | ◉ headlining? | 💲 rev per ticket |
|---|---|---|---|---|
| 1 | New York, NY - S.O.B.'s - 10-19, Thu | 400 | headliner | $35.92 |
| 2 | Boston, MA - Great - 10-20, Fri | 275 | headliner | $28.00 |
| 3 | Washington, DC - 9:30 - 10-21, Sat | 1200 | opening act | $8.40 |
| 4 | Philadelphia, PA – Johnny - 10-22, Sun | 250 | headliner | $28.20 |
| 5 | Baltimore, MD - Crown - 10-23, Mon | 385 | headliner | $24.50 |
| 6 | Atlanta, GA - Masquerade - 10-25, Wed | 2300 | opening act | $8.30 |
| 7 | Athens, GA - 40 - 10-26, Thu | 500 | headliner | $18.50 |

*Figure 8-22. Listing the revenue per ticket for each show.*

When we headline a performance, this usually means we will take significantly more revenue per ticket than if we are the opening act. As we can see in Figure 8-23, when we group records by the "headlining?" field and then sort them in ascending order by "rev per ticket," we make much more on the shows where we are a headliner.

| | *fx* Show | 💲 rev per ticket | ☰ C |
|---|---|---|---|
| ▶ | HEADLINING?<br>opening act | Count 11 | Mdn $8.00 |
| ▶ | HEADLINING?<br>headliner | Count 23 | Mdn $24.50 |

*Figure 8-23. Grouping records by whether the band is headlining, or the opening act, to understand the median revenue per ticket.*

We will make two estimates of ticket sales, one being a low estimate and another that we consider to be our best-case scenario. Let's start with the low-end estimate.

If only half of the tickets in a venue sell for one of our shows, we hope that's on the low end of outcomes for the tour. We can create a simple formula that multiplies the revenue for each show by the capacity and then use the multiplication formula operator to calculate half of this number in the next formula. We'll also use the ROUND() function to give us a rounded result. By wrapping the entire equation within the ROUND() function, we will round the result of everything we're multiplying together:

```
ROUND({Capacity (from Venues) (from Cities)}*{rev per ticket}*.5)
```

Now, let's make a formula to calculate what we think is a best-case scenario for each show. After all, 100% of the tickets never get sold since some are given away for promotional reasons and some are guest list spots. Therefore, it's likely that we will only sell 90% of the available tickets. We can use the exact same formula that we just did for our low-end scenario but substitute 0.9 for 0.5, as in this formula:

```
ROUND({Capacity (from Venues) (from Cities)}*{rev per ticket}*.9)
```

Using the summary bar at the bottom of the browser window, we can see that based on our calculations, there is a median low-end estimate of about $6,300 for our tour, and our best-case scenario has a median average of over $11,000 per show, as shown in Figure 8-24.

| $ rev per ticket | Capacity (f... | headlining? | $fx$ ticket est. – low | $fx$ ticket est. – best case |
|---|---|---|---|---|
| $35.92 | 400 | headliner | $7,184.00 | $12,931.00 |
| $28.00 | 275 | headliner | $3,850.00 | $6,930.00 |
| $8.40 | 1200 | opening act | $5,040.00 | $9,072.00 |
| $28.20 | 250 | headliner | $3,525.00 | $6,345.00 |
| $24.50 | 385 | headliner | $4,716.00 | $8,489.00 |
| $8.30 | 2300 | opening act | $9,545.00 | $17,181.00 |
| $18.50 | 500 | headliner | $4,625.00 | $8,325.00 |
| $10.30 | 1100 | opening act | $5,665.00 | $10,197.00 |
| Mdn $22.65 | | | Mdn $6,351.50 | Mdn $11,432.50 |

Figure 8-24. Estimating a median best case and worst case for Ticket sales, using the summary bar.

Now that we've touched on three major types of data that have their own formula functions and operators—text, dates, and numerical data—we can look at more of the logic functions that complement the IF() function we've already seen.

# Logical Functions

Logical functions such as IF() give us the ability to analyze and generate results from our data in a way similar to a programming language like JavaScript or Python. Using logic in Airtable formulas is especially helpful with complex business questions. For example, let's assume that we will need to buy insurance for certain tour performances.

## Determining Whether to Buy an Insurance Policy

We can use a combination of functions to help us decide whether or not it's worth paying for an insurance policy for a given show. Since this is a complex decision, it can be helpful to write out what we're trying to accomplish and the parameters of how we will make the decision. For instance:

- We *need* to consider buying a policy if we are the headliner.
- We *want* to consider buying a policy if the average between our low-end estimate and best-case ticket revenue scenario is greater than $7,000 because of the cost of a policy.

We already have all the fields prepared to write a formula that can tell us whether or not we might need to buy a policy for each show. In the next formula, we will use the IF() function in combination with the AND() function. The AND() function measures whether all conditions being evaluated are true. As we can see in the following formula, we are passing two different arguments to the AND() function:

```
IF(
    AND(
        ({headlining?}='headliner'),
        (AVERAGE({ticket est. - low},{ticket est. - best case})>7000)),
    '⚪ need policy',
    '👍 n/a'
)
```

The first argument is related to whether we are a headliner for a show. This was our first business rule for this formula. The second argument is related to whether the average of our low-end and best-case ticket revenues is more than $7,000. We will use the numeric function AVERAGE() to find the average between these two estimates.

Since both of those statements are being evaluated by AND(), if both are true, then our formula will return "⚪need policy." If one or more condition is not true, it will instead return "👍n/a," as we can see in Figure 8-25.

| headlining? | Capacity ... | *f*ₓ ticket est. - low | *f*ₓ ticket est. - best case | *f*ₓ show insurance? |
|---|---|---|---|---|
| headliner | 648 | $7,452.00 | $13,414.00 | 🔵 need policy |
| headliner | 250 | $3,250.00 | $5,850.00 | n/a |
| opening act | 3300 | $12,375.00 | $22,275.00 | n/a |
| headliner | 588 | $8,438.00 | $15,188.00 | 🔵 need policy |
| headliner | 900 | $10,800.00 | $19,440.00 | 🔵 need policy |
| headliner | 400 | $4,600.00 | $8,280.00 | n/a |
| headliner | 500 | $8,125.00 | $14,625.00 | 🔵 need policy |
| headliner | 800 | $13,600.00 | $24,480.00 | 🔵 need policy |
| headliner | 300 | $3,675.00 | $6,615.00 | n/a |

*Figure 8-25. Creating a formula to determine whether we need an insurance policy, using multiple logic functions.*

Then, we can filter the results to only show us the records that have the result of the formula "need policy," as shown in Figure 8-26.

| ☰ Filtered by show insurance? | ⊞ Group | ↓↑ Sort | 🎨 Color | ≡I | 🔗 Share view | |
|---|---|---|---|---|---|---|

| headlining? | Capacity ... | *fₓ* ticket est. - low | *fₓ* ticket est. - best case | *fₓ* show insurance? |
|---|---|---|---|---|
| headliner | 400 | $7,184.00 | $12,931.00 | 🔵 need policy |
| headliner | 750 | $8,025.00 | $14,445.00 | 🔵 need policy |
| headliner | 800 | $9,000.00 | $16,200.00 | 🔵 need policy |
| headliner | 648 | $7,452.00 | $13,414.00 | 🔵 need policy |
| headliner | 588 | $8,438.00 | $15,188.00 | 🔵 need policy |
| headliner | 900 | $10,800.00 | $19,440.00 | 🔵 need policy |

*Figure 8-26. Filtering to show the performances that we need to buy an insurance policy for.*

## Using SWITCH() to Calculate How Many Days Off Between Shows

When we used `IF()` to calculate if we had an extra travel day, we only returned a simple emoji if we had at least one day between shows. We'd like to know how many days there are in each break in the schedule. We could do this using a nested `IF()` statement, as we just did with our data validation formula, but we would have to make multiple nested `IF()` statements, which can get confusing. Instead, we can make a more efficient formula to put in values depending on the value of another field.

The next formula demonstrates how this can work with `SWITCH()`. We create a new formula field titled "Days of rest" and use the `SWITCH()` function to reference our

"Days between" field, which calculated how many days between a show and the show before it:

```
SWITCH(
    {Days between},
    1,'',
    2,'1 😴',
    3,'2 😴😴',
    4,'3 😴😴😴',
    'n/a'
)
```

After we specify the "Days between" field, we now create a list of possible values and the corresponding value for the formula to return. If the value is "1," this means there are no extra days between shows, so we want to just return a blank value. However, if there is a 2, this number means there is one extra day between shows, so we'll return the number 1 and a single sleepy emoji. We can do the same if there is a 3 by returning two emojis and if it's a 4 by returning three emojis, as shown in Figure 8-27.

The last part of the SWITCH() function is a value to return if the field value for a given record doesn't match any of the options. In our case, we'll return a default value of "n/a."

*Figure 8-27. Using the SWITCH() function in lieu of nested IF() functions to determine how many days, if any, between performances.*

In Figure 8-27, there's no previous show for the very first record. In this case, our "Days between" formula returns an error value of "n/a," which is an error message that means "not applicable." The "Days between" field returns "NaN," which is an error code that stands for "not a number."

# Using Nested IF() Statements for Data Validation

Although our dataset of 31 shows on the tour is pretty manageable, we can imagine a time when we have so much data in an Airtable base that we can't simply eyeball it for accuracy or completeness. In these cases, logical functions can help manage data.

We have used the IF() function before to analyze whether a piece of data meets a condition. We can also put an IF() statement with another IF() statement to do a secondary check. For example, we can first check to make sure that each record in the Show table has a city in the Cities linked field. Secondly, we can check to make sure that the Cities linked record also has a venue associated with it.

The first IF() statement is to check to see if we have a linked record from the Cities table so we can pass the argument asking whether the field Cities is BLANK(), as shown in the following formula:

```
IF(
    Cities=BLANK(),
    'no city',
        IF({Venues (from Cities)}=BLANK(),
        'no venue',
    '☑')
)
```

If that function returns as true, it means that we don't have a linked record in the Cities table for that show. Therefore, the formula will output "no city."

If there is a linked record for a show from the Cities table, then our nested IF() statement comes into play. If the "Cities" linked record field is not blank, then the formula checks to see if the "Venues" field is blank. As a reminder, this "Venues" field is a Lookup field that is dependent on being a linked city's record.

If the venue is also blank, then the formula will return "no venue." However, if both the city and the venue are present for a record, then the result of the two IF() statements is a check mark.

Our database design, which links each show to a city rather than a specific venue, allows us to easily incorporate and track the logistics of new cities as we plan the geographic route of our tour.

The existing shows will all have check marks, but let's add a couple of new records. We would love to play a show along the Pacific Coast Highway in Big Sur. So, as shown in Figure 8-28, we've added a new record for this location in the Cities table, but it doesn't have a venue. The next new record doesn't have a city at all, so we can see the formula has returned a value of "no venue" for the Big Sur record and a value of "no city" for the record without a linked city record.

| | *fx* Show | | ⛌ cities | ⛌ venues (from c... | *fx* Venue and city check |
|---|---|---|---|---|---|
| 1 | #ERROR! | | Big Sur, CA | | no venue |
| 2 | #ERROR! | | | | no city |
| 3 | New York, NY - S.O.B.'s - 10-19, Thu | | New York, NY | S.O.B.'s | ☑ |
| 4 | Boston, MA - Great - 10-20, Fri | | Boston, MA | Great Scott | ☑ |
| 5 | Washington, DC - 9:30 - 10-21, Sat | | Washington, DC | 9:30 Club | ☑ |
| 6 | Philadelphia, PA - Johnny - 10-22, Sun | | Philadelphia, PA | Johnny Brenda's | ☑ |
| 7 | Baltimore, MD - Crown - 10-23, Mon | | Baltimore, MD | The Crown | ☑ |
| 8 | Atlanta, GA - Masquerade - 10-25, Wed | | Atlanta, GA | Masquerade | ☑ |
| 9 | Athens. GA - 40 - 10-26. Thu | | Athens, GA | The 40 Watt | ☑ |

*Figure 8-28. Understanding the status of whether records in our Show table are missing a venue or a city or both.*

As seen in Figure 8-29, our primary field has an error. Normally, if we're referencing another field in a formula to display the contents of that referenced field, the absence of a value would just result in a blank space. But in this case, we are referencing a formula ("Formatting show date") we use to format our date and clean it up for easier reading without a date.

When this "Formatting show date" field references our two new records that don't have dates, it generates an error message of its own. Then, when the primary field pulls in these three fields and there's an error message on that date formula, it also triggers an error message.

| *fx* Show | *fx* City without quotes | *fx* Formatting show date | *fx* using IF() venue name |
|---|---|---|---|
| #ERROR! | Big Sur, CA | #ERROR! | |
| #ERROR! | | #ERROR! | |
| New York, NY - S.O.B.'s - 10-19, Thu | New York, NY | 10-19, Thu | S.O.B.'s |
| Boston, MA - Great - 10-20, Fri | Boston, MA | 10-20, Fri | Great |
| Washington, DC - 9:30 - 10-21, Sat | Washington, DC | 10-21, Sat | 9:30 |

*Figure 8-29. Getting an error in a formula in the primary field for two records that have errors in another field that the primary field references.*

In this chapter on formulas, we explored the functionality and capabilities of Airtable's Formula field. We learned how to manipulate text, dates, and numerical data using a variety of functions and operators, allowing us to perform calculations, format data, and combine values with ease.

We also explored the power of Airtable formulas to manipulate and analyze data. We learned about the different types of data that can be manipulated, such as text, dates, and numerical values, and how to use functions and operators to perform calculations and transformations. We also looked at logical functions that allow us to make decisions based on conditions. In the next chapter, we will delve into Airtable's Rollup field, which expands our ability to combine and aggregate data from linked records.

# CHAPTER 9

# The Rollup Field

Like the Lookup and Count fields, the Rollup field is another tool used in combination with a Linked records field. It's the most complex of the three and the most powerful.

Fundamentally, the Rollup field does two things. First, it looks up data values from a linked record field in the same table. Second, it can then answer a question about these values using a Rollup function.

## What Does It Mean to "Roll Up" a Field?

Once we have a Linked record field in a table, we can create a Rollup field. This Rollup field references a field from the record(s) we're linking to, as shown in Figure 9-1. (This is the same principle as looking up data from another table with the Lookup field.)

| Task name | Due date | Status |
|-----------|----------|--------|
| Task 1 | 2023-10-05 | In progress |
| Task 2 | 2023-09-30 | Completed |
| Task 3 | 2023-10-10 | Not started |
| Task 4 | 2023-10-15 | In progress |
| Task 5 | 2023-10-05 | Completed |

| Project name | Linked tasks | Rollup total tasks |
|--------------|--------------|--------------------|
| Project A | [Task 1, Task 2] | 2 |
| Project B | [Task 3, Task 4] | 2 |
| Project C | [Task 5] | 1 |

*Figure 9-1. Example of rolling up data from linked records in another field.*

Pulling in data about Linked records with a Rollup field allows us to do things like calculate the total of a group of orders in an orders table or find the highest-priced item in a table of items. We can use some of the same functions from Airtable's formula field in a Rollup field, such as SUM and AVG.

## Rolling Up Grocery Store Orders

Let's return to our grocery store example one last time before looking at an example from our Fall Tour Tracker. The grocery base has more records and will better illustrate how a Rollup field can offer insights, especially when data in your base grows beyond a couple of dozen records.

After choosing the linked table for your Rollup field, the Items table in this case, you choose which field in that linked table you want to roll up. As seen in Figure 9-2, we can choose the field from the table where the linked record lives.

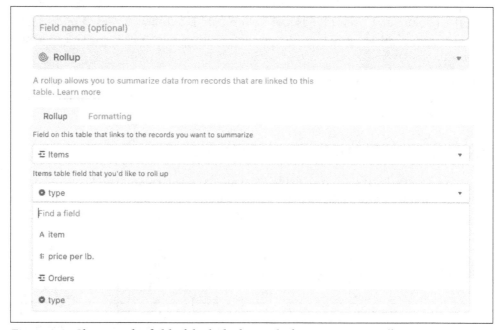

*Figure 9-2. Choosing the field of the linked records that we want to roll up.*

## Setting Conditions for Rollup Field

The Rollup field type mimics the sort of filtering we can do in the different views of a table. Instead of filtering in a view, we can set filter conditions that apply to the linked records whose data we're rolling up. Rather than applying a filter that would apply to all of the records in a table, we're just filtering which linked records (for all linked records that are linked in a given record) will be included in the Rollup field calculation.

We can toggle on the option and set a condition to only roll up fruit items, as shown in Figure 9-3.

*Figure 9-3. Creating a condition for the Rollup field that filters which linked records will be included in the rollup calculation.*

## Choosing a Rollup Function

After first choosing the linked record field and whatever filtering conditions we want, we can choose a function we'll use on the field we are rolling up. Depending on the type of data we're rolling up, we can choose various Rollup functions.

In this case, let's look at the most expensive type of vegetable in each order. We'll roll up the "price per lb." field with a condition that filters for vegetables in the "type" field. Next, we choose the MAX function, as shown in Figure 9-4.

*Figure 9-4. Determining the most expensive vegetable in each order with the MAX aggregator in a Rollup field.*

By choosing the MAX function, we have our new Rollup field that's calculated the most expensive vegetable for every order in the table, as shown in Figure 9-5.

| ☐ ‖ Order ID ⌄ | ☰ Items | ⌄ | ◉ type Rollup (from Items) | ☴ price per lb. (from Items) | ⌄ |
|---|---|---|---|---|---|
| 1 | 1 | Blood Oranges  Nectarines  Lettuce  ʌ | $3.70 | $3.02, $2.23, $2.62, $2.75, $3.70 | |
| 2 | 2 | Fava Beans  Mushrooms  Kumquats  ʌ | $3.85 | $2.93, $3.85, $3.75, $3.70, $3.60, $3.45 | |
| 3 | 3 | Plums  Apricots  Corn | $3.31 | $3.64, $2.75, $3.31 | |
| 4 | 4 | Nectarines  Cherries  Spinach  Blood | $3.63 | $2.23, $2.97, $3.63, $3.02, $3.45 | |
| 5 | 5 | Peaches  Morels  Apricots  Basil  Arti | $3.70 | $2.31, $3.09, $2.75, $3.18, $3.70, $3.45, $3.36, $3.60 | |
| 6 | 6 | Potatoes  Avocados  Basil  Arugula | $3.60 | $3.11, $3.36, $3.18, $3.60 | |
| 7 | 7 | Green Onions  Blood Oranges  Aspara | $3.45 | $2.53, $3.02, $3.45, $3.75, $3.18 | |
| 8 | 8 | Medjool Dates  Okra  Carrots  Articho | $3.70 | $2.45, $3.32, $2.13, $3.70 | |

*Figure 9-5. Finding the highest-priced vegetable from each customer with the MAX Rollup field function.*

# Rolling Up Costs from the Fall Tour Tracker

We can add a Rollup field to the Regions table in our Fall Tour Tracker base. Since we have a field of linked records, this is the opportunity to roll up values from those linked records using a Rollup field.

As seen in Figure 9-6, we can create a Rollup field that aggregates the sum of the promotional costs we've estimated for all cities linked to each region (since we didn't use any conditions to potentially filter out records from the rollup calculation).

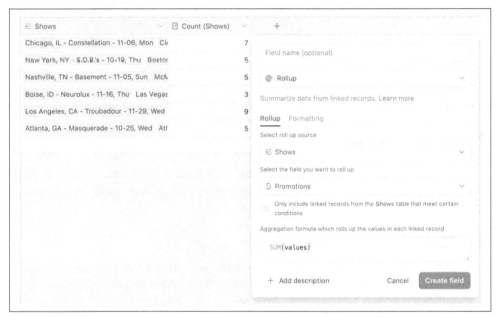

*Figure 9-6. Creating a Rollup field to sum together the values of the linked records for a particular field.*

The totals are shown in Figure 9-7.

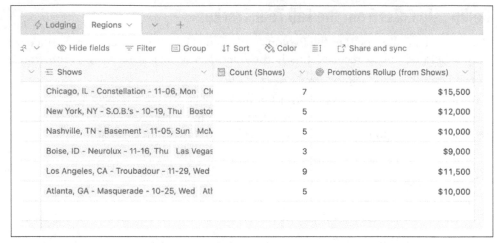

*Figure 9-7. A summary of the promotion costs by region, using a Rollup field.*

# Rollup Functions

As you'll see, the number of the Rollup field functions is the same as formula functions. Here's a rundown of the four different categories of functions we can use in aggregation formulas in our Rollup fields.

## Arithmetic Rollup Functions

Arithmetic Rollup functions are incredibly useful tools that allow you to perform calculations on a set of values from a linked record field in the Rollup field. These functions will provide you with valuable insights into the numerical data linked to each record.

### AVERAGE

One of the most commonly used arithmetic functions in a Rollup field is AVERAGE. This function calculates the average of all the values in the linked record field. By using the AVERAGE function in your Rollup field, you can easily find the average value of a specific numerical field from each linked record.

### SUM

SUM calculates the sum of all the values in the linked record field. By using the SUM function in your Rollup field, you can quickly determine the total sum of a numerical field from each linked record.

## MIN and MAX

The MIN function determines the minimum value from the set of values in the linked record field, while the MAX function identifies the maximum value. These functions are handy for identifying the smallest or largest value in a numerical field from each linked record.

# Logic Functions

Logical functions are essential building blocks when working with Rollup fields in Airtable. These functions allow us to perform various comparisons and evaluations on the data being rolled up, enabling us to gain insights into the linked records. Here are the three logic functions commonly used in Rollup fields.

## AND

The AND function evaluates whether multiple conditions are all true. It returns the value "true" if all conditions are met and "false" otherwise. In a Rollup field, this function can be used to determine if multiple criteria are simultaneously satisfied within the linked records.

Example: AND({Status} = "Complete", {Priority} = "High")

Result: Returns true if the Status is "Complete" *and* the Priority is "High".

## OR

The OR function evaluates whether at least one of several conditions is true. It returns the value "true" if any condition is met and "false" if none of the conditions are met. In a Rollup field, this function helps identify if any one of the specified criteria holds true within the linked records.

Example: OR({City} = "Berlin", {Country} = "Germany")

Result: Returns true if either the City is "Berlin" *or* the Country is "Germany".

## XOR

The XOR function stands for "exclusive OR," and it evaluates if an odd number of conditions is true. It returns the value "true" if exactly one condition is met and "false" if more than one or no conditions are met. In Rollup fields, XOR() can be employed when we want to find the presence of an exclusive condition that is isolated within the set of the linked records.

Example: XOR({Fruit} = "Apple", {Color} = "Red", {Taste} = "Sour")

Result: Returns true if only one of the conditions is met, either the Fruit is "Apple", the Color is "Red", or the Taste is "Sour".

## CONCATENATE Text Function

CONCATENATE is the only text Rollup aggregator function. It allows you to combine multiple values into a single string, making it especially useful when working with text or customer feedback data.

The benefit of using the CONCATENATE function in the aggregation section of a Rollup field is that it enables you to quickly create a consolidated view of the text data associated with linked records. Instead of manually copying and pasting each value or relying on complicated formulas, you can use the CONCATENATE function to automate the process and get an instant, well-organized summary.

CONCATENATE provides the option to include a delimiter between each joined value (a delimiter is a character or string that separates each value). By using a delimiter, we can visually distinguish between individual values within the merged string.

Imagine we have a table that represents a team of employees: John, George, and Paul. Now let's say we want to roll up all the team members' names into a single field using the CONCATENATE function in a Rollup field.

Without a delimiter, the names would be mashed together without any separation or distinction, making it difficult to distinguish one name from another. However, by utilizing the delimiter option in the CONCATENATE function, we can add a separator between each individual's name to make it more readable and organized.

Without a delimiter, the rolled-up field would look like this:

```
JohnGeorgePaul
```

Now, if we apply a delimiter, such as a semicolon (;) followed by a space, to separate each name, the rolled-up field would appear as follows:

```
John; George; Paul
```

## Array Functions

In addition to arithmetic, logical, and text functions, Airtable's Rollup field offers the power of array functions. These functions allow you to manipulate and analyze arrays of values that are rolled up from linked records. These functions are particularly useful when you are working with complex sets of data and want to extract specific information or perform calculations on the data.

### ARRAYCOMPACT

The ARRAYCOMPACT function is used to remove any blank or empty values from an array. This function is helpful when you only want to work with non-empty values in your rolled-up data. Once applied to an array, ARRAYCOMPACT returns a new array with all empty or blank values removed.

Example: ARRAYCOMPACT([54, , 38, ])

Result: [54, 38]

## ARRAYJOIN

The ARRAYJOIN function is used to concatenate the elements of an array into a single string with a specified separator between each element. This function allows you to easily display the contents of an array without having to manually concatenate the values together. Simply pass the array and the desired separator to the ARRAYJOIN function to get the concatenated string.

Example: ARRAYJOIN([John, Jane, Doe], "; ")

Result: "John; Jane; Doe"

## ARRAYUNIQUE

The ARRAYUNIQUE function is used to remove duplicate values from an array. This function can be helpful when you only want to work with unique values in your rolled-up data. Once applied to an array, ARRAYUNIQUE returns a new array with only the unique values from the original array.

Example: ARRAYUNIQUE([green, blue, blue, yellow])

Result: [green, blue, yellow]

With these array functions, you can further enhance the analysis of your rolled-up data. They provide robust manipulation capabilities and can help you derive meaningful insights by focusing on unique values, removing empty values, and joining array elements together.

In this chapter, we explored the Rollup field, a powerful tool that enables us to summarize and analyze data from linked records. By utilizing Rollup functions, we were able to gain valuable insights into our linked records and extract meaningful information from them.

# CHAPTER 10

# Extensions

Extensions are an easy way to take care of more specialized tasks in Airtable when working in Airtable's Data section. The ecosystem of Airtable extensions offers tools to clean up data, trigger a text message, import data from platforms like GitHub, find stock photos, and much more. Extensions are another way anyone in your organization can extend Airtable's powers to meet your goals without any programming abilities. (Although, if you do have the ability to write code in JavaScript, we will also look at how you can create your own scripts with the Scripting extension.)

Clicking "Add an extension" in the extensions dashboard on the right-hand side of the Data section opens up a selection of extensions and scripts from the Marketplace, as shown in Figure 10-1. With a few clicks, setting up an extension to enhance your Airtable experience is easy.

 Unfortunately, Extensions are only available on paid Airtable plans. (Previously, workspaces on the free tier were allowed one extension.)

*Figure 10-1. Choosing an extension from the Extensions Marketplace.*

In this chapter, we discuss the three major categories of Airtable extensions, show examples of using popular extensions in our tour tracker base, and show how to keep track of extensions. We will walk through several extensions in detail. But still, it's worth exploring the vast catalog in the Extensions Marketplace on your own.

# Three Major Categories of Airtable Extensions

We can bucket Extensions into three major categories:

- Extensions that manipulate data in your base
- Extensions that connect to third-party services
- Scripting extensions

The first category allows you to manipulate or display your Airtable data in a particular way. For example, you can create an organizational chart from data in your base, create a master calendar using data across different tables, or generate a visual schema showing how the fields and tables in your base relate to each other.

The second major category of Airtable extensions connect to third-party services, such as Google Hangouts and Shopify. Sometimes, these extensions are developed by the platform themselves, by Airtable, or by a third-party developer. Generally, these extensions allow you to import data from another service into your base, or use data in a table to do things like generate a PDF, send an email, or sync with a third-party service.

Lastly, the scripting extension is a general-purpose extension that allows anyone to develop an extension "script" that doesn't need to be published in the Extensions Marketplace. Scripting extensions are built with custom JavaScript that addresses your Airtable data via an SDK (software development kit). You can install and run scripts from the Extensions Marketplace without needing to customize any code, or you can build your own script to meet your particular needs.

Let's look at examples of these three categories before doing an in-depth walkthrough of some of the best extensions for the platform.

## Extensions That Work with Data in Your Base

Some of Airtable's extensions mirror functionality is now found in Airtable Interfaces. (We'll look at Interfaces in Chapter 12 and see how some of these features are analogous.) When Airtable launched the Extensions Marketplace, it had extensions with all different kinds of functionality. Let's look at a few categories of what Airtable developed for the community.

### Extensions for visual display

When extensions were launched, users didn't have an easy way to do visual reporting of Airtable data in Airtable. That has changed with the introduction of the Interface Designer (Chapter 12), but the following visual extensions can still be helpful when you're working inside the data section of a base.

 The Page designer allows you to create layouts of your data that can be exported as a PDF. We'll do a detailed walkthrough of Page designer later in this chapter.

**Chart.** The Chart extension is a workhorse that allows you to visualize your data in Airtable in a variety of ways. It's a perfect solution for anyone who wants to gain insights and make informed decisions based on their data. Whether tracking sales, analyzing survey results, or monitoring project progress, the Chart extension can help you better understand your data and uncover trends and patterns.

There are several types of charts, including bar charts, line charts, scatter plots, donut charts, and pie charts. Later, we will go through the different kinds of charts in the Chart extension using examples from the Fall Tour Tracker.

**Summary.** The Summary extension allows you to track and display high-level metrics from data in your base. With this extension, you can easily calculate and showcase important figures in your base, providing a quick overview of your data.

You have two main options for summarizing your data: count and summary. The count option gives you the total number of records in a specific field or view. We could use this in our tour tracker base for tallying the total number of shows on the tour, for example.

The summary option allows you to perform calculations on a specific field, such as sum, average, minimum, maximum, or other custom calculations. We could use this to find the average estimated attendance per show.

It calculates a value from a particular view and prominently displays that number on the right-hand side in the extensions dashboard, as shown in Figure 10-2.

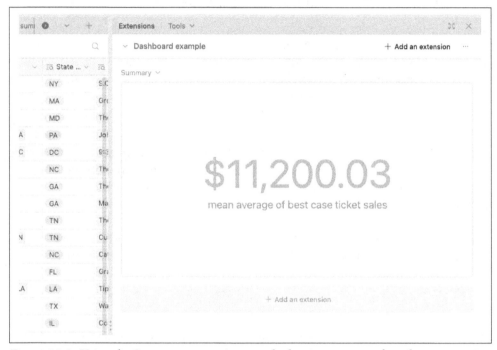

*Figure 10-2. Using the Summary extension to calculate an average of our best-case estimate for ticket sales.*

### Utility extensions

Airtable quickly understood that part of the user base deals with larger, more complex data and wants to manage it efficiently. Utility extensions are useful for Airtable users who are gaining more proficiency in understanding the platform.

**Dedupe.** Duplicate records can often be a headache, especially when dealing with large datasets. But with the Dedupe extension, you can quickly find and merge duplicate records, saving you time and effort.

You have the flexibility to choose whether you want to delete or merge the duplicates, depending on your specific needs. The Dedupe extension incorporates fuzzy matching to attempt to identify potential duplicates that aren't exactly alike. It takes into account various factors such as spelling variations, abbreviations, and common typos in an effort to ensure no potential duplicate records go unnoticed.

You can choose three levels of matching per field: exact, similar, or fuzzy, as shown in Figure 10-3.

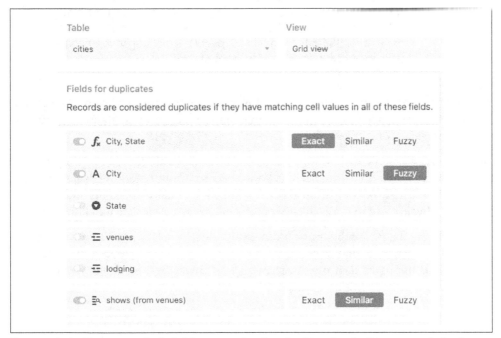

*Figure 10-3. Choosing which fields to search when looking for duplicate records in the Dedupe extension, and specifying how specific or fuzzy the search should be for each field.*

The risk with fuzzy matching in the Dedupe extension is that its algorithms are designed to strike a balance between precision and recall, meaning they aim to find as many potential duplicates as possible while minimizing incorrect matches. However, this balance is not always perfect, and there is always a trade-off between false positives and false negatives.

False positives occur when the Dedupe extension identifies records as duplicates that are actually different. This can happen when there are slight differences in spelling or formatting that the algorithm considers as similarities. False negatives, on the other hand, occur when the extension fails to identify actual duplicates, potentially leaving duplicate records in your base.

**Base schema.**   Base schema provides a comprehensive visual overview of the connections and dependencies between tables, making it easier to understand the structure of your base.

With the Base schema extension, you can see how tables are linked together through various types of relationships, such as linked records and Lookup fields, as shown in Figure 10-4. These relationships are displayed in a visually appealing and intuitive manner, allowing you to grasp the interconnectedness of your data quickly.

By visualizing the Base schema, you can easily identify relationships between tables, track data flows, and uncover any potential gaps or inconsistencies in your base design. This improves data organization and efficiency and enhances collaboration and decision making within your team.

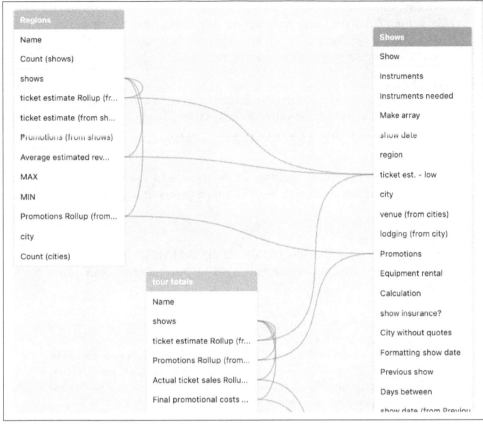

*Figure 10-4. Investigating connections between tables in the Base schema extension.*

**Batch update.**   The Batch update extension allows you to efficiently update multiple records in your base all at once. It is especially useful when you have a large dataset or when you need to make the same changes to multiple records simultaneously. To use Batch update, simply select the table that contains the records you want to update and choose the fields that you want to modify. Once you have selected your fields, you can perform various actions on each field individually. These actions include:

*Set to Number*
> This option allows you to set the selected field values to a specific number of your choice. For example, if you have a "Price" field, you can use this action to set all the prices in your records to a desired number.

*Set to Random Number Between*
> With this action, you can set the field values to random numbers within a specified range. It's great for adding a bit of variability or randomness to your data.

*Increment By*

This action allows you to increase the existing field values by a specified amount. For instance, if you have a "Quantity" field and want to increase all quantities by 5, you can easily accomplish that with this option.

*Decrement By*

Similar to the previous action, this feature allows you to decrease the existing field values by a specific amount. Handy for reducing quantities or adjusting other numerical values.

*Multiply By*

This action permits you to multiply the selected field values by a desired factor. Helpful in scenarios where you need to adjust prices or calculate totals based on existing values.

*Divide By*

Conversely, this operation lets you divide the field values by a specified amount. It's suitable for situations where you want to normalize or scale down certain values.

 While the Batch Update extension in Airtable offers convenience, there are risks of unintended errors and data inconsistencies if not used carefully. Double-checking actions and selecting the right fields is crucial to avoid potential data corruption or inaccuracies. Prioritizing backup measures and testing changes in a controlled environment are essential safeguards when using this extension.

By selecting multiple fields and applying different actions, you can make complex updates across multiple records efficiently and accurately. The Batch update extension takes away the hassle of manually updating each record individually and ensures consistent and streamlined changes. As shown in Figure 10-5, we can choose how to modify all records in a view.

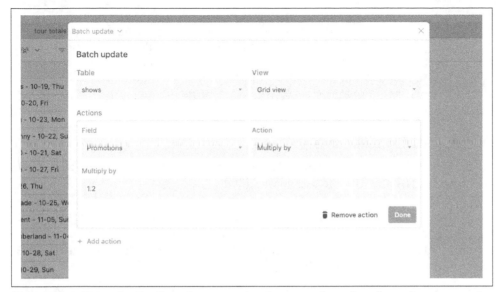

*Figure 10-5. Using the Batch update extension increases the values for each estimate of the promotion costs for all shows at once.*

## Extensions That Connect to Third-Party Services

Some extensions allow you to connect to another platform, such as Jira or Twilio, by connecting your account to the extension. These extensions are developed by third-party services. For example, the Loom screencast service has its own extension that allows you to preview a Loom video URL inside of Airtable.

Initially, Airtable partnered with a few companies, allowing Airtable to develop its own extension for its service. Some of these extensions have since been developed by Airtable, but the platform has also been opened up, and developers are welcome to submit an extension to be included on the Marketplace.

Independent developers are producing some of the most exciting and dynamic extensions. They are creating extensions that creatively use the strengths of Airtable to leverage the unique abilities of these third-party platforms. Instead of a large company having a relatively small initiative to build an extension, these independent creators are focused on bringing innovative extensions that can transform how people use Airtable. We will look at some examples next.

An API key is the most common way to connect your account on a third-party service to an extension that connects to the third-party service. These keys should be treated with the highest security precautions since they allow access to your account. Depending on how an extension has been developed, it's not uncommon that a user in your base can open a shared extension in your base and see your API key there.

### Examples of third-party extensions

Independent developers have created their own extensions for Airtable that aim to meet the needs of the Airtable user community.

**Data Fetcher.**  The Data Fetcher extension allows you to easily retrieve data from external sources and import it directly into your Airtable base. You can connect to various APIs, web services, and databases without any prior coding knowledge, making it a no-code solution for updating and integrating data.

One of the key advantages of the Data Fetcher extension is its simplicity. You don't need to write code or have any programming abilities to use this extension. Instead, all you need is an understanding of your data source's API or URL structure, which you can configure within the user-friendly interface.

Data Fetcher will perform automated requests to retrieve your desired data either on a regular basis or when specific triggers occur. From there, you can leverage all the other powerful features of Airtable to process and analyze your imported data.

**NoBull.**  Another useful extension is the NoBull extension, which was developed by Finsweet, a leading Webflow frontend web design studio. With this extension, you can use Airtable to manage data that feeds into a Webflow site via the Webflow content management system.

**On2Air Backups.**  The On2Air Backups extension provides automated, secure backups for your bases. You can schedule regular backups of your critical business data stored in Airtable and export your base data and attachments to popular cloud storage platforms like Google Drive, Dropbox, and Box. This means that you can easily send a backup of your Airtable bases directly to your chosen storage solution. It exports your data as CSV or JSON files and includes all your documents, images, and other attachments, preserving the format and size as saved in Airtable. This ensures that your data is always accessible when and where you need it.

On2Air Backups offers scheduling options for backups. You can choose from hourly, daily, weekly, or monthly backups depending on your needs. Additionally, the extension keeps a history log of all your backups. You can view the date and time of each backup, the destination of the backup, and how many bases, tables, records, and attachments were backed up.

# Scripting Extension

The Scripting extension is used to create more lightweight types of extensions. With a relatively novice understanding of JavaScript, anyone can create their own scripts for the Scripting extension to do most of the types of heavy lifting an extension can do. These scripts run inside of a generic container, the Airtable Scripts extension, which can be installed from the Scripts Marketplace just like any other extension. Often these scripts are used to perform a utilitarian task, like linking records or removing duplicates. As a result, there's an essentially infinite number of options when writing a custom script.

The scripting extension is, in some ways, just like any other extension. You install it into a base if you have creator permissions. But once you install it, you'll see that the scripting extension allows for JavaScript to be written directly into it using JavaScript.

You can write scripts to create and update records, call external APIs, or incorporate custom logic, which you can access with JavaScript in the scripting extension via the Scripting API.

Airtable offers three APIs: the Scripting API for custom JavaScript scripts; the Custom Extensions API for building integrated extensions that can be published in the Extensions Marketplace; and the Web API for programmatically interacting with Airtable from external applications. Appendix A is an introduction to these tools for the nondeveloper.

## Script examples

A primary value proposition of the scripting extension is to avoid manual repetitive work. The scripting extension allows streamlining a workflow that might otherwise involve many manual changes to records.

The scripting extension is powerful, so it's important to know that any user can press the "Run" button regardless of access level. However, Airtable still enforces permission levels. So if a user isn't authorized to create or modify records, for example, the script will stop once it encounters records that the user isn't authorized to modify.

Unlike other extensions in the Airtable Marketplace, the script extension allows totally customized code to run. The extension has access to your base's tables and records, so there's a near-infinite variety of what a scripting extension can do. Before we learn how to write scripts, let's look at some scripts we can use without manipulation.

**Convert URLs to attachments script.** Imagine that you are syncing a table from another base, and one of the fields has a link to the logo of a company you are researching in Airtable. There are a few ways to automate taking that URL and downloading the image as an image into an attachment field. The script for this task, which can be found in the Marketplace, is more direct and streamlined than setting up an automation.

If we install the script from the Marketplace and click "Edit Code," we see a preview of its JavaScript code on the left-hand side, as shown in Figure 10-6.

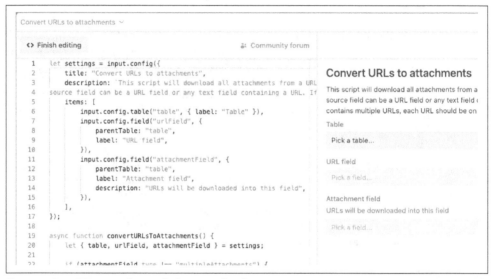

*Figure 10-6. Viewing the underlying code of a scripting extension.*

But don't worry. We can just use the simple user interface, as shown in Figure 10-7. That script allows us to pick a table, the field that has the URL, and the attachment field where we want the downloaded file to be placed.

*Figure 10-7. The user-friendly interface of a scripting extension we can use to import images from a URL into an attachment field.*

**Validate emails script.**   If we set up a form with Airtable and one of the fields is an email address, we could get some junk data submitted by users. This extension looks like an email field in a table and lists all values that are not formatted as email addresses.

Like the first example, we can preview a chunk of code after we open the script from the Airtable Marketplace. But once we install it, there's a simple user interface. As shown in Figure 10-8, we can pick any table in the base and then a field.

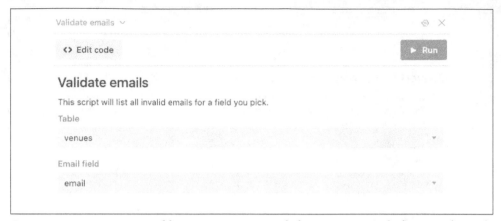

*Figure 10-8. Using an Airtable script, we can search for any improperly formatted email addresses.*

After clicking run, it will list the records by the primary ID and the cell value that should be formatted as an email address but is not, as shown in Figure 10-9.

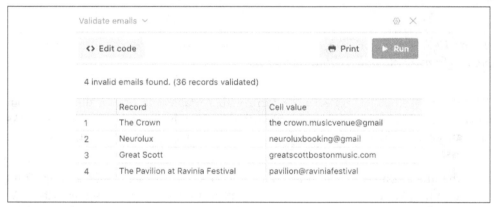

*Figure 10-9. The "Validate emails" script returning a list of improperly formatted emails.*

There are many ways to find code to put inside a scripting extension. Let's look at how we can install a script and find scripts.

## How to install a script

Users have two main options for using the scripting extension. The first is to install a script from the Airtable Marketplace, just like any other extension.

**Installing an extension from the Marketplace.**   To do this, click into the Scripts section of the Extensions Marketplace, as shown in Figure 10-10. You'll see a couple of dozen scripts that Airtable has curated, like the two previous examples. Simply click the "Add" button next to the script you want to install, and it brings up a simple user interface.

*Figure 10-10. Browsing scripts available in the Extensions Marketplace.*

**Installing custom code into the scripting extension.**   This time, instead of installing a script listed in the Extensions Marketplace, let's go to "Add an extension," and this time select the scripting extension itself. As we can see in Figure 10-11, the scripting extension window has three parts: the code, the interface on the right-hand side, and a series of options on the bottom left. These options include documentation of the scripting extension, examples of scripts, a reference for the scripting API, and, in an advanced section, the option to show the script code when sharing a base.

```
Scripting  ⌄

<> Finish editing                                                    Ask th

 1    // Change this to the name of a table in your base
 2    let table = base.getTable('Invoices');
 3
 4    // Fetch conversion rate from API - you could change this to any API you want
 5    let apiResponse = await fetch('https://api.exchangerate.host/latest?base=USD');
 6    let data = await apiResponse.json();
 7    let conversionRate = data.rates.GBP;
 8    output.text(`Conversion rate: ${conversionRate}`);
 9
10    // Update all the records
11    let result = await table.selectRecordsAsync({fields: ['Amount (USD)']});
12    for (let record of result.records) {
13        await table.updateRecordAsync(record, {
14            // Change these names to fields in your base

   Documentation  Examples  API  Advanced
```

*Figure 10-11. Viewing the code of a script extension.*

The upper left pane has an example of JavaScript that grabs the latest currency exchange rates.

Let's look at how we can use a scripting extension to take JavaScript code other people have written for the scripting extension and use it in our base.

## Where to find Airtable scripts

Aside from writing your own scripts, there are a couple of primary starting points for finding a particular script for a particular need. The first is the vibrant Airtable Community Forum. Searching for a specific need can bring up an answer from a community member who has pasted a short script to meet the need the original poster asked about.

Airtable also maintains a GitHub repository for extensions. In this repository's "Dependency graph," you'll find several hundred more repos of individual scripts built on top of the extensions code that people have made public. Unfortunately, these extensions can be added without any editorial oversight, so they might be unfinished or broken.

There are several other methods for obtaining scripts. You can hire a freelancer to create a custom script tailored to your requirements. There are Airtable pros, such as Kuovonne Vorderbruggen, who offer prewritten scripts available for purchase, which can provide a ready-made solution for various use cases. Additionally, with the advancements in generative AI, there are now tools available that can generate scripts automatically. (As with all things generative AI, the results are mixed but improving fast.)

 When looking at the many scripts listed in the dependencies for the extensions code, you can filter which GitHub repositories have a star or how many stars they have. It's an imperfect way to search, but it may tip you off about what scripts other people use and might be worthwhile.

Now that we've looked at finding prebuilt scripts, let's take some code and put it in the scripting extension.

### Putting code into the scripting extension

Some members of the Airtable community have published open source scripts on GitHub for public use. For example, Justin Barrett is a top contributor to the Airtable community and has a script in his GitHub that's a good example of when to use the scripting extension.

The script, "Reverse Attachment Order," addresses a niche problem that is perfect for the scripting extension's powerful flexibility. In this case, Airtable happens to track the order in which an attachment is added to the attachment field. That order is referenced when you're pulling multiple attachments through an automation or API call. If you have this problem, you would need to be dealing with lots of attachments, working with them programmatically, through either automations or the API. So this scenario is the sort of thing that will just apply to a small number of users.

Since there's not going to be a huge demand for a dedicated extension that reorganizes the order of attachments in an attachment field, someone can build it on their own, which Justin did. Let's look at his script and how we can use it in our base.

Justin's public repository (*https://oreil.ly/gfqX0*) is shown in Figure 10-12.

*Figure 10-12. We have navigated to Justin Barrett's "Reverse Attachment Order" script on GitHub.*

We can copy this code from GitHub and paste it into the scripting extension that we installed. Let's start by erasing the default "Hello World!" code. Now that it's empty, we can paste in the code from Justin's repository, as seen in Figure 10-13.

```
1   /**
2    * Title: Reverse Attachment Order
3    * Version: 1.0.0
4    * License: MIT
5    * Author: Justin Barrett
6    * Site: http://allaboutthatbase.tips
7    * Support: https://ko-fi.com/allaboutthatbase
8    * Source: https://github.com/justinsbarrett/airtable-scripts/tree/main/scripting-extension/reverseAt
9    *
10   * Description: Reverses the attachment order of files in a specified field.
11   * Only records with more than one attachment in the field will be updated.
12   */
13
14   const settings = input.config({
15     title: "Reverse Attachment Order",
16     description: "v1.0.0 - Reverses the attachment order of files in a specified field. Only records wi
17     items: [
18         input.config.table("table", {
19             label: "Table"
20         }).
```

*Figure 10-13. Pasting Justin's script from GitHub into an instance of the scripting extension.*

Now that we have pasted in the code, the interface that Justin developed for this extension is immediately visible in the right-hand dashboard, as shown in Figure 10-14. We can see the title of the extension as "Reverse Attachment Order," a short description of the extension, and the option to pick a table and then an attachment field.

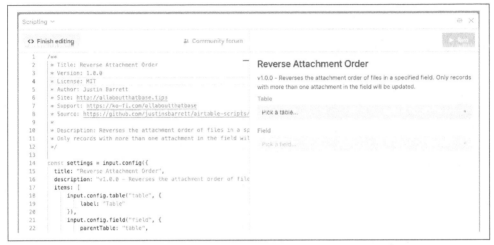

Figure 10-14. After pasting in a script, the applicable user interface appears in the scripting extension.

If we select a table with an attachment field and then specify that attachment field, the script gives us the option to run. In the case of this highly useful script, however, there is no warning telling us how many attachments will be reordered. Likewise, we won't find a warning that if we click this option, everything in the field we selected will be reordered.

In this case, it's probably not a big deal since we can simply rerun the extension to switch back to the original order. However, it's a good reminder that the scripting extension has fewer guardrails than other tools in Airtable. (For example, many extensions will warn you about the effect running the extension will have.)

 It takes a lot of skill to write a quality script. As you can probably imagine, there are scripts floating around that can have some serious unintended consequences. At the very least, it's a best practice to give a script a test run on some unimportant test data. If it's critical data, you may want to rule out using a script that hasn't been written by someone whose skills you trust.

Now that we've tried the extension, we don't need to edit the code or see the documentation in the lower left of the scripting extension window. So if we click "Finish editing," it closes the JavaScript editor and leaves us with the user interface. In our extensions sidebar on the right-hand side of the base, as seen in Figure 10-15, we now have drop-down menus to choose which attachment field to reverse the attachment order of and the button to run.

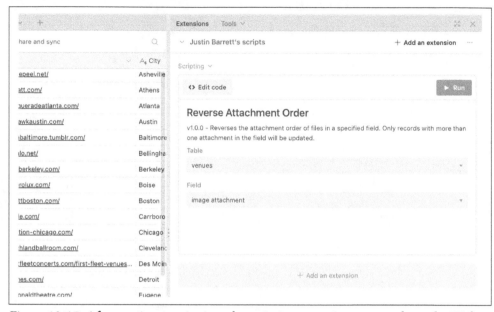

*Figure 10-15. After pasting a script into the scripting extension, we now have the UI for the script in our extensions dashboard to use, just like any other extension.*

Next, let's look at some popular Airtable extensions.

# Top Airtable Extensions

In this section, we look at some extensions that are broadly applicable and can be helpful in most Airtable projects. First, we will look at the Web clipper extension, which enables grabbing data from any web page you visit and putting it straight into your base. Next, we will examine how the Page designer extension can allow you to build custom layouts of your records data. The Chart Extension allows us to use a number of different graphical elements to display our data visually. Lastly, we will close the section by demonstrating how to connect Google's Translate API to the Translate extension to demonstrate how to easily leverage an external API service to transform data in our base.

# Chart Extension

The chart extension provides several ways to visualize data in your base. This extension mirrors the functionality of Airtable Interfaces, which we will look at in Chapter 12. First, let's explore the chart extension by looking at the best-case scenario we've estimated for each show in our Fall Tour Tracker base.

In Chapter 8, we created a formula field titled "Ticket estimate - best case." The formula multiplies the capacity of each venue by the revenue we are due to receive for each ticket sold, and then multiplies that number by 0.9. The assumption is that even in the best-case scenario, at least 10% of the tickets will be given to special guests or the press, for example.

## Bar chart

After installing the chart extension, we can choose the bar chart type. First, let's select the Shows table and a view created for this example titled "Chart extension." As we know from other extensions, such as the Page designer, the ability to choose a view allows us to choose a subset of records in a table if that view uses a filter. For this "Chart extension" view, nothing has been filtered out, and each show in the table is accessible for the chart.

First, we need to choose what to put on the x-axis. Since chronology is a common measure on the x-axis, let's use the show date and choose to show the access label as pictured in Figure 10-16. Next, we want to order the x-axis by the value that we've chosen. In other words, we want to order the records along the x-axis by the date in ascending order.

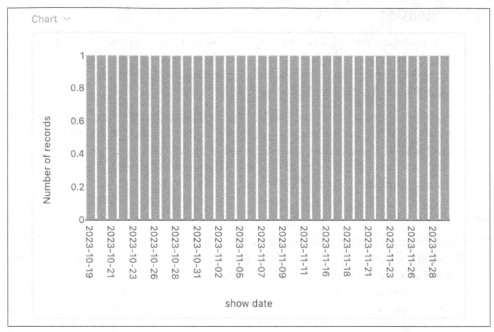

*Figure 10-16. Building a bar chart by first adding shows to the x-axis, ordered by date.*

On the y-axis, we're going to measure another field. So the first option would be to count the number of records for each item or category in the x-axis. But since we only have one show per date, that would not be a very interesting chart.

In Figure 10-17, we can now see a nice bar chart of ticket estimates that start with the first show in the middle of October and run through the end of November when the tour ends. Because we've toggled on "Show access label," we can see that the highest estimate is north of $25,000 and the lower estimates are just above $5,000. We can also mouse over any of the bars to reveal the exact x- and y-axis values.

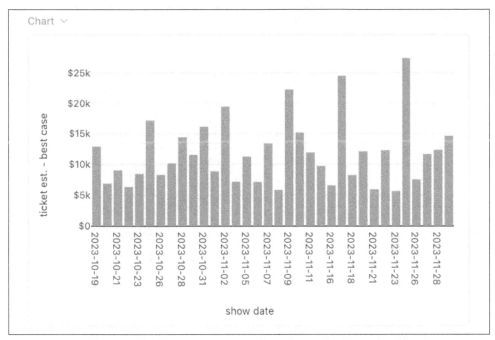

*Figure 10-17. Charting the best-case scenario for tickets sales for each of the shows in our bar chart.*

Let's do one more thing and group these records in a way that will help us meaningfully distinguish them. For example, we can choose "Group by" and select the "Regions" field, allowing us to see each show grouped by region as a different color, as shown in Figure 10-18.

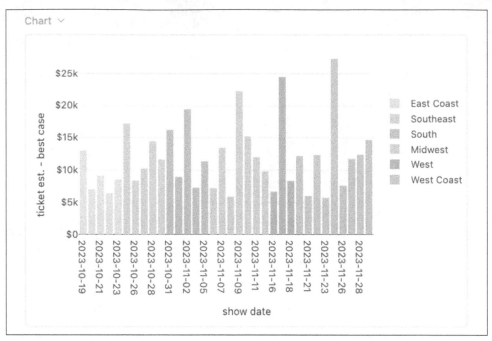

*Figure 10-18. Grouping the shows by region with color coding.*

## Line chart

Making a duplicate of our bar chart and simply choosing the line chart type gives us a less intuitive graph. Since we've grouped by region, we have six distinct groups of lines that track the trajectory of estimated ticket revenue per show by region, as shown in Figure 10-19. These figures are broken out by color, similar to our grouped bar chart.

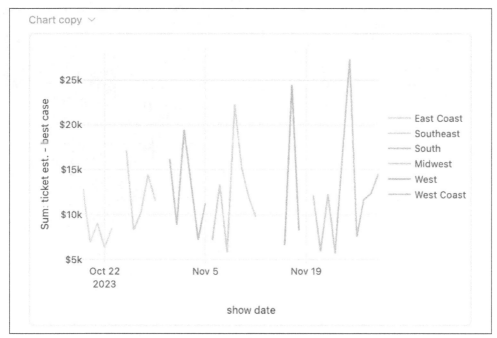

*Figure 10-19. Converting our grouped bar chart to a line chart shows disconnected lines.*

If we're interested in seeing the continuous ups and downs of our estimated ticket revenues, it may make sense to get rid of the grouping. So let's toggle off "Group by," which will show us a continual line chart of our expected ticket revenue over the six-week tour, as shown in Figure 10-20.

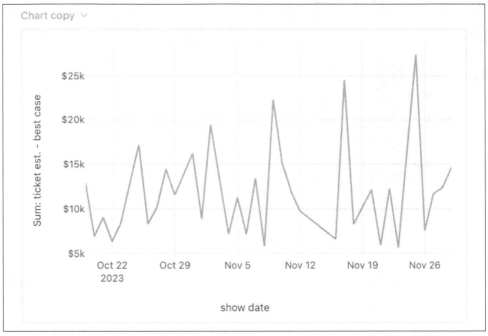

*Figure 10-20. Removing grouping by region for a continual line graph to see the ups and downs of the best-case scenarios for ticket sales.*

### Scatter plot chart

Duplicating the first bar chart we created and choosing this scatter chart type, we see a relatively chaotic group of chart points, as shown in Figure 10-21.

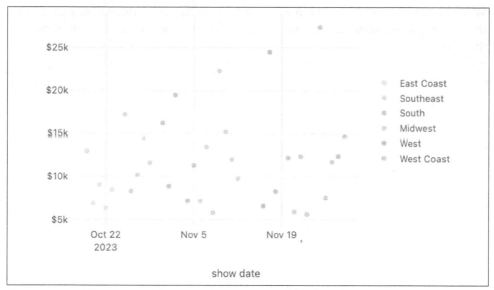

*Figure 10-21. The result of changing the chart type from bar chart to scatter plot.*

While the scatter plot is doing its job, it's hard to see anything meaningful, so let's try bucketing these values, as shown in Figure 10-22. This feature groups date values such as our show dates. It will be more helpful to view the range of potential earnings for these shows if we group them by week.

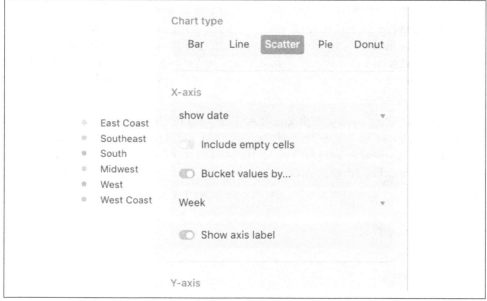

*Figure 10-22. Bucketing values in a scatter plot chart.*

When we do this, as illustrated in Figure 10-23, we can see a distinct line of dots on the scatter plot showing us the range of potential ticket revenues for a given week of the tour.

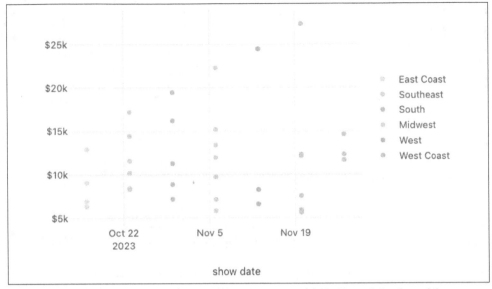

*Figure 10-23. Bucketing values in a scatter plot organizes the visual display of data points in the chart.*

### Donut chart and pie chart

The donut and pie charts are functionally the same, except that the donut chart has a note in the donut hole explaining what the chart is measuring. The pie and donut charts can measure a maximum of 25 entities. In the case of our tour, we have more than 25 shows. So instead of measuring shows, we'll group them by region to use these charts' capabilities.

In the values section, we will choose the same field of "Ticket estimate - best case," and we will choose to "Sum" the values, meaning adding up the values that fall into each category/region, as seen in Figure 10-24. This option gives us a bird's-eye view that compares ticket revenue from shows in the Midwest with those on the West Coast.

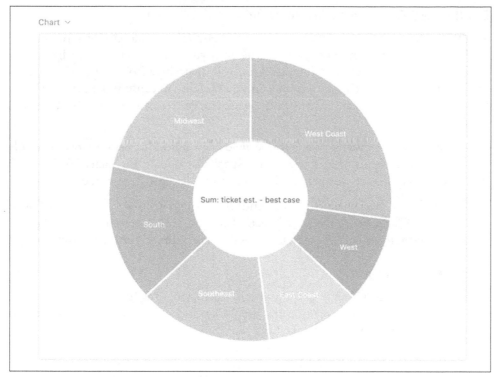

*Figure 10-24. Using a donut chart to create a visual comparison of our best-case scenarios of ticket sales by region.*

# Web Clipper Extension

Chapter 5 looked at how to bring data into Airtable in bulk via a spreadsheet or a connection to a data source like Google Sheets or GitHub. But what if you want to grab data on the web to put it into your base as you find it? The Web clipper extension is an easy way to quickly import data from a web page into a predefined table with the push of a button. The clipper can grab things like a page's name and URL and automatically push them into your base to save you time, be precise, and stay organized.

### The two components of Web clipper

Airtable's Web clipper is an extension just like the others, except it needs another component for it to work. Along with the extension itself, we need to install Airtable's Chrome extension to pull information from the page you are visiting into our base. So we should start by installing Web clipper from the Extensions Marketplace. Next, search for the Airtable Web clipper in the Google Chrome store and accept the permissions to install it.

### Data that the Web clipper extension can capture

The Web clipper extension is a halfway point between automated web scraping and the norm of just copying and pasting data into your base. Web clipper has clever defaults for the information you most likely want to archive from a site you're tracking. For example, Web clipper has built-in functionality to capture the title of a page, the page's URL, and whatever text on the page you've selected before activating Web clipper.

If your base has attachment fields, these fields can hold a screenshot of the whole page, a smaller screenshot you select, or a specific image on the page. We'll look at how to do this task once we open up the clipper after it's been configured.

For those with a background in frontend web design who are comfortable with HTML and CSS, it's also possible to specify CSS and HTML selectors to grab either text or images automatically based on where they are in the structure of a web page.

### Setting up the Web clipper

Let's return to our Fall Tour Tracker base and start generating ideas of where we may want to have dinner while we're on the road. First, we can create a new table called "Restaurants" and create new fields. Let's start with an attachment field called "Restaurant picture," a text field called "Description," a URL field, and a field titled "Yelp rating." So we have our primary field name, restaurant picture, description, URL, and Yelp rating. Let's also add a field for the appropriate city that will link to our Cities table.

After you've installed the Chrome extension, let's install the Web clipper extension, as shown in Figure 10-25. We are first asked to choose the table, which is Restaurants. Airtable then makes some educated guesses about what defaults you may want. We can set up a record name to be the page title, which is likely the restaurant's name if we're looking at a review site like Yelp.

*Figure 10-25. The initial fields Airtable suggests for our Web clipper.*

The URL will be the page URL, and when we're in the Web clipper itself, we can decide what we want to use for the restaurant picture. Let's add a couple more. For "Description," let's choose "selected text" for the Yelp rating. And for "City," which is a linked record, we can leave it without a default value since we'll choose to link that record.

We have six fields in this Web clipper extension we are mapping to the restaurants table. Let's title this Web clipper "Yelp restaurants for the tour."

## Using the Web clipper

New York City is the first stop on our tour. Luckily, we already have an idea of where we may want to have dinner, saving us from sifting through thousands of possibilities. So let's navigate to the Yelp page for the famous Katz's Delicatessen on the Lower East Side. If we click the Web clipper, we can see that it's filled in the name of the page and the URL of the listing. And since we've scrolled down and selected the description from the business owner before we selected it, that description is also captured in our Web clipper.

The restaurant picture field allows us to choose an area to screenshot, take a screenshot of a whole page, or select an image on the page. Let's choose the second option and get a screenshot of the entire page into our "Restaurants" table. Next, we can go to "City" toward the bottom of the clipper and select "New York," as shown in Figure 10-26, which will create a linked record once we add this record to the restaurant's table via the Web clipper. The last item is the Yelp rating we specified in the

Web clipper. We were going to grab that information from a CSS selector. But since we haven't set that up yet, let's just manually enter "4," which is what we see here on the page, and then click "Add record."

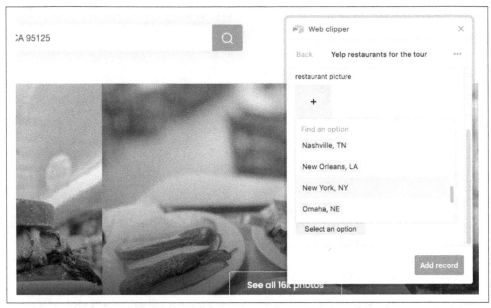

*Figure 10-26. Choosing a city to link to the new restaurant record for Katz's Delicatessen we are creating with the Web clipper.*

Returning to our new "Restaurants" table, we can see an entry for Katz's Delicatessen with the screenshot of the Yelp page. It includes the text description we selected, the Web clipper, the URL, the page, and the rating we entered. And it's linked to New York, too.

Suppose we wanted to grab the Yelp rating automatically whenever we use this Web clipper. In that case, we could go into developer tools in Chrome, find the CSS selector of the rating, then paste that information into the Web clipper configuration and its extension. Then, it would automatically pull that value every time we activate the Web clipper.

### Advanced Web clipper options

Using a CSS selector, we could preconfigure what image will go into an attachment field via the Web clipper. For example, every Yelp page has a "Popular dishes" section. So we could find the CSS selector for the first item image and automatically pull, in this case, a pastrami sandwich from the Katz's Delicatessen Yelp page.

# Page Designer

We've looked at many ways you can get data into Airtable and how to manipulate that data once it's there, but it can be just as important to get data out of an Airtable base to a customer or colleague. In Chapter 12, we'll look at the Interface Designer, which provides a way to build simple web interfaces on top of the data in your base. Another common way to share data is by creating a PDF layout. Page designer is one of the first extensions developed by Airtable, and it does a good job of allowing you to control the design of a template for records in your base to be captured in a PDF.

## What you can put into Page designer

Any layout in the Page designer extension is based on the data in a single table. So if a table has most but not all of the data we need for a Page designer layout, a lookup field and a linked record can bring that data from another table into the table we're creating the Page designer layout for.

The Page designer dialogue lists the table's fields on the left-hand side, as shown in Figure 10-27. This list includes all of the different kinds of fields in the table containing text and attachments.

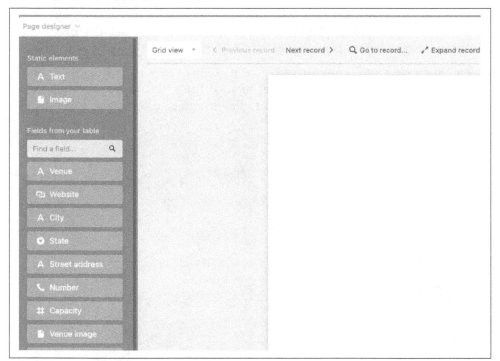

*Figure 10-27. All the fields from a table that contain text or attachments are listed on the left-hand side of the Page designer extension.*

### Static and dynamic elements

After opening Page designer, you see a left-hand sidebar with two groups of options. The first group includes static elements—either static pieces of text or static images. But what does this mean? With the static text element, you can add fixed text such as titles, headers, or descriptive paragraphs to your layout. For example, we might put a title at the top of a Page designer layout, like "Invoice."

Counterintuitively, the static text element also has the ability to include dynamic data from your base. This means that you can include the content of o a "static" text element, ensuring that the information is automatically updated whenever the underlying data changes. For example, you can include the name of a customer, the date of an event, or any other relevant information from your records directly in the static text element.

When you add a static image element to your Page designer layout, you have the option to select a specific image or logo that remains the same for every record. We could add a static image of the band's logo that would stay the same for each page, for example.

But, similar to the static text element, the static image element in Page designer can also include dynamic data. Let's say you have a table with records that include an attachment field for images. With the static image element, you can link this field and display the corresponding image for each record in your layout.

Below "Static elements," as shown in Figure 10-28, we can see the fields in the Shows table. This particular table has many of its own fields, linked records, and lookup fields. A search box located above the list of fields can be used to find a field instead of scrolling through the options.

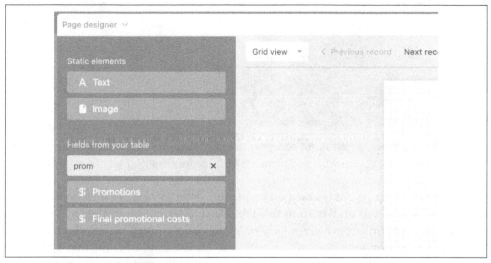

*Figure 10-28. When you have many fields in a table, the search function in Page designer can help you quickly find the field you want to include in your layout.*

### Available fields and records in Page designer

There are two different variables for determining what base content will be available in a Page designer layout. The first variable is your table itself. For instance, go to the upper left-hand corner, click the down arrow, and then hit "Settings." You'll see a dialogue box that notes from which table you're pulling data, as shown in Figure 10-29.

**Settings**

Table

shows

Record size

Letter (8.5 × 11 in)

Record orientation

Portrait        Landscape

Done

*Figure 10-29. Choosing the table for your layout in Page designer.*

The second key variable, as shown in Figure 10-30, is the view and therefore records that will be brought into your layout.

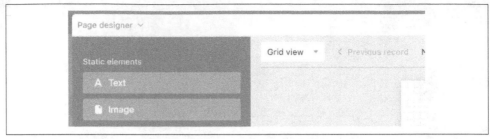

*Figure 10-30. The upper left-hand corner of the Page designer extension as a drop-down menu to choose the view, which will dictate which records it will create layouts for.*

Each Page designer layout is based on one table's data, so next we want to determine which records we can display from this table. The filter option in the Grid view can remove some records from a given view's display. A drop-down menu is located at the top of the extension interface with an option to choose any views for that table. This selection will determine which records can be displayed in that layout. For example, if we filter all the shows that are in the Northwest and then print each of these records, Page designer will only print records of shows in the Northwest.

To see which records are available and compare the layouts next to that drop-down menu, you can click between "Next record" and "Previous record" or press "Go to record" to search for a record to view in the layout. It's also possible to make changes to a record, as shown in Figure 10-31, by clicking "Expand record," which brings up the same expanded record dialogue we are used to from the Grid view.

*Figure 10-31. Clicking "Expand record" to edit any editable fields for a given record.*

### Positioning elements on the page

Let's pull the "Static text" option from the top of the left-hand menu. In the content section, which is now green, type in "Tour summary," as shown in Figure 10-32. For a text element, there are a number of options, including the position on the page with XY coordinates, the width and height of the box, the rotation, the font and font size, the text alignment within the box, the font color, and whether there is a background color or borders around the element.

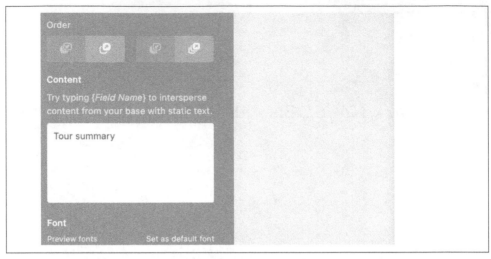

*Figure 10-32. Adding static text to our layout.*

Let's center the text horizontally and vertically, as shown in Figure 10-33. When we make the box larger, it will keep the text in the center of the box. It's worth remembering that we could have more text or larger text that the box can't accommodate for certain records; we'll see this situation when we review dynamic text and image elements. Let's leave the tour summary box at the top of the page and increase the font size to 20 and the weight to 700.

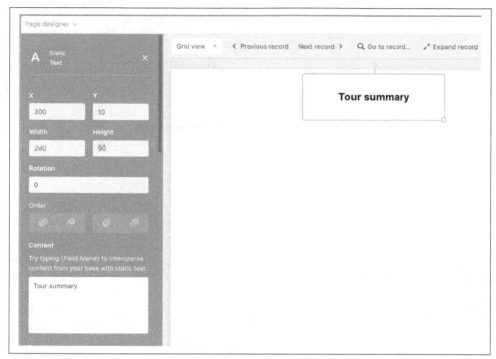

*Figure 10-33. Formatting a static text element in the Page designer extension.*

Now let's pull our primary field "Shows" into the Page designer canvas. We can already see that the text is wrapping onto the next line, so we can increase the default width from 200 pixels to 400. Next, let's change the color of the text to blue and put a border on the bottom of the text box. We can make the box shorter, too, as shown in Figure 10-34.

 We've made the element holding the show's name fairly wide, so none of the text is being cut off, as shown in Figure 10-34. However, this is something to look out for in Page designer. While one record might have plenty of room for a field in the element, the next record might have too much text, so the element overflows and you can't see everything for that record. It's important to spot-check records after building the layout to ensure that each element can hold all the text for every record that needs to be seen.

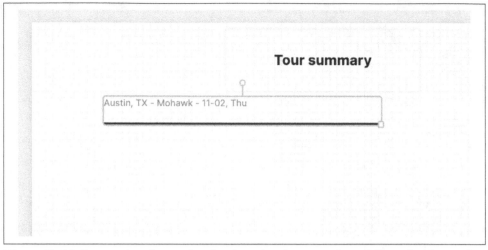

*Figure 10-34. Formatting the text box by changing the text color, adding a border on the bottom, and widening the box.*

Let's add one more element. Every show has a performance venue, and in the venue's synced table, we have an image for every venue. Unfortunately, we don't currently have those images accessible in the Shows table, so let's create a Lookup field to pull them into this Page designer layout. After creating a lookup field, we can open up Page designer again and search for the venue image in the search bar on the left-hand side. Then, drag that field to the Page designer canvas. The default size for new elements is 200 pixels wide by 150 pixels high. This size is a reasonable middle ground for bits of text, but we want to showcase what the venue looks like, so let's make the image larger and increase it to 500 wide by 300 high.

In the Page designer extension, all measurements are exclusively in pixels. Other units of measurement like centimeters or inches are not available, so users will need to adjust to working solely with pixels for sizing and positioning elements in their designs.

If we're referencing an attachment field with more than one image, we can display just the first image or all the images. If the latter, Page designer will put them on a grid. Users have three ways to put an image inside its box. If we "Fit" it, then there will be whitespace. If we "Fill" it, then part of the image will be cropped out. And if we "Stretch" it, it will fill the box but be stretched beyond its original proportions.

Let's select "Fit" mode and put a red background behind the image, as seen in Figure 10-35. Now we can look through the records in the view and see if the layout works for us.

*Figure 10-35. Making the image of each record fit into the box and adding a red background, which shows empty space in the box.*

### Printing from Page designer

Clicking "Print" in the upper right-hand corner allows you to print just the current record in Page designer or print all the records in a view. Of course, you can also choose the view from this print dialogue.

Printing more than one record at a time is complex if you want to have more than one record on a page. For example, imagine we want four shows listed on each 8.5″ × 11″ sheet of paper. In this case, we would want to print the records using the "In a list" option. But in "Settings," the record size would need to be set to a custom size represented in pixels.

The width of a page is represented in pixels, and the width of a page in Page designer is 927 pixels; the height is 1,199. So if we wanted four records on a page, we would need to make records with a custom size of the standard 927 pixels wide but round the height to 300 pixels.

### Drawbacks of Page designer

Page designer is far from perfect. As we saw, printing layouts with multiple records on a page can get complicated and cumbersome. For example, if you wanted to print 2″ × 3″ mailing labels from Page designer, it's possible, but it'll take some arithmetic and patience.

The other primary drawback of Page designer is that it cannot be connected to an API or automation. In other words, you can't trigger a Page designer to print a newly created record or create a PDF for all the records created in the last week. For many users, Page designer is very helpful, but ultimately users hit a wall when they need to automate the creation of PDFs. In this case, Airtable users tend to migrate to a third-party PDF creation service.

## Translate Extension

Airtable extensions allow you to leverage other robust services and bring those capabilities into your base. For example, Google's Cloud Translate service is the backbone of the Translate extension developed by Airtable, which can be easily set up to use Google's translation capabilities on text in your base.

### Setting up the Translate extension

As with any third-party service you want to integrate with Airtable, you need to first set up an account on that service. In the case of Google Translate, this is a part of the Google Cloud platform, so you'll need to set up a GCP account, create a project, and create an API key, which is the way to link your Google Cloud account to an Airtable base.

### Configuring the Translate extension

After entering your API key, select the table with the field you want to translate. It's essential to remember that this extension works by reading the text of records in a view from one field and entering the translated text into a different field.

You can limit unnecessary translations, which cost money, by using filters in a view to only translate the text in a field for certain records. For example, if you have 20 records you've already translated, you could filter to show 10 new records that still need to be translated. Otherwise, you'll be charged for translating all 30 records, 20 of which would be performing the same action again with no added benefit.

### Creating a translation

Let's return to our *Simpsons* episodes base to translate the name of episodes from English into other languages. Since this is a test, we'll create a new view titled "Translate test" and filter just the episodes in Season 1. In this view, I'm going to hide all of the existing fields, leaving us with just the primary field "Episodes."

Now we need to let the Translate extension know what text we need to be translated. We choose the "Episodes" table and the newly created "Translate text" view with just the Season 1 episodes. The source field is the "Episode" field—our primary field—and of course the source language is English. We'll create a new field titled "episode title - French," as shown in Figure 10-36.

*Figure 10-36. Setting up a new field for the translated episode titles.*

Choose that field in the extension and mark the destination language as French, as seen in Figure 10-37.

*Figure 10-37. Configuring the Translate extension.*

When we press "Translate with Google," we receive a warning dialogue that this particular batch of translations contains 258 characters and will cost us about one penny, as shown in Figure 10-38.

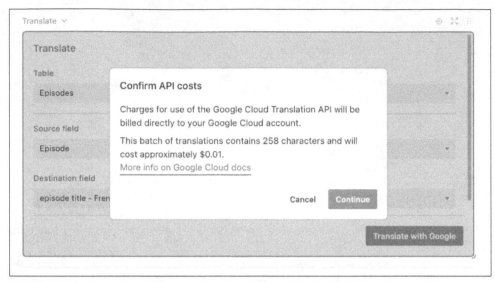

*Figure 10-38. A preview of the cost for translating with the Google API.*

After clicking "Continue," it displays all the records that will be updated and the number of records updated (13), as we can see in Figure 10-39.

*Figure 10-39. Previewing the translated title before the records are modified.*

Clicking "Save" then writes the translation data to our new "episode title - French" field, as shown in Figure 10-40.

| | A Episode | | A episode title - French | |
|---|---|---|---|---|
| 1 | Simpsons Roasting on an Open Fire | | Simpsons rôtir sur un feu ouvert | |
| 2 | Bart the Genius | | Bart le génie | |
| 3 | Homer's Odyssey | | L'Odyssée d'Homère | |
| 4 | There's No Disgrace Like Home | | Il n'y a pas de honte comme à la maison | |
| 5 | Bart the General | | Bart le général | |
| 6 | Moaning Lisa | | Lisa gémissante | |

*Figure 10-40. The translated data is written to the new field.*

# Keeping Track of Extensions

As you use more extensions and scripts in your base, your team may need help keeping track of everything. Fortunately, Airtable has different ways to track what extensions are installed in your base and how to find them.

When you're not using an extension in full-screen mode, it sits in the extensions dashboard on the right side of the browser, as shown in Figure 10-41. You can click the upper-right corner to see the different dashboards that contain extensions. Renaming these dashboards is easy, so you can easily group extensions by type or function.

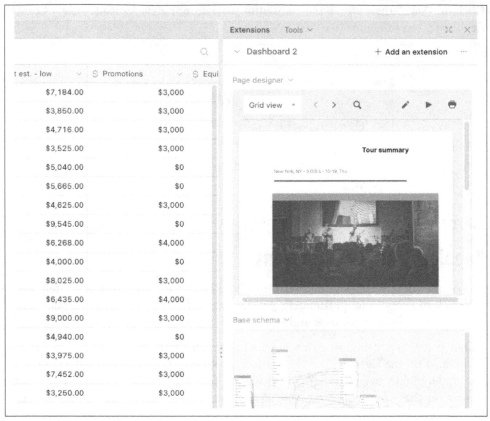

*Figure 10-41. Viewing a dashboard of extensions in the right-hand side of the browser in the Data section.*

For the extensions themselves, clicking the down arrow next to the extension's name allows you to do several things. You can rename the extension, give it a description, disable it, delete it, or move it to a different dashboard using the menu in each extension's upper right corner, as shown in Figure 10-42. In addition, you can mouse over the extension to see two small columns of dots that allow you to change the placement of extensions in a dashboard.

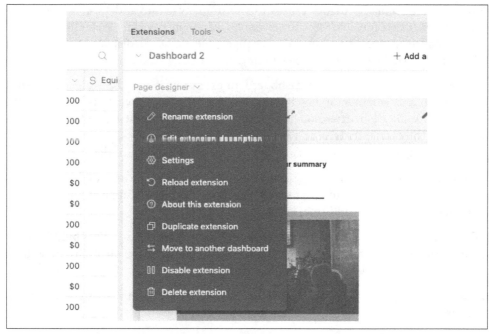

*Figure 10-42. Each extension has a menu to make adjustments like duplicating, disabling, or deleted the extension.*

# The "Manage Extensions" Dashboard

If you have a lot of scripts and extensions in your base, even sorting them into different dashboards may still not give you an easy way to understand who installed an extension and when. Airtable's "Manage extensions" function is a dedicated pop-up window listing every extension currently installed, as shown in Figure 10-43. To get to the "Manage extensions" window, go to your list of dashboards and click on the gear icon below.

*Figure 10-43. Viewing the extensions in a base.*

"Manage extensions" provides a list of extensions by name and type, which is the name of the extension itself. So, for example, we might have the Web clipper extension installed in our base, but we've changed the name to display as "Restaurant ideas." However, the extension type still stays the same as Web clipper.

This window also tracks which dashboard an extension is in, who added it, when it was added, and whether or not it's enabled. In "Manage extensions," all the same functionality for each extension is accessible on the far right side of the window under the three dots. As with the right-hand pane of extensions, you can rename an extension, duplicate it, move it to another dashboard, disable it, or delete it.

At the top of the list in "Manage extensions" is a search bar in case you have so many extensions that you need to use a search function. And in the upper right-hand corner, there's an option to add an extension, too.

We've seen a spectrum of extensions, including prepackaged extensions built by Airtable, creative third-party extensions, and, finally, the ultimate flexibility of writing custom JavaScript code into the scripting extension.

In the next chapter, we'll look at Airtable Automations, which allows complex software workflows to be built without any coding knowledge.

# CHAPTER 11

# Airtable Automations

Until now, we have focused on the Data section in Airtable. However, as Airtable has developed new features, it's become a full software platform. It includes a way to build user interfaces (the Interface Designer) and Airtable Automations, which are accessible no-code workflows you can run to automatically modify or create data based on conditions in your base.

Automations can reduce your busywork and the potential for human error in simple tasks. For example, you might be copying and pasting values from one field to another for records in a table. However, Automations can change values based on the conditions you set up. So you can think of Automations as your personal army of copy-and-paste robots.

Not only do Automations effectively copy and paste data from one place to another inside your bases, but they also interface with third-party services like Gmail and Google Sheets. In this chapter, we will walk through the options for connecting these external services to trigger and execute actions in Airtable automations. Connecting third-party services without writing code is an example of the no-code software development that Airtable enables for nondevelopers.

## Airtable Automations Versus Other Connector Software

Years before Airtable's Automations were released, tools like Zapier and Make (*http://make.com*) (formerly Integromat) were already connecting different software tools using a no-code interface. Using Airtable Automations instead of these tools has both advantages and drawbacks, which we will examine in more depth in Chapter 13. First, let's consider the high-level differences between the built-in no-code Airtable Automations and external tools like Zapier.

## Advantages to Connecting Airtable via Airtable Automations

Triggering no-code automation flows inside of Airtable has distinct benefits and drawbacks. On the plus side, the integration between the Airtable platform and Airtable Automations is unparalleled. Everything happens within one tool, and the data is always kept up to date. Information, like what fields are available to reference in a table, is always current. Last but not least, there's almost no lag between something triggering an automation and the automation firing off the actions associated with it. (Services like Zapier "poll" your connected applications for changes that might cause a trigger on a certain time interval, which can be up to 15 minutes between polling.)

A final advantage is that it's often more economical to use Airtable Automations than external connector tools. After all, Airtable allows 25,000 automation runs per workspace per month on the Team plan and 100,000 on the Business plan; workspaces on the Free plan have only 100. Airtable also uses a different model than third-party services like Zapier, which charges you based on the number of steps run inside of each automation flow. For example, if we wanted to copy some data from one field to another and then send it in an email, we would take three steps against a quota in a system like Zapier. In an Airtable Automation flow, though, we could have up to 25 steps, and Airtable will only count the workflow overall.

## Disadvantages to Connecting Airtable via Airtable Automations

A big disadvantage of Airtable Automations is significant if you're interested in integrating with third-party services. Currently, Airtable only has native integrations in its Automations platform with a few dozen services. Airtable Automations integrate with some of the most well-known applications, but compared with Zapier's thousands of services, Airtable is more limited in that respect. It's an apples-to-oranges comparison. So if the integrations for triggers and actions we discuss in this chapter do not include services you expect you'll need to integrate through no-code automations, you'll want to consider using a service like Zapier or Make (*http://make.com*), which will be discussed in Chapter 13.

Another significant limitation to note is that Airtable does not offer the option to purchase additional automation runs if you exhaust your monthly allotted amount. This constraint may prompt you to explore using a third-party service, despite the availability of native Airtable automation options. Additionally, Airtable's native automations do not support complex logic or calculations, including simple math operations, without the use of JavaScript code inside an automation. Third-party services generally offer more advanced functionality in this regard.

# The Basics of Airtable Automations

You'll need creator- or owner-level permissions to create and modify Automations in a base. However, once an automation has been built and turned on, any users with creator- or editor-level permissions can activate a trigger's automation.

Each base can have up to 50 different automation flows. And since each automation flow can have up to 25 actions, plus the trigger, you might benefit from combining small, discrete flows into larger workflows with more steps to stay under the limit of 50 automations per base.

Most steps in an automation, whether trigger or action, reference a single table for that step. If you need to reference a field in that table and data from another table for the same step, we can use a lookup field to pull data from the second table into the table you're referencing for that step.

## The If/Then Logic of Automations

A fundamental concept in software is the if/then statement, which simply notes what should happen if something else happens. If/then logic is the basis for every automation. The "if" statement is a trigger, and the actions that follow that trigger are the "then" portion. In other words, a trigger consists of conditions that must be present to start an automation. If those conditions are met, then the action consists of one or more steps programmed to happen after the trigger is activated.

Next, we will look at some simple automations to understand what tools are available to build no-code workflows using Airtable Automations.

In Airtable automations, the general if/then logic is the foundation of every workflow. Conditional logic takes if/then statements to another level by introducing specific conditions that must be met for certain actions to run. This allows for more precise control over the flow of the automation based on the results of previous triggers or actions. We'll look at conditional logic later in this chapter.

Although we can have up to 25 actions that follow the trigger of an automation, let's start by looking at a couple of simple two-step automations that have one action after the trigger.

# Simple Automation: When a Record Is Updated

Every automation starts with a need to understand or change data in a base. The trigger "When a record is updated" fires the automation based on criteria about records in a specific table that has specific fields modified. When those fields are updated, the actions of the automation are triggered:

- Trigger: "When a record is updated"
- Action: "Send an email"

### Setting up the trigger

Let's return to our preparation for the fall tour; we want to monitor our promotional costs closely. These costs can change often, as a result of negotiations with the venue, and the negotiations can be contentious.

So the goal of this automation is for the tour manager to receive a notification email if anyone on the tour planning team checks a box. To start, we've created a checkbox field, "promotion change," as shown in Figure 11-1, that's meant to be checked by a teammate when a venue has proposed an increased promotions budget.

| Show | show date | Promotions | promotion change email | |
|---|---|---|---|---|
| New York, NY - S.O.B.'s - 10-19, Thu | 10/19/2023 | $3,500 | | |
| Boston, MA - Great - 10-20, Fri | 10/20/2023 | $3,000 | ✓ | |
| Baltimore, MD - Crown - 10-23, Mon | 10/23/2023 | $3,000 | | |
| Philadelphia, PA - Johnny - 10-22, Sun | 10/22/2023 | $3,000 | | |
| Washington, DC - 9:30 - 10-21, Sat | 10/21/2023 | $0 | | |

*Figure 11-1. Creating a checkbox field to serve as a trigger for a simple automation.*

Tracking the costs of the concert promotion is an ideal use case for the "When a record is updated" trigger, as shown in Figure 11-2, because we want an action to happen when the team makes an update to an existing record in the Shows table.

In the configuration of the trigger, we choose that trigger and then we select the "Shows" table.

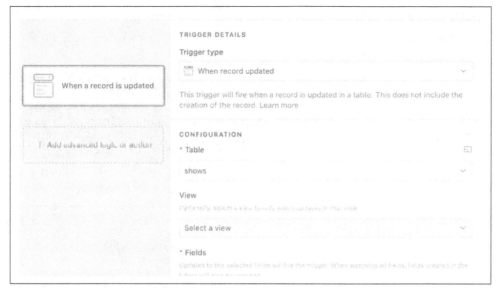

Figure 11-2. Selecting a table for an automation trigger.

## Choosing the field to monitor

Lastly, we open the "Select fields" button to toggle on the "promotion change email" checkbox field. When this Checkbox field is checked (or unchecked) for any record, it will trigger the actions we'll set up in the next step, as shown in Figure 11-3.

Figure 11-3. Watching a particular field to trigger an automation.

### Testing the step

Now that we've configured the trigger, we will test it by pulling a record into the automation that meets the criteria of the trigger.

We have two options in this test step section. "Use suggested record" grabs a record from the view of the table you've specified that meets the criteria.

Suppose Airtable is able to find a record that meets the conditions from the "Use suggested record" option. In that case, it will display "Step successful" in the "RESULTS" section of the "Property" sidebar, as shown in Figure 11-4. Or if you prefer to test the automation with a specific record that meets the criteria (in this case, of having the "promotion change email" field checked), use the "Choose record" option.

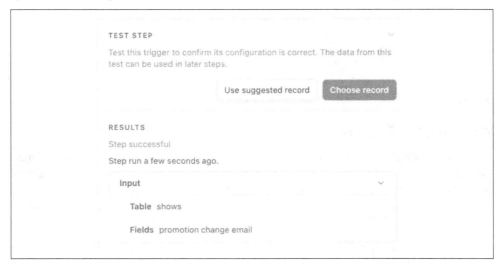

*Figure 11-4. Letting Airtable find a record that matches the criteria in your trigger with "Use suggested record."*

However, if no records in the view meet the criteria, then we see an error. If, for example, we are using a trigger that has specific conditions of records that none of the records meet, we will see an error such as "Table does not contain any records that match the provided filters."

### Setting up the action

Our goal with this automation is to send an email to the tour manager, which we've decided will happen when a team member checks the "promotion change email" checkbox whenever the promotion costs for a show change.

Users have a few ways to send emails in Airtable Automations. The easiest is sending an email directly from Airtable's built-in email service, which is the "Send email" action shown in Figure 11-5. (Later, we will look at the other two options, which tie to Gmail or Outlook Mail.)

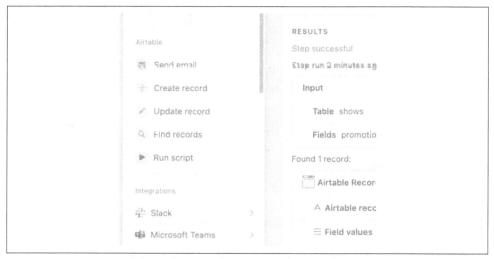

*Figure 11-5. Choosing to send an email from Airtable in an automation.*

Although it's not possible to name a trigger, you can add a description to each action step in an automation. Let's title this action "Cost alert to tour manager."

### Static and dynamic data

When we built page layouts in the Page designer extension in Chapter 10, we could have static elements, such as a logo on an invoice, or dynamic elements, like the total cost for a specific invoice. The same principle applies in Automations.

In our example, the cost alert email will go to the same person regardless of what show record has changed. So we'll put the static email address into the "To" field, where we could add additional emails if needed. As we will see in later steps, we can also dynamically pull an email address from a record in an earlier part of an automation.

Similar to the email recipient, we'll start with a static email subject in this automation step, as shown in Figure 11-6.

*Figure 11-6. Using static values in an email action of an automation.*

Using the "Send an email" action allows Airtable to deliver an email with Airtable branding in the email. Later in this chapter, we will look at how you can send emails from your own email account using Gmail or Outlook mail and customize them without this branding.

If we click "Show more options," we could also add emails for the CC and BCC fields, a specific sender name, and a reply-to address.

### Pulling dynamic data into the action

While we used a static value for the email recipient and the subject of these emails, let's now use some dynamic data. We don't just want to know that one of the shows had a change in the promotion costs: we want to know which show and what the new value is. So in the "Message" box, we can click the plus sign to bring up a pop-up box with two columns, as shown in Figure 11-7. The first column is labeled "Use data from." In our case, we only have one step in this automation before our current step, so that's the source we'll pull dynamic data from.

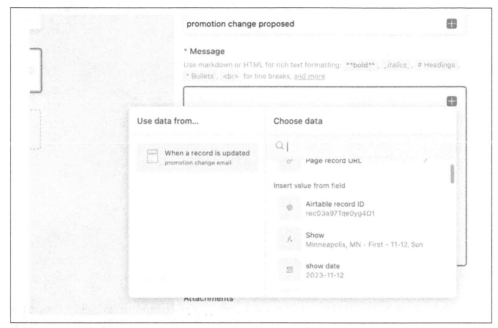

*Figure 11-7. Choosing which step to use data from in the automation. (In this case, there's just one step previous: the trigger.)*

The right-hand side includes a "Choose data" column. It's a list of all the fields we can pull dynamic record data from and include in the automated email. We've grabbed a few key fields and included each on a separate line in the email, as shown in Figure 11-8. (Since the currency field's formatting isn't imported, we've added a $ symbol before the variable to signal that it represents the latest cash value that's been proposed.)

The last item isn't a field value per se but rather a link that will take the user directly to the "expanded view" of the record they're being notified about.

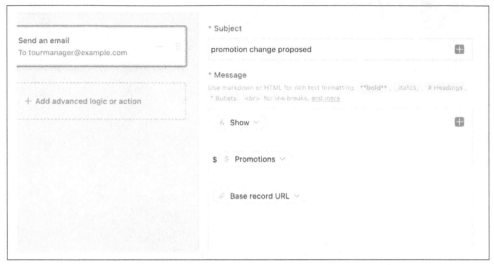

*Figure 11-8. Including several relevant fields in an automated notification email.*

Alternately, if we scroll to the bottom, we'll see a couple of options under "Insert the whole record as…" The first option is "List," and the second is "Grid." Both of these options take the result from the trigger and cleanly format it for us, and we can choose which fields are placed into the list or grid layout, as we see in Figures 11-9 and 11-10. We've toggled on the option for the record name ("Show"), the "Promotions" currency field with the latest proposed amount from the venue, and a link to that specific record in our base.

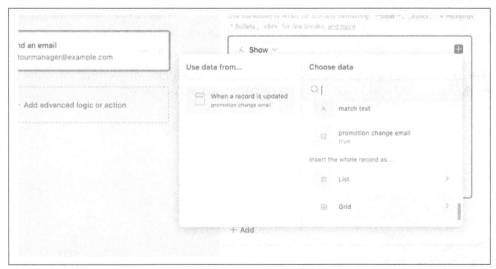

*Figure 11-9. If you want to include field values of a record(s) included as a grid or list of one or more records.*

*Figure 11-10. Choosing which field values to display when inserting records as a list or grid.*

### Testing the action

In the "Test step" section of the "Property" sidebar, we can now click "Generate a preview," as shown in Figure 11-11.

*Figure 11-11. Previewing how the email automation will look.*

After generating the preview, we can review it later in the final results section by clicking the "View result" button. Below that button, we also see the field values that created the test. Figure 11-12 shows the result of running the automation in the "Test step" section.

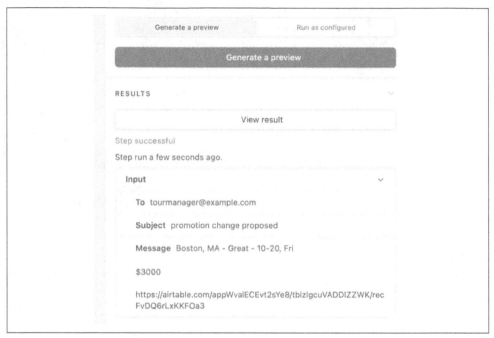

*Figure 11-12. Viewing the results of a preview of an automation.*

We can also choose "Run as configured" and then the "Run test" button, which will actually perform the action. So, in this case, the test would send a test email to the tour manager with our test record.

### Running the automation

If everything has gone well, we can then toggle on the automation. Whenever a team member checks the "promotion change email" checkbox to signal there's a new proposal from the venue that's been entered for the tour manager to review, it will send the tour manager an email.

This automation of sending an email to the tour manager is a simple way to show how automations work, but perhaps it's too simple. If someone were to uncheck the "promotion change email" checkbox field, that would also update the record, though not as we originally envisioned. This could lead to confusion if the tour manager receives emails about promotion budgets that haven't been updated.

# Simple Automation: When a Record Matches Conditions

In the last automation, we had the option to limit the records that could trigger "When a record is updated" by choosing a (presumably filtered) view. However, the "When record matches conditions" trigger considers all records in a table, regardless of the view, but with a set of predetermined conditions:

- Trigger: "When record matches conditions"
- Action: "Slack: Send a message"

Using conditions instead of a view can save time and confusion by not creating a specific view just to trigger a particular automation. It also keeps the logic for what records will trigger automations discretely contained inside the automation trigger itself. It is not dependent on a view configuration that a teammate could inadvertently change.

For this second automation, let's assume that the band and the tour management team are using Slack for internal communications. Slack channels are set up for both critical discussions and channels for less important things, like choosing where to eat in each city. The team has dedicated a Slack channel for discussing restaurant options that are pulled into Airtable through the Web Clipper extension (as we set up in Chapter 10 with the Katz's Delicatessen example).

### Choosing a trigger

We have several options to trigger an automation after someone uses the Web Clipper extension to pull restaurant information into our tour planning base. For example, we could use the "When record is created" trigger, since it's logical that we will want to talk about a new restaurant in our Slack channel after someone creates a new record in the "Restaurants" table.

However, we want to maintain quality control over which records get pushed into Slack. It would be confusing if someone isn't using the Web Clipper to get all the restaurant information, or just isn't putting in key information when manually entering a record into the Restaurants table. This potential for missing data is why we'll use conditions to ensure that we have all the right information about the restaurant before it gets sent to the Slack channel for discussion.

### Setting up the trigger

After selecting the "When record matches condition" trigger, we choose our "Restaurants" table in the tour planning base. Again, since we don't have the option to choose a view, any record in this table could potentially trigger the automation.

Airtable Automations are forward-looking. If we set up an automation triggered by records matching conditions, the trigger will not look at all existing records that match those conditions, just records that newly match the conditions. The good news is that you can't inadvertently trigger thousands of automations on existing records, but the bad news is that you can't perform an action based on a condition that an existing record already meets.

Below the table we've chosen, we can begin to add conditions, as shown in Figure 11-13. Although the Web Clipper we configured has six potential fields, just a few are crucial for now. We want to make sure there's a restaurant name, the city it's in, and, perhaps most importantly, a value in the URL field so we can click through to see reviews of the restaurant. (If this was a more advanced automation, we might run a conditional action to ensure that the value in the URL field was properly formatted and linked to Yelp. We will look at conditional actions later in this chapter.)

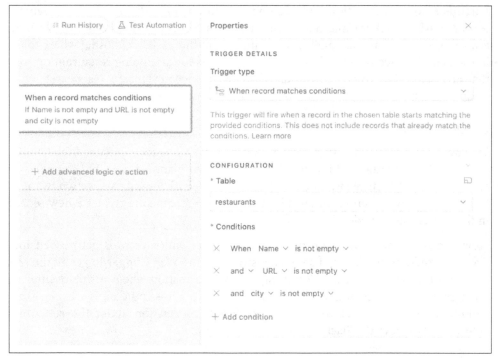

*Figure 11-13. Adding conditions to the trigger.*

## Testing the trigger

In the test step section below the configuration section, we can click "Use suggested record" and see the "Step successful" message, which means that Airtable found a record that met the specified conditions. However, as before, if no records in the table meet the criteria, we would receive the error message "Table does not contain any record that matches the provided filters." In that case, we'd need to go back and create a test record or modify an existing record so that there is a record in the table that meets the conditions in the trigger and is therefore able to be used as a test.

## Setting up the action

Now that our trigger is set up and we know there is at least one record for a test, we can move on to building the action of sending a message to a Slack channel. We can also add a description for this action called "send new restaurant for discussion," as shown in Figure 11-14.

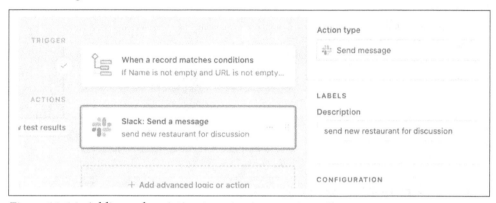

*Figure 11-14. Adding a description to a step in an automation.*

Let's use dynamic data again. We could choose just one aspect of the record to insert, which might be more useful if we had multiple steps in an automation before we sent the Slack message and we wanted to combine the steps in a single Slack message. But in this simple automation, like our cost alert email, we're just passing along one piece of data. So the best option is "Insert the whole record as…" and then choose "List," as seen in Figure 11-15. We will toggle on all the fields by clicking "Select all" and then "Insert."

There are a few additional Slack-specific options, such as customizing the Slack bot's name or adding an icon for the bot. Since our team knows this information is coming from Airtable, we'll keep the defaults as is.

## Testing the action

Let's try testing the step by generating a preview. As we see in Figure 11-15, the six fields are listed in the Slack message preview. It also shows the Slack channel where the message was sent. While the information is all there, it does not include the image itself in the preview or in the Slack message.

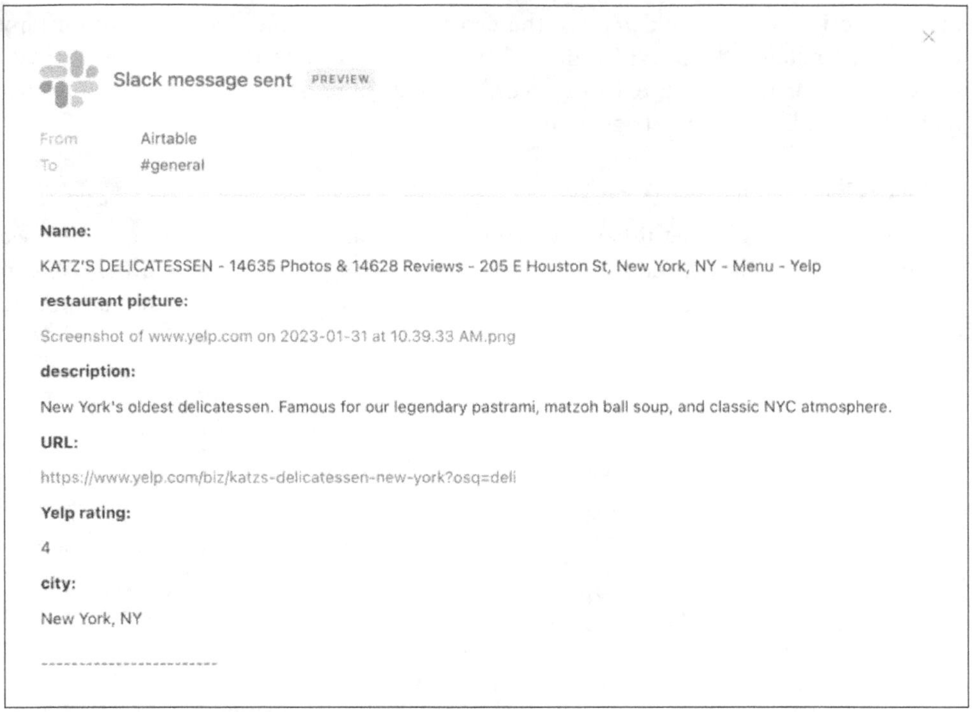

Figure 11-15. Preview of Slack message action.

 If we click the image link in one of our Slack alerts, it displays the image in a new tab, but we must be logged in to Airtable just to see it. If we click out of the image, we'll be in the expanded view for that record in the "Restaurants" table.

These two examples illustrate how we can monitor for changes to data in our base and pass that data along to other places. Next, we'll look at some more in-depth Automations that start to display the power of more complex, and valuable, scenarios. And finally, we'll review all of the different triggers and actions we can utilize to build Automations.

## Advanced Automations

We've seen a couple of simple Automations with one trigger and one action. Let's look at more advanced Automations with more than one action step and incorporate some advanced functionality, such as the "Find records" feature.

## Advanced automation: daily ticket sales update

The triggers we've looked at so far have been activated when a certain event happens, such as updating a record. The "At a scheduled time" trigger works independently of changes to records and allows you to set an interval for how often the trigger should activate the automation. Let's use the "At a scheduled time" trigger to check if we had changes in ticket sales in any of the six regions of our tour in the previous day. This alert will give us peace of mind about where ticket sales stand, and it also will reduce the team's impulse to constantly check the ticket sales totals.

- Trigger: "At a scheduled time"
- Action: "Find records"
- Action: "Slack: send a message"

**"At a scheduled time" trigger.** We'll first set up our "At a scheduled time" trigger to fire off every morning at 10:00 a.m., as shown in Figure 11-16. The "At a scheduled time" trigger also allows us to specify intervals in minutes, hours, weeks, months, or just one time on a specified date and time.

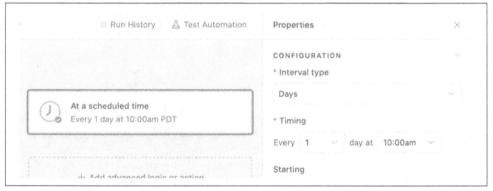

*Figure 11-16. Configuring a daily trigger.*

Instead of emailing a specific team member, we want an update to go out to everyone. So just as we did with our new restaurant idea notification, we're going to send ticket sales updates to a specific channel on Slack called #ticket-updates.

But unlike the new restaurant idea example, we aren't going to immediately send the data after the trigger. First, we will have a "Find records" action that will search through records to see if we had any new sales in the last 24 hours. To get started, we need to prepare some data in the Regions table using linked records data from the Shows table.

**Tracking ticket sales in last 24 hours.** We need to calculate the number of tickets that have sold in the last 24-hour period. To do this, we will go to the Shows table and use a "Last modified" field to calculate how many hours have elapsed since this field was modified.

We already have our "Actual ticket sales" field. We will add a "Last modified time" field and choose the "Actual ticket sales" field to monitor, as shown in Figure 11-17.

*Figure 11-17. Tracking when only the "Actual ticket sales" field was last modified.*

Now that we know when the number of tickets sold changed, we can write a simple formula to understand how many hours have passed since the value in that field changed. We do this using the DATETIME_TIME() operator:

```
DATETIME_DIFF(
NOW(),
{ticket sales last modified},
'hours'
)
```

The formula for this is shown in Figure 11-18.

*Figure 11-18. Calculating how recently the tally of tickets sold for each city in the Shows table has been modified.*

Calculating the time difference using the NOW() function in Airtable poses certain risks. The NOW() function, which is intended to provide the current time, is subject to different update intervals depending on the usage of the database. If the database is actively being used, the NOW() function will update roughly every 15 minutes. However, if no collaborators are using the base, the NOW() function may refresh only every hour or two. This lack of reliability can undermine the accuracy of calculations that rely on precise time differences. However, we've set our trigger to activate at 10 a.m., by which time our team will be working in Airtable.

**Rolling up ticket sales.** Let's create a new Grid view, "tour totals," in the Regions table for calculating ticket sales. We need to aggregate all ticket sales by region with a Rollup field, as shown in Figure 11-19. The SUM(values) aggregation will add up the sales for shows linked to each region.

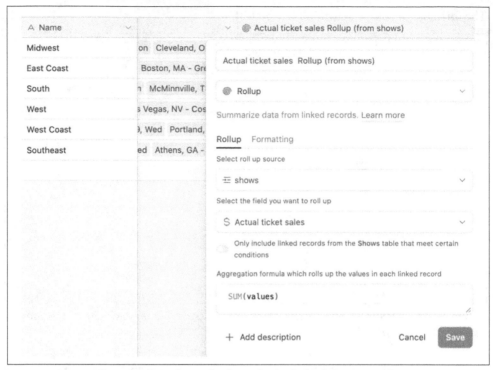

*Figure 11-19. Rolling up the values of ticket sales by linked show records.*

This Rollup tells us the ticket sales by region, but we want to build an automated daily notification of what sales have happened in the last 24 hours. Let's create a second Rollup field that adds a condition based on the "hours since ticket sales change" formula we just made in the Shows table. We'll initially set it up to be the same as our other Rollup field, pulling values from Shows records linked in Regions, and rolling up the "Actual ticket sales" field. But now, we will use the "Only include records from" option for records in the Shows table that meet certain conditions.

As shown in Figure 11-20, we add a condition to the new "Actual ticket sales Rollup - 24 hours" Rollup field that only sums values that have been calculated as occurring in the last 24 hours.

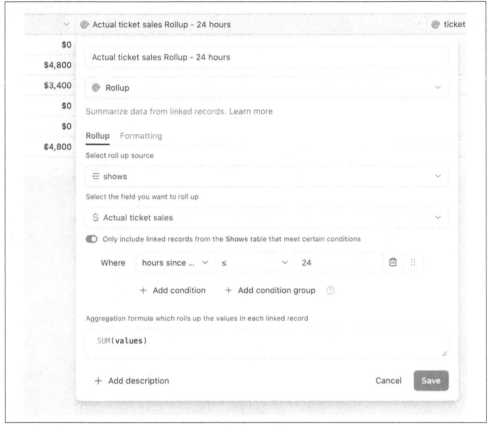

*Figure 11-20. Creating a Rollup field with a condition.*

**Finding regions with recent sales in automation.** In the "Find records" action, as shown in Figure 11-21, we've chosen our table to find records based on a condition. The condition is based on the "Rollup" field we created in the "Regions" table, "Actual ticket sales Rollup - 24 hours." If the value exceeds $0, it will meet the condition.

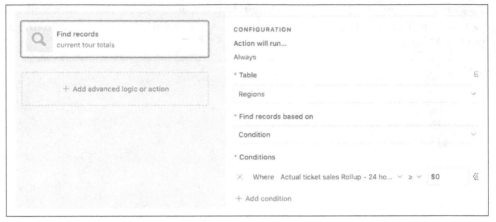

*Figure 11-21. Searching for records in a "Find records" automation action that meet a condition.*

Clicking "Test action" will bring up the two regions where we've had ticket sales in the last 24 hours: the South and the West. Airtable pops open a small table, as shown in Figure 11-22, with every field in the table.

*Figure 11-22. Results of "Find records" action step in automation.*

We've referenced a "Last modified" field in a "Formula" field in the Shows table. In a Rollup field, we've created a condition to have the "Find records" action just return regions with ticket sales in the last 24 hours.

---

**Ticket sales notification in Slack.** Let's pass these results into the Slack message for our team. As we set up before, we can choose the "Send a Slack message" action. This time, we will send the message to the #ticket-updates channel in Slack, and we need to put the results of the "Find records" action into the message of the "Send a Slack message" action.

Clicking the plus sign in the message box allows us to choose where to pull data from, which should be the "Find records" action we just configured, as shown in Figure 11-23. We can insert these records as a list and then choose the fields we want to include. In this case, let's include the region's name, the "Actual ticket sales" data, and the ticket sales in the last 24 hours.

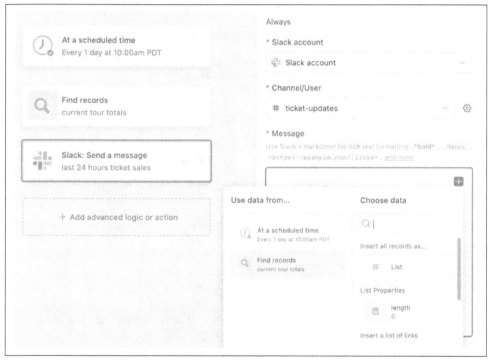

*Figure 11-23. Inserting records from the "Find records" step into a Slack message.*

If we click "Generate a preview," as shown in Figure 11-24, we can see the list that this action creates. The list of regions from the "Find records" step includes the region name, the overall ticket sales, and the sales that occurred in the last 24 hours.

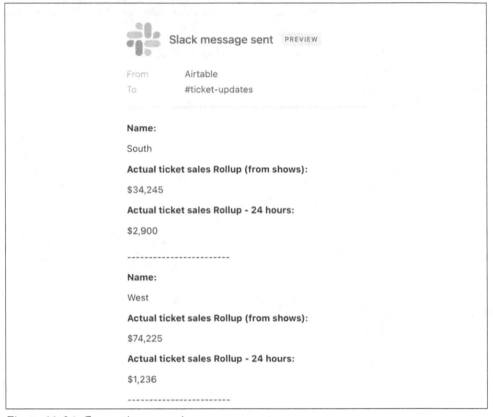

*Figure 11-24. Generating a preview.*

Similarly, let's click "Run test," and we can see that it successfully sent the same message to our Slack channel, as shown in Figure 11-25.

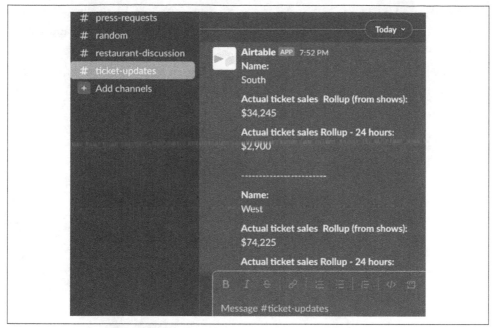

*Figure 11-25. Receiving an automated Slack message with an update about ticket sales.*

### Advanced automation: Managing press requests with automations

Dealing with inquiries from the media is time-consuming, and we want to create an effective automation workflow to streamline these requests. We will set up a form and use the "When a form is submitted" trigger to kick off an automation that will let us know when a member of the media is reaching out and perform an automated filtering process to know if the journalist is from a press outlet we hope to get coverage from.

- Trigger: "When a form is submitted"
- Action: "Send an email"
- Action: "Gmail: Send email"
- Action: "Find records"
- Action: "Update record"
- Action: "Slack: Send a message"

**Creating a new table with a form.** We've created a table, "Press requests." The table has fields for the news outlet, the name of the reporter, the reporter's email, and a message they can add through the form.

Let's now create a new form view, which has just these four fields from our table; all are required, as shown in Figure 11-26.

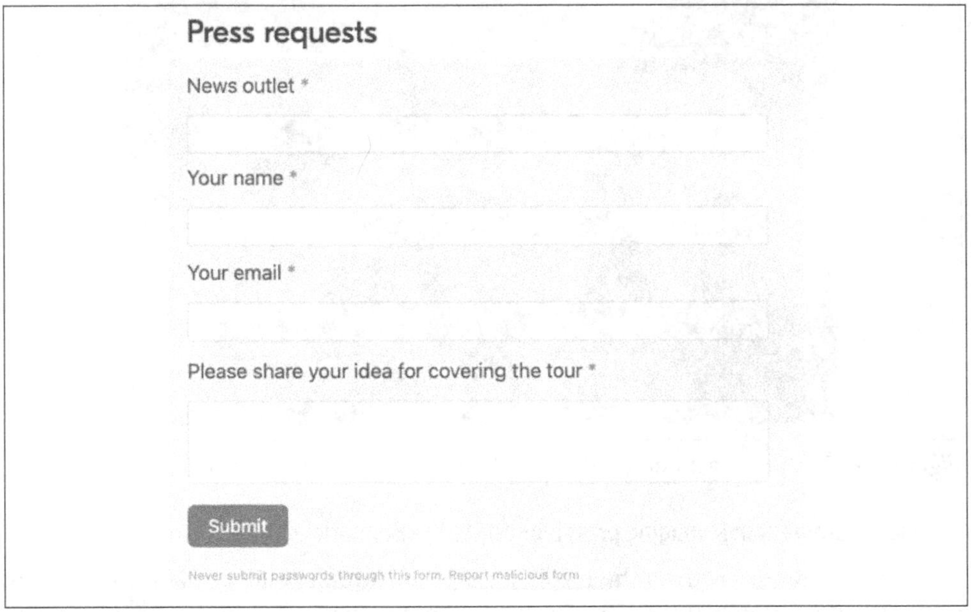

**Press requests**

News outlet *

Your name *

Your email *

Please share your idea for covering the tour *

Submit

Never submit passwords through this form. Report malicious form

*Figure 11-26. Creating a simple form to manage inbound press requests.*

**"Send an email" action.** Going back to our automation, let's set up a series of actions to occur whenever the form is submitted. First, let's use Airtable's "Send an email" action to alert the tour manager; it's an internal email, and it doesn't matter that it has the Airtable branding or that it's coming from Airtable. It's just more convenient to use Airtable's "Send an email" action in this case.

In the "Configuration" section on the right-hand side of the Properties area, we can add the static variable of the tour manager's email and then pass some dynamic variables in the subject line. We've added a "Created time" field type to the "Press requests" table and a simple formula showing the day and month it was submitted. The following formula is a simple way to use Airtable time formatting to show an abbreviated month and day:

```
DATETIME_FORMAT(created,'MMM DD')
```

This formula is shown in Figure 11-27.

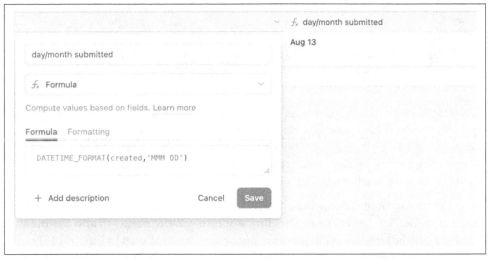

*Figure 11-27. Creating a simple formula to simplify the submission's date.*

In the subject line of the email to the tour manager, we're going to insert the dynamic variables of the name of the primary record, which is a formula concatenating two fields, the publication and the journalist. We will add the formatted day and month the form was submitted in the message box below. As shown in Figure 11-28, let's also add the name of the form submission record, when it was submitted, and what the message was.

*Figure 11-28. Adding field values from a form submission to the email notification.*

Airtable allows for using markdown to format text. Let's put double asterisks on either side of "Message:" in the email body. As shown in Figure 11-28, we've added the markdown notation for bold, **, so the email notification we'll receive clearly distinguishes what the journalist has written to us in their form response.

**"Gmail: Send email" action.**    Now, let's set up an action that will send an automated reply to the journalist who fills out the form. Since we want this message to come from one of our own email accounts and not the Airtable email server, we'll use the "Gmail: Send email" action. The setup is essentially the same as the "Send an email" action, except we need to connect a Gmail account.

Now that the account is connected, we will pass the dynamic variable of the reporter's email into the "To" field. The subject line will be a generic message, and the message box itself will be a mix of static text and customization, as shown in Figure 11-29.

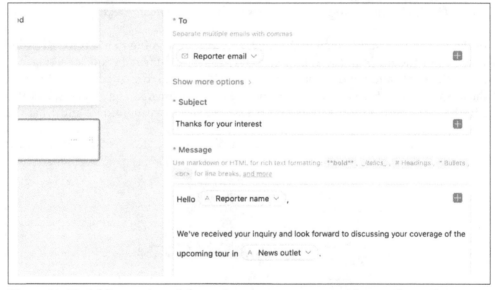

*Figure 11-29. Adding static and dynamic text to an autoresponder email sent from Gmail.*

Now we can generate a preview, as shown in Figure 11-30. The preview assures us that the email will go to the address the journalist submitted and that our dynamic variable of the journalist's publication does show up correctly in the email that we'll automatically send with the "Gmail: Send email" action.

*Figure 11-30. Previewing the Gmail action in our automation.*

**Adding conditional actions.** Whenever a journalist submits an inquiry form to do a story about the band, we'll always alert the tour manager via Airtable. We'll also automatically send the journalist a thank-you email from our Gmail account. But not all publications are created equally, and if a journalist from one of our top publications reaches out, we want to be notified so we can proactively schedule an interview. To do this, we'll use a conditional action, which takes the result of a trigger or previous actions and, if the conditions are met, adds subsequent actions to the automation.

Before we set up the condition, we need to use the "Find records" action again; we will use it to match information from what the journalist submitted. With a list of our top publications in our base, we've created a new table, "Top publications," with fields for the name and website of the news outlet, as shown in Figure 11-31.

| | A Publication | | ⊘ Website | | ƒ extract domain | |
|---|---|---|---|---|---|---|
| 1 | The Fader | | https://thefader.com | | thefader.com | |
| 2 | The Washington Post | | https://washingtonpost.com | | washingtonpost.com | |
| 3 | Stereogum | | https://stereogum.com | | stereogum.com | |
| 4 | Spin | | https://spin.com | | spin.com | |
| 5 | Rolling Stone | | https://rollingstone.com | | rollingstone.com | |
| 6 | Pop Matters | | https://popmatters.com | | popmatters.com | |

Tabs: Shows · Cities · Regions · Tour totals · Restaurants · Press requests · Top publications ⌄

Toolbar: ☰ Views · ⊞ Grid view ⌄ · ⊛ Hide fields · ⚑ Filter · ▤ Group · ↕ Sort · ⬥ Color · ▤ · ⬈ Share and

*Figure 11-31. A new table of publications to link with press requests.*

Our goal is to compare the email domain of the email address the journalist submitted with the domain of one of these top publications. Let's start by isolating the domain of the publications. We create a simple formula that uses three formula operators to extract everything from the website field that comes after "https://":

```
MID(
    Website,
    FIND(
        "//",
        Website)+2,
    LEN(Website)-8
)
```

This formula is shown in Figure 11-32.

*Figure 11-32. Stripping out the "https://" from the website address.*

Next, let's set up something similar in our "Press requests" table of form submissions. Here is a similar formula that extracts the text after the ampersand ("@") symbol in the email, leaving just the email address's domain:

```
MID(
    {Reporter email},
    FIND(
        '@',
        {Reporter email})+1,
    20
)
```

This formula is shown in Figure 11-33.

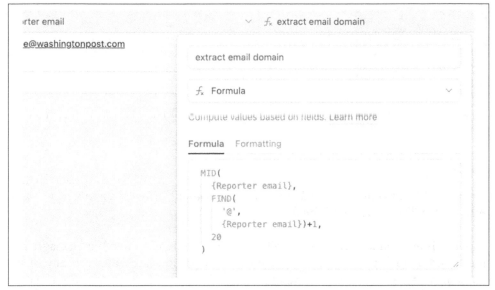

*Figure 11-33. Creating a formula to extract the domain from an email address.*

**Matching journalist with publication using "Find records" action.**   Now that we have the domain from the journalist's email address and the domain of the publications we hope to get coverage in, we can use the "Find records" action to determine if we have a match to these publications from any of our press inquiries coming through the form submission.

After adding the "Find records" action, we will choose the "Top publications" table. Since we've already brought in data from the "Press requests" table, we can compare values from the two tables. We can either search records based on those visible in a view or find records based on a condition. Conditions in "Find records" are similar to how we might filter fields and records in a view.

In our condition, we're first going to choose a field from the table we are searching within, which is our "Top publications" table. We want to search the extracted domain of these publications and see if any match the email domain of the journalist who submitted the request. Therefore, we can choose the "extract website domain" field, choose the operator "Is," and select the "extract email domain" field for the email domain of the journalist, as shown in Figure 11-34.

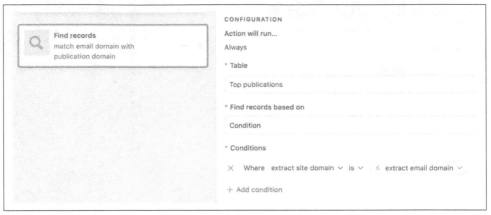

*Figure 11-34. Searching for records from "Top publications" where a domain of a website matches the journalist's email domain.*

When this automation triggers, we will first send an email to the tour manager and then send a stock thank-you email. And lastly, we will search to see if any of the domain names of the top publications match the domain name of the journalist's email.

If we click "Test action," we see that we found one *Washington Post* result from the "Top Publications" table, since the journalist domain matches that publication in our list. We can now set up actions that are only triggered if the conditions we set are met.

**Configuring conditional logic.**　There are a number of actions we want to take if the journalist who submitted the form is from one of the publications we're targeting, but only if there is a match. So we can set up a condition to predicate this second set of actions on that match happening.

First, we choose "Conditional logic" from the list of available actions. In the "Config-uration" section, we can add a simple condition, as seen in Figure 11-35. We can choose to "Use data from…" either the form that was submitted or the "Find records" action.

Since the "Find records" action is the mechanism that matches the journalist with the publication, we want to start this new set of conditional actions based on the results of that "Find records."

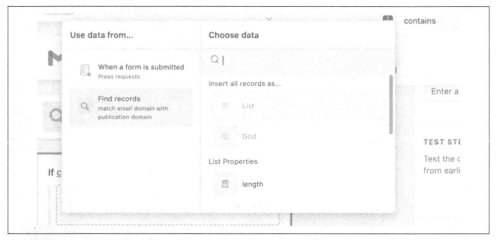

*Figure 11-35. Choosing to base the conditional logic on data from the "Find records" action instead of data from the form.*

After we select to use data from the results of that "Find records" action, we have a few different options under "Choose data." First, we can insert all records as a list or a grid, which we did when sending the updated ticket sales by region to our ticket sales Slack channel.

The second option, "List properties," gives us a value for how many records the "Find records" action returned. We don't know the result of the "Find records" action, but we do know that if there's a match, we want to move forward with the conditional actions. Let's base the condition on the length of results being 1, as shown in Figure 11-36.

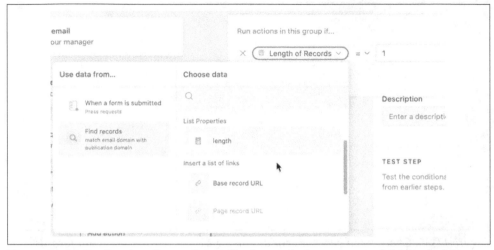

Figure 11-36. Predicating the conditional logic on whether one record is returned from "Find records."

Our condition is "Length of records" equals 1. The only other possible value for this condition is zero, which is because there are no matches between the journalist's email and our top publications. And since only one email can occur per form submission, there's no chance of having more than one match in this particular automation.

Airtable automatically labels our condition with the terms of the condition. As shown in Figure 11-37, we can test the step.

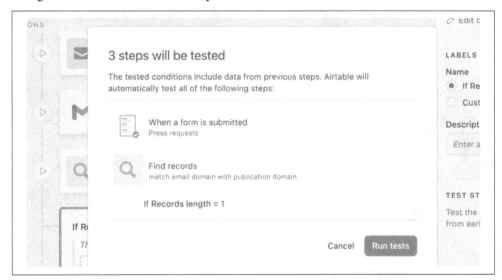

Figure 11-37. Testing conditional logic.

The input of the fourth step in our automation, the "Find records" action, did return one item. This result means the record length equals 1, and since there's one item in the length of the list, we have success and can move forward to the other actions.

**"Update Record" action.**  When a journalist is from one of our top publications, we want to update the journalist's form submission record using the "Update record" action.

After updating the description of the action, we choose the table where we're collecting the form submissions, "Press requests." We also need to specify which record we're modifying in that table. This record is, of course, a dynamic value under "Record ID."

We can choose data from either the form submission or the "Find records" action, as shown in Figure 11-38. Since we're updating the form submission, we want to choose Press Requests and pull in the first option, which is the record ID of the press request record from the press request table.

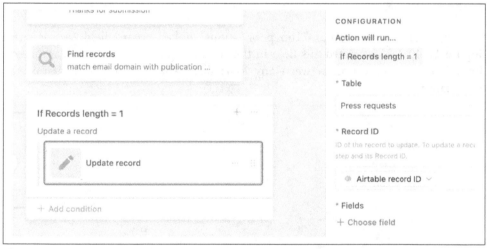

*Figure 11-38. The first action under a grouping of conditional actions is to update a record.*

We've set up a single-select field to rate the priority level of the different press requests we received for any records matching our top publications. We will use this "Update record" step to update the priority to "High priority." This static value will be the same for any record that is in the set of conditional actions, as shown in Figure 11-39.

*Figure 11-39. Marking form submissions that match with top publications as being high priority.*

We also want to update our "Top publications" linked record field, as shown in Figure 11-40. We've created this field in the "Press requests table" so we can make a linked record connection between any journalists who are from one of our top publications.

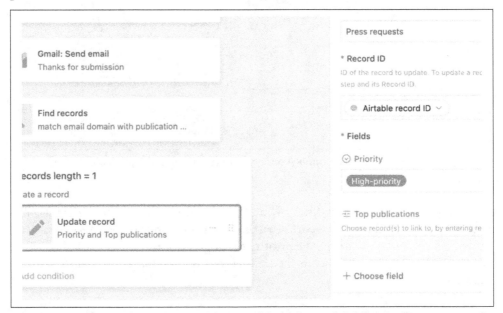

*Figure 11-40. Updating the "Top publications" linked record field in the "Press requests" table.*

Since the publication of every journalist will vary, this value is dynamic. We can pull the publication from the results of the "Find records" action, where we searched through publications to find a match with the journalist's email domain in the "Choose data" section.

We don't want to insert a list or a grid, and the number of records ("length") returned doesn't matter to us. Instead, we want to get the record ID to link this form submission with the publication.

The last set of options is "Make a new list of…" The first choice is "Airtable record ID," which feeds the dynamic record ID of the result from the "Find records" action step. Although Airtable is describing a list, we don't need to search through more than one record of results because we have a maximum of one record that can be passed through this automation. Therefore, we can simply choose "Airtable record ID," as shown in Figure 11-41.

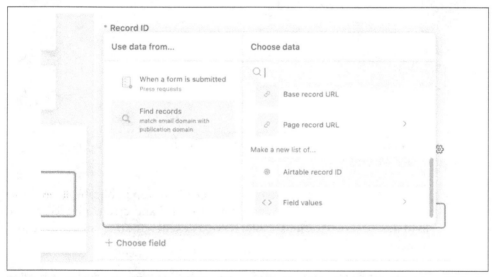

Figure 11-41. Inserting the record ID of the publication into the Top Publications linked record field in the Press Requests table.

After clicking "Generate a preview," we see our two fields that have been updated by being outlined in green. The priority of this submission has been changed to "High priority." We also see the name of the publication, the *Washington Post*, in the "Top publications" linked records field. Airtable has taken the record ID passed from the "Find records" action step and created a linked records connection between Ben Bradlee's form submission and the *Washington Post* record in the "Top publications" table, as shown in Figure 11-42.

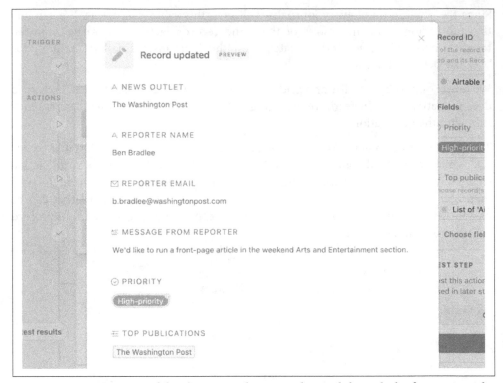

*Figure 11-42. A preview of the changes to the original record through the first action of the conditional logic group.*

For any form submissions that we can match to one of our top publications, we've set up an "Update record" action to mark as "High priority" and create a linked record relationship to the "Top publications" table. Next, let's generate an email that will connect the journalist with our PR team.

**"Gmail: Send email" from press representative.**   Since this isn't an internal notification email where we might use Airtable's "Send an email" action, let's use the "Gmail: Send email" action instead. But we will use a different Gmail account than our first "Gmail: Send email" action. Earlier in this automation, we sent a thank-you note from the tour manager to anyone who submitted the form. However, this email is going to come from our PR liaison, and we only want it to go to journalists that match one of our top publications.

Let's add another "Gmail: Send email" action below our "Update record" action of "Conditional actions" and give it a description. The next step is to add the Gmail account of our PR liaison. We'll need access to their email account so that we can authenticate with Gmail.

We can set up the "To" field exactly like we did with our first "Gmail: Send email" action, where the recipient of the email is taken from our "Reporter email" field. In this case, we are also going to add the tour manager in the CC field, so they're aware and can monitor replies between the journalist and our PR representative, as shown in Figure 11-43.

*Figure 11-43. Routing the personalized email to the reporter from a publication in our top list.*

The subject field will be static, but the message should be customized to make a strong impression on the journalist.

Let's customize the message field box in a couple of ways. First, we can add the journalist's name as a dynamic value pulled from the original form submission in the greeting, which is the trigger for our automation.

We also want to mention the journalist's publication. So we'll also add the publication as a dynamic variable, which is "News outlet" from the form submission trigger, as shown in Figure 11-44. The last piece of our short and sweet email is an ask to schedule time to talk.

*Figure 11-44. Customizing email to a reporter asking for a meeting.*

We want to ensure that our customized email is working correctly and we don't have any glitches. Those mistakes would undermine our credibility, so we can "Generate a preview" to see that both the reporters' names and the publication are coming through as hoped, as shown in Figure 11-45. The next time we have a form submission from a reporter with one of our top publications, they will get an email from our PR liaison to debrief before setting up an interview with the band.

*Figure 11-45. Previewing the Gmail outreach to the journalist.*

**Slack message to the team.**   The team is enjoying using Slack to organize tour updates, so let's send everyone a message when we get an inquiry from an important journalist. As we've done before, we will add a "Send a Slack message" action, connect it to our Slack account, choose the appropriate Slack channel, and then fill in the message. Let's also put a dynamic variable in the Slack message, the list of results from our "Find records" action, as shown in Figure 11-46.

*Figure 11-46. Setting up a Slack message for the team to know we have interest from a top publication.*

Clicking on "Generate preview" shows us that the Slack message will come through with the name of the *Washington Post* in the message, as we see in Figure 11-47.

*Figure 11-47. Testing the dynamic content in the Slack alert for our team.*

The automation we just completed has a total of seven steps. You might remember that Automations in Airtable can have up to 25 steps. So even as complex as this set of Automations has seemed, we are really just scratching the surface of Airtable's capabilities.

In this automation, we triggered the flow with a form submission, alerted the tour manager, and sent an automatic thank-you email. Then, if we can match the journalist with one of our top choices for press coverage, we can update that journalist's request to be a top priority and link them to the publication. We can also send an email from our press representative to schedule a time to discuss when they can interview the band. And finally, we let everyone in the tour planning group know that we've received an inquiry from one of our top picks for press coverage.

# Triggers

In this section, we will look at Airtable's own triggers and then examine triggers to connect to other applications.

## Airtable Triggers

Airtable's own triggers are designed to interact only with records.

### "When a record is updated"

This trigger allows you to specify which fields in a table to watch. When a value changes in any of those fields, the changed records trigger the automation.

 This is not a good trigger to use in fields where users are making multiple key-presses for making a full update, like text fields, date fields, or number fields. As soon as the first letter of a word is typed, the trigger would be activated. Instead, it's better use the Single select, Checkbox, or Rating fields, where the update takes place in a single action.

### "When a record is created"

Any records created in a table you choose from your base will start the automation workflow for this trigger. It's important to note that the automation starts as soon as a new record has been added, not when you've finished entering data in that new record. So if you manually enter data for a record that you might need in a later step of the automation flow, this may not be the best choice for you. A better choice is probably "When a record matches a condition."

### "When a record matches a condition"

As we saw with "When a record enters a view," it's possible to have an automation fire off before everything you need for the entire flow is in place. Triggering a flow with "When a record matches a condition" ensures that everything you need for the rest of the flow is already in place.

### "When a record enters a view"

Using filters on a view can narrow down the records you may want to access for a certain reason if you're filtering records on a few variables. This action can be a way to trigger a workflow when a record meets the filters in the view.

 Although "When a record enters a view" is similar to "When a record matches a condition," it has additional risks. Since the logic of what triggers the workflow is based on the filters in the view, it's possible those filters could be accidentally changed by you or a colleague. However, this automation could be a good option if you feel confident that the filters will be kept from being accidentally modified. (This is a good use case for locking views.)

### "When a form is submitted"

Airtable forms tightly integrate into your base, and the "When a form is submitted" trigger takes advantage of that connection. Whenever a form in your base is submitted, the "When a form is submitted" trigger will fire the automation, pass details from the form submission, and make them available for actions in the flow.

### "At a scheduled time"

The five previous Airtable triggers were activated when a record changed. The trigger activates when a record was created, was updated, enters a specific view, matches a condition, or was the product of a form being submitted. The "At a scheduled time" trigger is different because it runs at a certain time interval but doesn't necessitate any change in any records to be triggered. The trigger can be scheduled for a certain number of minutes, hours, days, weeks, or months beginning on a specified date and time. It can also be triggered just once at a specified date and time.

### "When a webhook is received"

Using webhooks to trigger Automations with the "When a webhook is received" trigger is a more technical option.

This trigger will allow your automation to receive a webhook, which is a simple packet of data that can come from an outside application. This trigger dramatically broadens the data you can push into an automation flow. Since many applications generate webhooks, the data sent with the webhook to the "When a webhook is received" trigger can be passed through to subsequent steps in the automation flow.

### "When a button is clicked"

In the next chapter, we will look at Airtable's Interface Designer. The "When a button is clicked" trigger connects a button element from the interface to an automation flow. The automation flow is triggered when users click the button in your interface. As we build out Interfaces, we will look at this button option in the next chapter.

## Third-Party Triggers

Airtable has a small group of triggers that connect to Google Workplace and Microsoft Office products.

### "Outlook Email: When email is received"

The "Outlook Email: When email is received" trigger is the only trigger to start a workflow based on an email being received. This automation allows new emails to an Outlook inbox to start the trigger and pass data from the email to subsequent actions in the flow.

### "Outlook Calendar: When event created" and "Outlook Calendar: When event changed"

There are two ways to trigger a workflow from an Outlook calendar: when an event is created or changed. When either of these triggers is activated, the event data—like its starting time, location, or creator importance—is passed along to the workflow's actions.

### "Google Calendar: When event created," "Google Calendar: When event changed," and "Google Calendar: When event canceled"

Calendar triggers for Google Calendar are similar to Outlook. The Google Calendar triggers include when an event is created or changed. However, you can also trigger a workflow using the "Google Calendar: When event canceled" trigger, which will fire off an automation for a canceled event.

### "Google Sheets: When a row is created"

When a new row is created in Google Sheets, this action can trigger an automation flow with the "Google Sheets: When a row is created" trigger. Once triggered, the column values of the newly created row are available for subsequent actions.

The "Google Sheets: When a row is created" trigger doesn't always work as expected. It only triggers for a new row added to the bottom of the sheet, and it needs to be a net new row. If you have 100 rows total and remove five, you would not activate the trigger until you add back those five rows plus another one. Also, if you have a hundred rows but are filling in data for blank cells in row 21, for example, this does not create a new row as the trigger defines it.

### "Google Forms: When a new response arrives"

Google Forms has more functionality than Airtable's form builder, so it may be advantageous if the form you need is complicated. In the Google suite of tools, all form submissions are new rows in a Google Sheet, similar to how Airtable forms write to an Airtable table.

Since the "Google Forms: When a new response arrives" trigger is ultimately monitoring a Google Sheet, the same requirements of what qualifies as a new row are applicable in the "Google Forms: When a new response arrives" trigger as in the "Google Sheets: When a row is created" trigger.

# Actions

While each automation can only have one trigger, we can have up to 25 actions. So any automation can have many tasks it's performing by its actions.

## Airtable's Actions

Five actions concern only data inside of your Airtable base. All of these actions can be triggered without needing to connect to third-party services or accounts.

### "Create record"

The "Create record" action allows you to create new records in any table of your base. In addition, you can pass data from other Airtable records or other sources, from either a third-party trigger or an action.

### "Update record"

Like the "Create record" action, the "Update record" action allows you to add new data to a field of records in your base.

We can update more than one record in Automations, too, with the "Repeating groups" capability in an automation flow.

### "Send an email"

You have three options for sending emails with an Airtable automation action. First, you can connect to a Google or Microsoft Outlook email account and directly send an email from that account. Or you can use the "Send an email" action to email someone via Airtable's mail service.

As you'll see in this chapter's examples, the upside of the latter is that there's less configuration, but the downside is that the email is branded as being sent by Airtable. So if the goal is to send an email via an automation from your own email account, you'll want to use either the "Gmail: Send email" or the "Outlook Email: Send email" action.

### "Run a script"

In Chapter 10, we looked at the Scripting extension, which provides a way to create interactive applications that users can access in the data portion of Airtable. The "Run a script" action uses the same SDK to access the data in your base, but there are some key differences.

The "Run a script" action runs in the background and has no interactive elements, such as a drop-down menu. Instead of a user entering values like in a scripting extension, you can pass values from the trigger or previous action steps into your "Run a script" action.

Using this action has some defined limitations, though. First, scripts can run up to 30 seconds in Airtable. However, API calls timeout after 12 seconds. What's more, scripts can use up to half a gigabyte of memory. Third, scripts can make 50 fetch requests and 30 select record queries. (Developers should note that some function calls that are supported in scripting extension are not supported in automation scripts.)

### "Find records"

As we saw in the examples in this chapter, the "Find records" action is a critical tool for building complex Automations. It enables you to search through records either with a condition or by a view. The conditions can be made up of static or dynamic values, most often from a previous step in the automation flow.

The "Find Records" action in Airtable has a limit of returning 100 records, regardless of the number of records in the view or the number of records that meet the specified conditions.

### Conditional logic in Automations

Conditional logic in Airtable automations allows you to incorporate dynamic decision making into your workflow. It allows you to create sequential groups of automation actions where each group is executed based on the results of a previous trigger or action.

For example, let's say we need to assign different tasks to team members based on the region of the concert. We can use conditional logic to automate this process. We would set up a trigger when a new concert is added to our base and then create a series of conditional groups of actions.

In the first group, we would set a condition that if the concert is in the East Coast region, we assign the task to our team member Sarah. In the second group, if the concert is in the West Coast region, we assign the task to John. In the third group, if the concert is in the Midwest region, we assign the task to Lisa. And so on for each region.

This way, whenever a new concert is added, the automation will run through each conditional group and assign the task to the appropriate team member based on the region of the concert. Conditional logic like this in automations allows you to create workflows that adapt based on specific conditions or criteria.

### Repeating groups in Automations

The repeating groups feature in Airtable Automations is a powerful tool that allows for the automation of repetitive tasks in a simple and streamlined manner. You can create a set of actions that will be applied to a group of records, iterating through each record individually.

Let's consider the task of sending personalized emails to all the venues that we are considering for the tour. By using the repeating groups feature, you can create an automation that will iterate through each venue record and send customized emails based on their information.

In another example, if you want to schedule follow-up calls with all potential venues that have not responded within a week, you can use a repeating group action to iterate through the records and create corresponding tasks for your team members. Each team member will then receive a customized task notification with all the relevant information.

Overall, the repeating groups feature streamlines repetitive workflows and greatly reduces the need for manual intervention.

# Third-Party Actions

Airtable has compiled a small group of actions that connect to third-party applications compared to services such as Zapier, which we'll look at in Chapter 13. The list is relatively limited, but it at least covers the most commonly used applications.

### "Send a Slack message"

The Airtable automation action is robust. If your organization communicates on Slack, you can use the "Send a Slack message" action to send messages that mention users by username or Slack user ID, send messages to a channel, or send users a direct message. Values from previous steps can be passed dynamically into the message.

### "Send MS Teams message"

The "Send MS Teams message" action is tailored to organizations. Personal accounts cannot use this action because of a Microsoft restriction. The "Send MS Teams message" action has functionality similar to the "Send a Slack message" action, including direct messages, clickable links, and sending to different channels.

### "Gmail: Send email" and "Outlook Email: Send email"

Airtable's own "Send an email" action sends email from Airtable's transactional email account with Airtable branding. However, if you'd like to send email directly from your own email account, you can use either "Gmail: Send email" or "Outlook Email: Send email" actions.

These automation actions allow you to have static or dynamic data for the email's recipient, the email's subject line, and the email's message. Plus, both allow adding attachments, adding recipients in the CC and BCC fields, and customizing the "From" address and "Reply to" fields.

### Google and Outlook Calendar actions

Users of Google Calendar and Outlook Calendar can both create and update events. Outlook users can trigger the "Outlook Calendar: Create event" and "Outlook Calendar: Update event" actions to create or update new events. Likewise, Google Calendar users can use "Google Calendar: Create event action" and "Google Calendar: Update event action" to create and update events.

### "Google Sheets: Append a new row to a spreadsheet"

If you need to push data to Google Sheets, the "Google Sheets: Append a new row to a spreadsheet" action allows you to choose a spreadsheet and worksheet you can access and to choose what data you'd like to go into the various columns of the worksheet.

It's important to note that the worksheet you choose must have a header row with names for the columns, or this action cannot be configured.

While it's not possible to actually create a form response for a Google form, Airtable has a workaround that builds off of the "Google Sheets: Append a new row to a spreadsheet" action. When you configure the "Google Forms: Create a new response action" action, you're actually specifying the Google Sheet tied to the Google form. Once you've selected the spreadsheet that collects the form responses of your Google form, you follow the same steps of choosing the worksheet and columns to insert data into for the new form.

### "GitHub Issues: Create issue" and "GitHub Issues: Update issue"

Teams that use GitHub Issues can update and create issues through automation actions using "GitHub Issues: Create issue" and "GitHub Issues: Update issue." When creating or updating these issues, it's possible to modify the title, body, milestone, labels, and assignee.

### "Twitter: Post Tweet"

With this action, you can automate sending tweets with attachments, like images and videos. In addition, the "Twitter: Post Tweet" action connects to a single Twitter account, and you can pass data from the trigger or previous actions into the body of the tweet. Unfortunately, it's not possible to mention other Twitter users in tweets generated with "Twitter: Post Tweet."

### "Facebook Pages: Create a new post"

While it's not possible to automate posting to a personal Facebook page profile, you can create a post for Facebook pages with this action. After connecting to a Facebook page or business manager account, you can use dynamic data to craft the post in "Facebook Pages: Create a new post." If you'd like, you can also add a link or an image or video attachment.

### "Hootsuite: Schedule post"

Regardless of which social media platforms you are using, Hootsuite is a good tool for scheduling those posts in advance. In Airtable, you can use the "Hootsuite: Schedule post" action to create those posts. You can define the scheduled time, the message itself, attachments for the message, and tags for the post. Then, Hootsuite can post to Twitter, Facebook, LinkedIn, and personal Instagram accounts with the Airtable "Hootsuite: Schedule post" action.

We've seen how Automations can save you time by defining triggers and actions that change data in Airtable and other connected services. Next, we'll look at how we can abstract away the intricacies of a base with custom, user-friendly applications in Airtable's Interface Designer. We don't need to write any code, and it connects directly to our data; we can even trigger an automation and do much more from within an interface.

# CHAPTER 12

# Interface Designer

Over the past 11 chapters, we've progressed from using Airtable as a simple spreadsheet-like table to using it as a complex system for entering, storing, and moving your data. Still, Airtable can feel overwhelming for someone who isn't familiar with the platform. And besides, it might be too difficult to train everyone in your organization to understand Airtable's finer points. Luckily, we can build simple web app interfaces and tailor the Airtable experience to each user's needs with Interface Designer.

Conceptually, Interfaces are not unlike the views we first looked at in Chapter 4, where each view allows you to view some amount—and aspects—of your data. You can remove records from the view without deleting records if they are filtered out of a view, for example. However, Interfaces can have more customized, interactive components.

Interface Designer makes it easier to work with Airtable and allows you to limit what data users can access. Even more importantly, Interfaces allow you to customize how you interact with your data. For instance, someone on your team might need to create a content approval workflow or enrich information in your CRM. Whatever business function needs to be accomplished, this chapter examines how to build a custom interface to meet your colleagues' needs.

In this chapter, we will delve into the various layout options and examine the different elements available in Interface Designer, including text elements, record picker elements, filter elements, number elements, chart elements, and more. We will walk through three practical examples to solidify our understanding of Airtable Interfaces, including building a full-page interface with customized views for tracking our tour, creating a reporting dashboard interface for monitoring ticket sales and revenues, and constructing an interface that integrates multiple tables and enables email automation for managing deposits from venues. Finally, we'll explore the permission levels for collaborators to whom you may be giving editing, commenting, or just viewing access to an interface and the underlying base.

# Interfaces as a Frontend

Interfaces provide a highly flexible and customizable frontend to your data, similar to a web application. Like a view, each interface uniquely displays base data. For example, the data can be filtered and sorted before it reaches what the user sees in the interface. That is, we can craft a subset of our data to be available in any particular way that's relevant to the end user of an interface. The data in our Airtable base is still our single source of truth, and any modifications we might make to the records in our base using an interface connect back to the Airtable database.

## Why Use Interfaces?

At a high level, Interfaces are beneficial because they make collaboration more tailored to specific users.

More specifically, Interface Designer allows create accessible software tools for your collaborators that support the workflows you need to achieve. To illustrate, let's go back to our tour example and a scenario in which we need to deal with a contract for our tour. The booking agent is the first person to submit the contract. Then the band's manager needs to sign off on it, and finally, the attorney needs to give it a look and be sure that it's ready to sign. These tasks could all be tracked using a Kanban board in the Data section of Airtable. But with Interface Designer, we can create a special page for each person in the workflow that only gives them the information they need to do their part of the job. Interfaces make approval processes more streamlined and less prone to confusion or errors.

Last but not least, Interfaces can give your organization reporting insights. In Chapter 10, we looked at the Chart extension, which gives a visual representation of data in a base. But the data visualization aggregation tools in Interface Designer offer far more customization and flexibility. And again, these tools can be customized for each user or group of users who only need to log in to see the interface. Furthermore, users never need to open the Extensions pane to look at a chart.

## How Do Interfaces Work?

Airtable's Interface Designer is another example of the platform's no-code functionality. You don't need to know any programming to use this feature. To build an interface, drag and drop elements onto a page and configure them in a simple editor on the right-hand side of the screen, as seen in Figure 12-1.

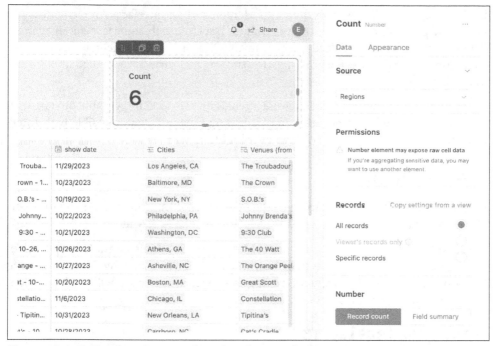

*Figure 12-1. A Number element selected in the Interface Designer.*

Just as we can do with Automations and the Page Designer extension, we can use static or dynamic data in an interface. Most often, we will link to dynamic data from a table that can be filtered, sorted, or grouped as needed.

Interface Designer allows us to pick and choose which fields are editable by users. The tour manager might only need to access a handful of fields in the contract approval process; and of those fields, the manager might only need to modify one or two fields. With Interface Designer, we can define which fields are visible and restrict users to modify specific fields related to the approval flow.

## What Makes an Interface?

Airtable's interface designer has three main hierarchical components: interfaces, pages, and elements. First, there is the interface, which is a group of pages. You can think of each page as its own mini-application. A base can have multiple Interfaces that contain multiple pages. Each base can have up to 50 Interfaces, and each Interface can have up to 50 "pages" (what most would think of as a very simple application).

Users with creator permissions can create Interfaces, but anyone can use them.

In this chapter, we'll closely examine the elements of an interface. An element could be a static piece of text with instructions about how to use the interface, or an element could be a field from a record selected in the "Record picker" element, as we'll see later. Some elements are versions of views, such as the "Grid," "Calendar," and "Timeline" elements.

To build an interface, you can either use a template provided by Airtable or start with a blank canvas. Let's look at these templates to understand what's possible with Interface Designer. And afterward, we'll go over building interfaces from scratch.

# Creating Interfaces

Let's create Interfaces so we can work with the data for our fall tour. As the tour gets closer to kicking off, the team needs to stay on top of a few key metrics.

We need to track when each venue has paid the deposit. We also want to keep track of ticket sales because we want to track how much profit we're making. We also want to know if the venue is effectively promoting the concert, which we will track by calculating the hours since the last ticket sale.

## Creating Full-Page Layouts

As we've seen, a full-page layout is beneficial because you can use one of six views to let your users understand various aspects of your data, usually from a single table. Later in this chapter, we will build an example from scratch using data from multiple tables.

When we first choose a layout, the options such as "Calendar," "Kanban," and "List" are at the top of the dialog, as seen in Figure 12-2. The options below the list of full-page layouts are more flexible, including "Dashboard" and "Record review," which are not full-page layout options. We will build a couple of examples using those types of layouts later in this chapter.

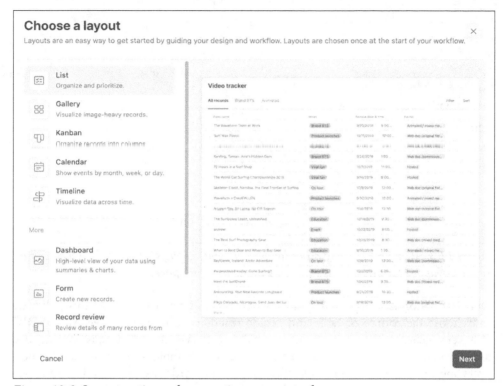

*Figure 12-2. Layout options when creating a new interface page.*

Let's start with the List layout and specify that we want to use data from the Shows table. In this full-page layout, Airtable will grab a handful of fields for this List view, as seen in Figure 12-3.

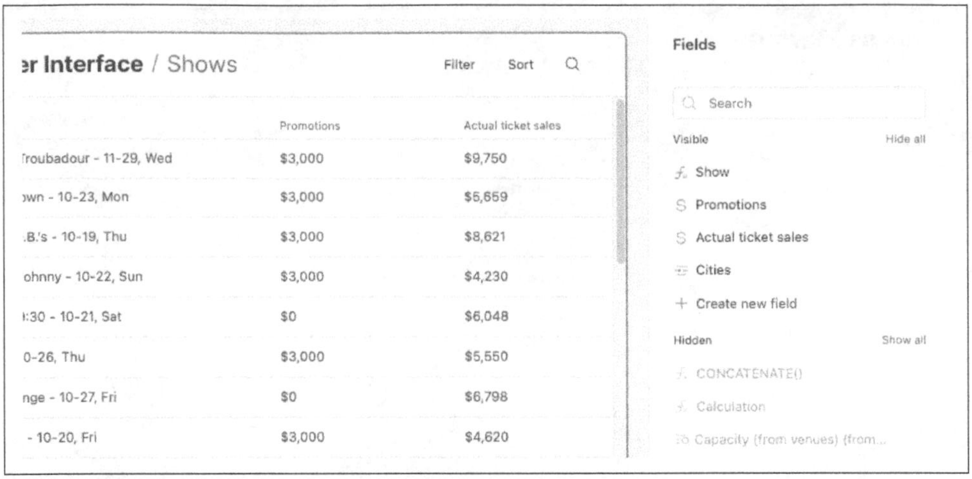
ər Interface / Shows
Filter
Sort
Promotions
Actual ticket sales
Troubadour - 11-29, Wed
$3,000
$9,750
ɔwn - 10-23, Mon
$3,000
$5,659
.B.'s - 10-19, Thu
$3,000
$8,621
ohnny - 10-22, Sun
$3,000
$4,230
:30 - 10-21, Sat
$0
$6,048
0-26, Thu
$3,000
$5,550
nge - 10-27, Fri
$0
$6,798
- 10-20, Fri
$3,000
$4,620
Fields
Search
Visible
Hide all
Show
Promotions
Actual ticket sales
Cities
Create new field
Hidden
Show all
CONCATENATE()
Calculation
Capacity (from venues) (from...

*Figure 12-3. After first creating a List layout, Airtable displays a few fields, which can be kept or swapped for other fields to display in the interface page.*

Our first option is in the right-hand sidebar under "Users can see." At this point, we can choose the source or table and decide whether we want to show "All records," "Viewer's records only," or "Specific records." In this case, the interface is not intended to show data specific to one group of our users, for example, so we will want to show everyone all the shows. Therefore, let's choose "All records," as shown in Figure 12-4.

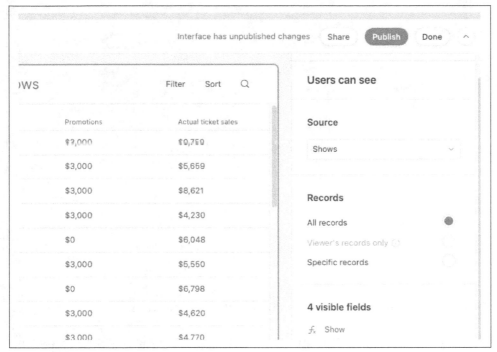

*Figure 12-4. Choosing which records to display in a list layout.*

In the next section of the right-hand sidebar, as seen in Figure 12-4, we have five additional options besides our List to display the data if we toggled on "Allow users to switch visualizations." We can also choose additional views. For this example, we'll use List, Gallery, and Calendar, as seen in Figure 12-5.

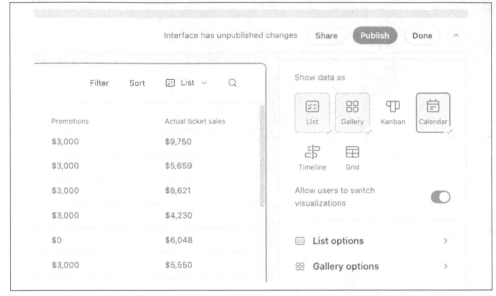

*Figure 12-5. Selecting which views users of the interface can access.*

Setting up each view, we've chosen three different ways to have our users view the data, including List, Gallery, and Calendar. For every view type you allow your users to switch between, options are specific to that view. For example, the List option allows us to sort the data, change the row height, and perhaps most importantly, choose the fields that are visible.

For this List view, it's important that we have the primary field of the Shows table, which is our concatenation of the city venue and date. We'll also have the "Show date" column field and will display field values for "Deposit match," "Actual ticket sales," "Hours since sale," and "headlining?"

As we set up the Gallery view as seen in Figure 12-6, we can choose to show the image of the venue in our base and the "Actual ticket sales" field.

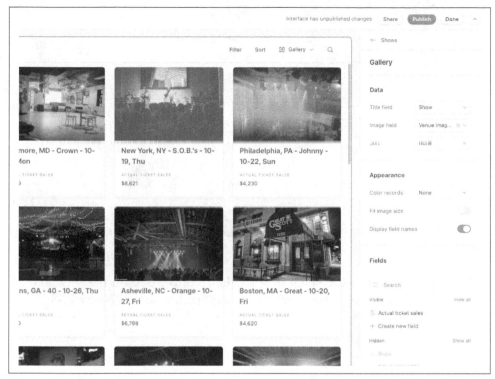

*Figure 12-6. Specifying the image field and other visible fields for a gallery layout.*

Our third view, which is a Calendar view, displays the shows on a simple calendar. If we click any of the records in Figure 12-7, we can view more information about that particular record. Furthermore, we can display the data as either a side sheet or a full screen. We can also choose the fields that are visible and which of those fields are editable by users, giving us a highly granular level of control.

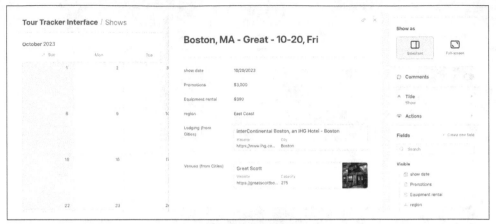

*Figure 12-7. Clicking into a record in the calendar layout to see more fields that we can specify.*

In this Calendar view, we're going to color the records based on the "headlining?" field so we can quickly see when we are the opening act, as seen in Figure 12-8.

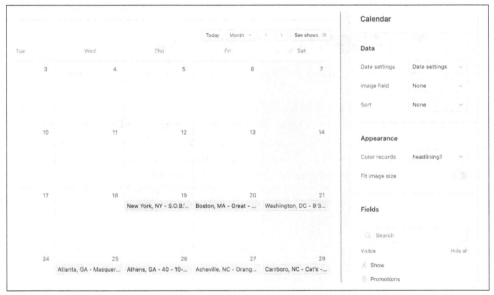

*Figure 12-8. Coloring records in a calendar layout using a single select field.*

## Setting global preferences for full-page interfaces

Below the specific options for the List, Calendar, and Gallery views, there is a set of options that apply to every layout we make available to our users. The first option is the records filter that we looked at earlier.

We can choose between not having a filter or having a filter with tabs or drop-downs. In this example, we'll use tabs to give us quick access to understanding our data. After all, we need to track some important metrics, including what shows we are headlining and when we've received a deposit.

Let's start with a default tab based on what we set up with "Users can see." In our case, we allowed users to see all the records in the Shows table, so we automatically have an "All shows" tab. Let's set up two more tabs. The first is based on the "Deposit match?" field. If the value is unpaid, those records will appear in this "Deposit unpaid" filtered tab. As we can see in Figure 12-9, all of the shows in this "Deposit unpaid" filtered tab have "Deposit unpaid" as the value for "Deposit match?"

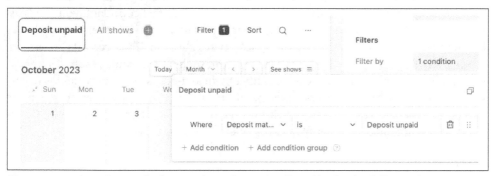

*Figure 12-9. Specifying which records to show in a filtered tab of a full page layout.*

Similarly, the Headlining tab that we set up simply filters for records that have a value of "Headliner." In our Calendar view, the "headlining?" field is color-coded. The only shows visible on the calendar are the ones we are now headlining, as seen in Figure 12-10.

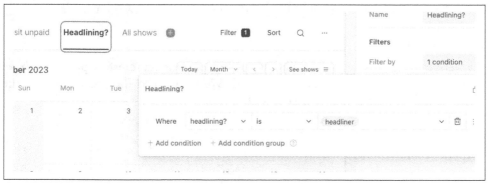

*Figure 12-10. Filtering which records are visible in a set of layouts for an interface.*

### "Click into record details"

There's only so much information we can easily view in an interface without requiring our users to scroll a lot. So the "Click into record details" option for our full-page view is a way to give access to more data for each record. As we've seen before, we can choose and create different templates for what data is seen. Inside each of these templates, we can toggle fields on or off and choose which of those fields are editable.

### "Find records"

One reason to use Interfaces is to avoid accidentally changing or deleting data. The data section of Airtable gets complicated, and it's better to put guardrails around your data by using Interfaces for novice users. However, if you feel confident, you can trust your users to be careful with what they do in Interfaces. For instance, it's possible to let them edit records directly in an interface. By toggling on "Find records," users can modify any field in a view that's not a calculation, such as a formula result. It's important to note, though, that users can't modify any field, because not every field is necessarily visible in a view. If users have the ability to click into a record to get more details because you've activated "Click into record details," those fields can be designated to be editable or view-only on a peripheral basis.

### "Add records"

It can be useful to have the option of "Add records" so that users can quickly add new records that might pertain to their work. For example, if you have a customer service agent who needs to generate a new ticket based on a phone call, allowing them to do that from an interface will certainly be helpful. However, in our case, any shows that might get added to the tour base should be completed by just one or two people managing the team's Airtable. After all, we don't want to activate "Add records" and run the risk of someone accidentally adding a show that would skew our calculations.

### Adding a button

As seen in Figure 12-11, we can choose an action to go to an interface page, which we will link to our next interface, a dashboard. We'll return to this interface once the dashboard is complete in order to connect the two.

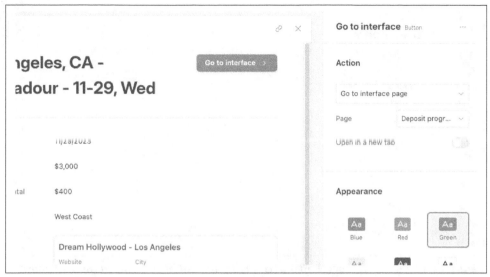

*Figure 12-11. Setting up a button to go to another interface page from "Click into record details."*

## Creating a Dashboard Interface

Let's create an interface that is more flexible than the full-page interface we just configured. Airtable gives you countless ways to build a reporting dashboard in Interface Designer using the different available elements with the blank layout option, but let's start by using the Dashboard layout.

After choosing the Dashboard layout, we will pull data from the Shows table. The next dialog gives us options to customize the six default elements, as shown in Figure 12-12. The Dashboard layout has a "Filter" element that we can connect to one or more of the other elements, including the three "Number" elements and the two "chart" elements.

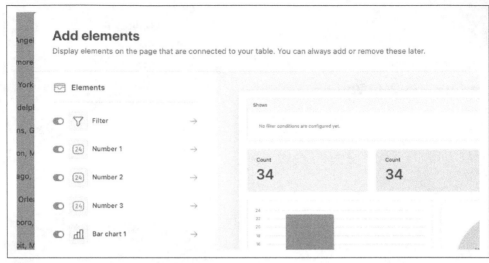

*Figure 12-12. Options to toggle off and configure the initial elements in the dashboard layout.*

If we click on the first Number element, we can see that Airtable has defaulted to counting the number of records in our Shows table, as seen in Figure 12-13. Let's leave this option as is.

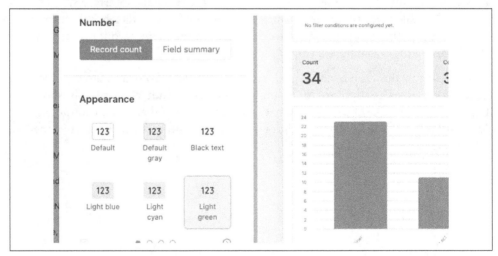

*Figure 12-13. A default configuration to count records to be displayed in a Number element.*

For the second Number element, Airtable also defaults to a record count. Let's change it. Instead, let's choose "Field summary" and change the field to "Actual ticket sales."

In the summary type, we have a list of options related to number-based fields. Let's choose "Sum" to see the total amount of ticket sales to date, as seen in Figure 12-14.

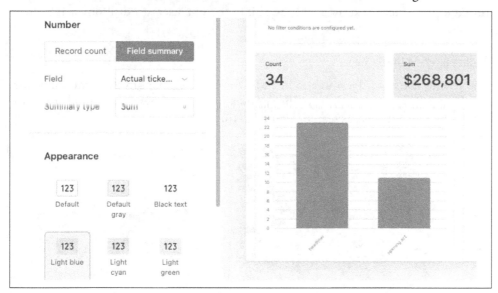

*Figure 12-14. Configuring a number element to display the sum of values in a field in a table.*

Before moving to the dashboard to configure the other elements, let's configure our last Number element here in the setup dialog. Let's again choose "Field summary," and we'll choose "Actual ticket sales" again as the field. And instead of summing all of the ticket sales across all the shows, let's average the revenue per ticket field, as seen in Figure 12-15.

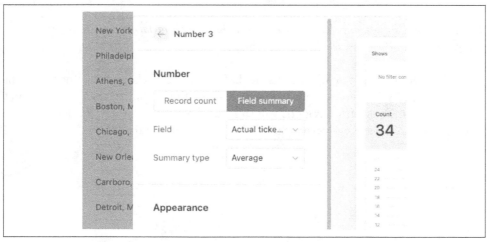

*Figure 12-15. Averaging values across records for a given field.*

Now we have three Number elements that give us high-level key metrics, including how many shows are on the tour, the total number of ticket sales, and the average revenue per ticket. Next, let's add the ability for our users to drill down into these figures.

## Adding filters to the dashboard

The default Dashboard layout also includes the Filter element in the right-hand sidebar. Under data, we can add two filter options identical to what we would see in the data section of Airtable, as seen in Figure 12-16.

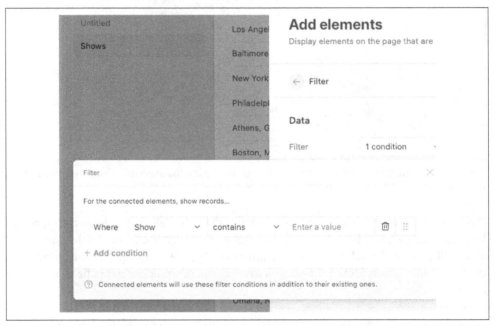

*Figure 12-16. Configuring the filter element with a user interface that is similar to the filtered views in the Data section.*

We will select the Show and Regions fields for the filter. Users can either type the name of a show or choose a linked record from the Regions table. For example, choosing "East Coast" from regions will show us five shows, the ticket sales for those five shows, and the average revenue per ticket, as seen in Figure 12-17.

*Figure 12-17. Choosing two fields to include in a filter element.*

Adding charts to the dashboard is easy. Let's add two different charts to round out this reporting dashboard. Remember that the Dashboard layout also comes with two Chart elements: a bar chart and a pie chart. Let's keep the bar chart but swap the pie chart out for a scatter plot.

### Bar chart to measure ticket sales by region

All elements we configured in this dashboard are linked to the Shows table. For this bar chart, we'll use the Linked record field Regions to sort shows by area.

The point of this bar chart is to look at ticket sales by region. Let's have the x-axis be the Regions field, as seen in Figure 12-18.

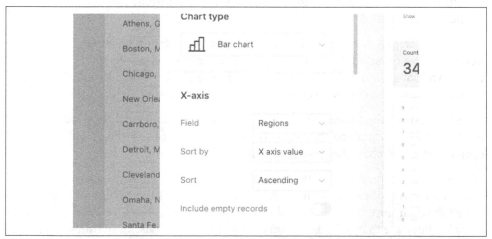

*Figure 12-18. Specifying the field for the x-axis of a bar chart.*

For the y-axis, we'll use a rollup field of the "Actual ticket sales" field that the regions linked to from the Shows table. All we want to do is add up these values, so we'll use the sum operator and toggle on "Start at zero," as seen in Figure 12-19.

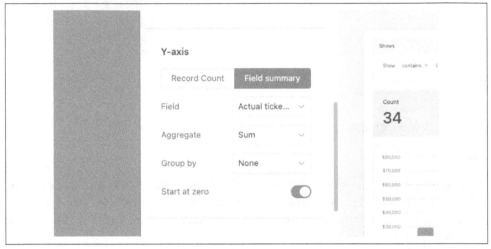

*Figure 12-19. Configuring the y-axis of a bar chart and summing the values for the x-axis grouping.*

### Setting up a scatter plot

The other default chart for the Dashboard layout uses the pie chart option. In the upper right-hand corner of the pane, we can simply switch this to scatter plot. (Because we chose the Shows table when we initially set up this layout, it will default all the elements to link to that table.)

In this scatter plot, we want a bird's-eye view of how many hours it's been since a ticket sale was reported. Since no two shows fall on the same date and time, we'll put the shows along the x-axis. We have the chance to bucket shows by another field or value, but we want to measure each show individually, so we will just bucket by day.

On the x-axis of the scatter plot, we do not want to only count how many records relate to each show, since that value is one. We want to use the "Field summary" option instead, to chart the "revenue per ticket."

With these six elements—a Filter, three Number elements, and two chart elements—we've built fairly robust reporting to understand the tour's financials and how quickly tickets for each show are selling, as shown in Figure 12-20. Next, we will build a more complex interface that pulls data from different tables and uses a button to trigger an automation.

*Figure 12-20. Configuring a dashboard with three number elements, a bar chart, a scatter plot comma, and two filters.*

# Creating an Interface with Multiple Tables and Buttons

The first interface example in this chapter used the full-page layout option, which already has most of its functionality baked in. In the second example, we took the dashboard template and swapped out one of the charts. For this example, we will start using a "Blank" layout and create the interface we need from the ground up.

### The business case

Our first two dashboards give us insights into what's happening during the tour and generate metrics about the tour's revenue. In this next interface, we will focus on the deposits we will receive from the venues. Because this interface will have lots of functionality, like emailing venue representatives, we're putting it in a different place.

The first interface we created had two pages, including the "Shows" full-page layout and a tour metrics dashboard. However, we will create a second interface consisting of just this one page. We will only share it with the tour manager and our accountant. From the main "Interfaces" tab, we will click "Create new" and title this interface "Deposit progress." We will start with a clean slate and use the Blank layout option, as shown in Figure 12-21.

*Figure 12-21. Starting with a blank interface layout.*

In this interface page, we will allow users to view which shows have a paid deposit. Plus, we want to give them the ability to send emails to the venues asking them to send the deposit and including notes about the amount due.

### Interface functionality

We can start by thinking of the elements we will include in this interface page. First, we want to see a list of all the shows without a paid deposit. Then, we want to be able to view those records in more detail. We want the ability to email the venue, and we also want to know the individual deposit amounts received. Sometimes, a venue will send partial or multiple payments.

Let's start by listing the venues still needing to pay a deposit. First, we can choose the List element. If we hover above the element, as seen in Figure 12-22, we can change the width to "Wide." This formatting change will be helpful since we need all the real estate we can get on this page.

*Figure 12-22. Opting to make our List element the full width of the page.*

Now let's customize the fields. We want to include only the bare minimum information to make room for other elements on this page. In addition to our primary field with the city venue and show date, let's also add the "Deposit match?" field. The value of this field results from a formula that results in either "Deposit paid" or "Deposit unpaid." Since we aren't concerned about shows with a paid deposit, let's filter these out and set a simple filter condition where "Deposit match?" is not "Deposit paid," as seen in Figure 12-23.

*Figure 12-23. Setting a filter for our List layout.*

Since we will squeeze a lot on this interface page, we should allow users an option to easily see more about each show. So let's toggle on "Allow users to open record details." We will show this record detail as a side sheet and leave the key fields in place, as shown in Figure 12-24.

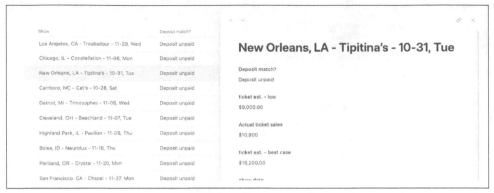

*Figure 12-24. Allowing users to open more details about a record as a side sheet.*

To make room for more elements, let's resize this List element to be on the left side of the page, as seen in Figure 12-25. With this extra space we now have on the right, let's add a "Record picker" element. Let's also add the same filter so that we only show records where the field "Deposit match?" returns "Deposit paid."

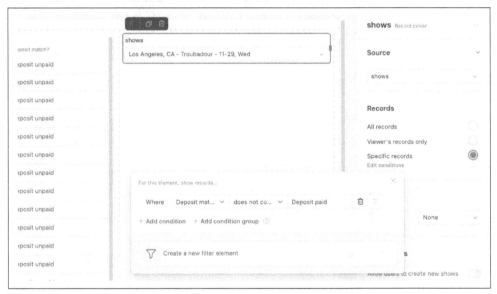

*Figure 12-25. Adding a record picker with the same filter as the List view on the same layout.*

The tour manager or accountant will use this interface, and they'll only need a handful of fields when digging into a show that doesn't have a deposit paid yet. Let's add fields for "Deposit match?," "show date," "email," and "number." Let's also add the rollup field, which aggregates all the deposits paid thus far from the venue, if any.

## Adding buttons

Buttons will give this interface more interactivity. Let's start with adding buttons so the user can move back and forth between records that don't have a paid deposit. After dragging two "Button" elements to the right-hand side of our page, we can also put an empty "Text" element between them so they're spaced evenly on either side, as seen in Figure 12-26.

Every button needs an action. Let's choose the "Go to previous/next record" option for these two buttons. We'll make the button on the left navigate to "Previous record" and the one on the right navigate to "Next record," as shown in Figure 12-26. In the "Appearance" section, we can change the color and change the button's name.

*Figure 12-26. Configuring buttons to allow us to move through records.*

## Adding fields

If we're going to use the buttons to search through the records, we will want to see field values for those records. Let's add fields for the show's day, email address of the venue, and the venue's phone number, as shown in Figure 12-27.

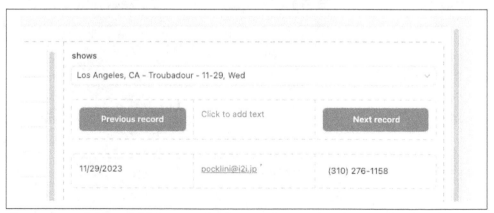

*Figure 12-27. Adding field elements for the record selected in the record picker element.*

And now, let's step it up a notch with another button. This button will eventually trigger an automation to send an email. We'll place it below the information about the record, as seen in Figure 12-28, and choose the "Run automation" action for the button.

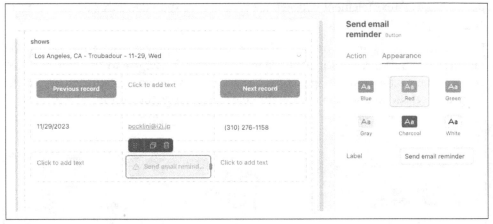

*Figure 12-28. Configuring the action for a button.*

In the "Appearance" setting, we can color the button red, and we'll change the name to "Send an email reminder," as seen in Figure 12-29. Now we need to build an automation for this button.

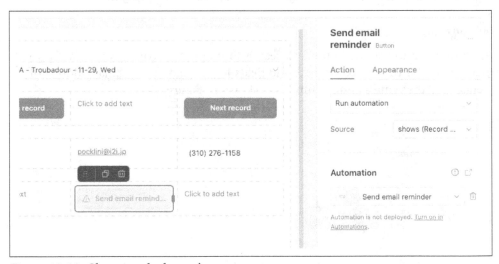

*Figure 12-29. Changing the button's appearance.*

## Building an automation for an interface button

Let's create a simple automation using the trigger "when a button is clicked" and choosing the "Gmail: Send email" action. Since we already have our Gmail account tied to our Airtable base, we simply need to configure the "To" field of the Gmail message to pull from the email listed in the record, as shown in Figure 12-30. We'll also add a simple note in the subject and message portions and a dynamic variable for the amount of the deposit due and the amount paid so far.

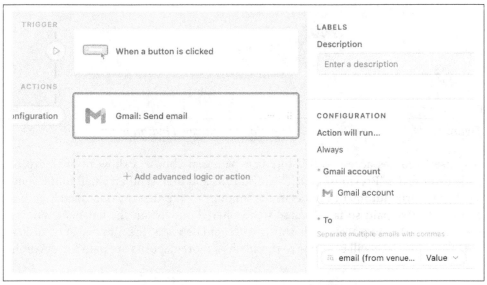

*Figure 12-30. Setting up an automation to run when a button is pressed in an interface page.*

Back in the interface that we are configuring, we can choose that automation, as shown in Figure 12-31. Once we turn it on in Automations, our button will be live.

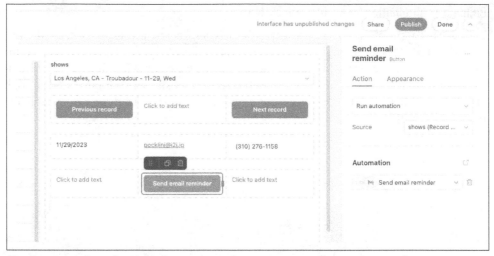

*Figure 12-31. Specifying the live automation to activate a button in interfaces.*

Any user who has access to this interface page can choose a show from the record picker or use the "Previous" and "Next" buttons and then send an email to the venue. That email will automatically detail the amount of the deposit due overall and the amount they've paid so far. Because we've filtered our list on the left-hand side and the record picker to only include shows with paid deposits, the number of records we see in this interface will continue to diminish as more deposits are paid for upcoming shows.

In the next section, we will look at more Interface layouts and elements in detail.

## Interface Layouts

Airtable has many interface layouts, one of which is the blank canvas we just used. Sometimes, these layouts give you a head start by connecting key functionality to fields in a table; this is the case with the "Record picker" element that's built into the Record summary layout. Other layouts have specific functionality that can't be created from scratch, such as the "Form" layout.

After choosing a layout, Airtable will prompt you to connect to one of the tables in your base unless you choose the blank layout. You can always filter and sort records in an interface at any time for your users, but this initial setup step allows you to filter or sort if you already know how you want to do that.

## "Record review" layout

As seen on the left side of the screen in Figure 12-32, we can view a list of the records accessed in this interface. This "Record list" element is only accessible using the "Record review" layout. All other components can be applied to a blank canvas.

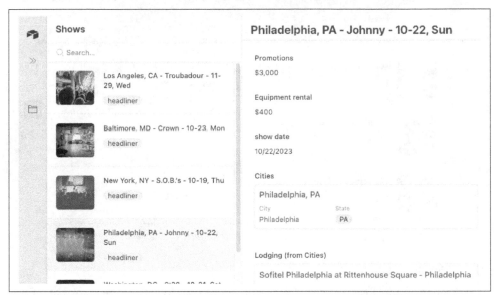

*Figure 12-32. The record review layout is the only way to have a "Record list" element in interfaces.*

The "Record review" layout allows you to scroll or search for a record. You can look at it in more detail from that left-hand navigation. Once you find the right record, you can click on it to see select details in an editable layout on the right-hand side. You can also choose the number of fields to display, which can be editable or view-only.

You'll see a few novel options in the left-hand "Record list" element. For instance, we can enter text about a record name in the search bar to find it. We can group those records by a Single select field and expand or collapse them as we do in the Grid view. The record list can also display a preview of three fields for each record that you can choose and order however you'd like. In the example shown in Figure 12-33, the shows from our tour base are grouped by the geographical regions where the shows take place.

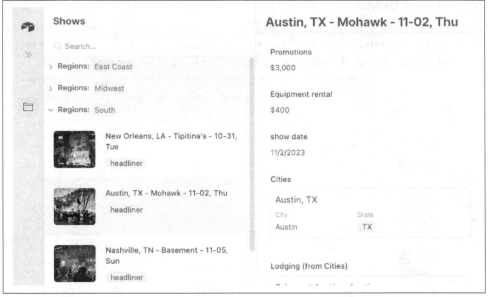

*Figure 12-33. Grouping records in the record list element of the record review layout.*

### "Record summary" layout

The essence of the "Record review" element layout is to focus on one record at a time. The "Record summary" layout has the same goal. There is a drop-down menu at the top of the interface where we can either search or scroll to find a specific record and its details, which is the "record picker" element.

The "Record picker" element is crucial in the "Record summary" layout. The interactive element allows users to select whatever records are available for that interface, as seen in Figure 12-34.

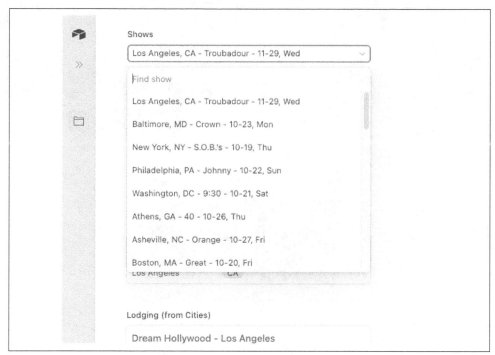

*Figure 12-34. The record picker element is the interactive component in the record sum-mary layout.*

### Dashboard layout

Stakeholders in any organization want to know how different initiatives and metrics are progressing. It's possible to build highly customized Interfaces to report our data, and the Dashboard layout is a good place to get started.

The Dashboard layout uses the Filter element for interactivity, as we saw earlier in this chapter and as shown in Figure 12-35. The Filter element can be used in any kind of interface for a multitude of use cases, and it gives users a simple but restricted ability to add the same type of filters on what they see in the interface, as we would in a Grid view, for example.

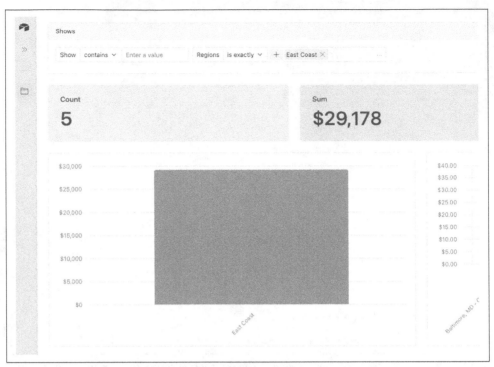

*Figure 12-35. Using the filter element to narrow the calculations in the dashboard only to shows in the East Coast region.*

The chart element is a last major component of the Dashboard layout. These charts are identical to what we've seen in the chart extension and include six options for visually representing data. From earlier in this chapter, as seen in Figure 12-36, there are chart options that include bar charts and scatter plots.

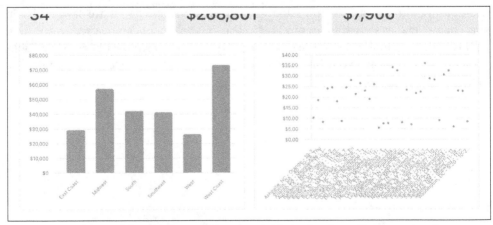

*Figure 12-36. Two of the six chart options available in the chart element.*

The Dashboard layout also includes several Number elements. Similar to a chart, it displays a figure but can't be edited and isn't a field value. (In this way, it is similar to the summary bar and the "Summary" extension.)

## Form layout

Interfaces are valuable because you can highly constrain what data a user sees and can change. However, in certain cases, you might want colleagues to be able to add records to a base; the Form element layout offers a way to do this.

In Chapter 5, we looked at the Form view, which created a form that anyone on the web could access with or without a password. The Form layout has the advantage of keeping a form completely behind your Airtable login, and access to it can be more granularly limited than just a one-size-fits-all password for the Form view. In terms of functionality, the Form layout in Interface Designer is very similar to the Form view.

The Form layout and the Record review layout have specific elements that aren't available if you build your own interface. Essentially, any editable field type from a table can be optionally included in the Form layout to create new records.

 While the Form element itself is only accessible in the Form layout, adding records in other ways is possible, as we'll see later. The Record picker element has the option to allow users to create new records.

## Full-page layouts

Full-page layouts essentially mimic the views from Airtable's data section. We can choose one or more of these views for each page.

As seen in Figure 12-37, we can show just one of these views or offer all six to the users of the interface page. We can choose from the Grid, Calendar, Timeline, Gallery, List, and Chart views by toggling on "Allow users to switch visualizations." We can then select more than one view option; each option has its own set of options specific to that view type.

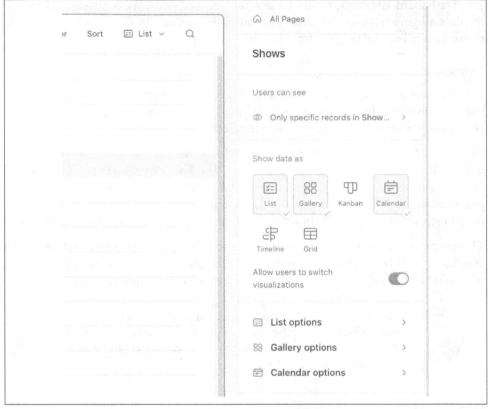

*Figure 12-37. Choosing one or more ways for users to view data in a full page layout.*

For example, in the Gallery view, we can choose the field we want to stack the cards by whether there's an image field and if we want to color records.

These full-page layouts have less granular controls but are more intuitive for novice Airtable users or users who would benefit from highly preconfigured data. In the "Allow users to switch visualizations" area on the right-hand side of the screen, we can set up a number of preconfigured options so that a user can drop in and automatically see the exact data that would be most useful to them.

Now that we have a general sense of some capabilities of Interface Designer, let's look at the building blocks, which are the elements we can use to create our own Interfaces from scratch.

# Interface Elements

After looking at the default Airtable interface layouts, you may have some ideas of Interfaces you'd like to build. It's worth taking an overview of each interface element. The next section discusses elements modeled after the different view types in the data section of Airtable.

## View Elements

In Interface Designer, there are six elements that emulate the six Airtable views: Calendar, Gallery, Grid, Kanban, List, and Timeline. For all six, there's a similar flow, adding the element to the interface canvas, configuring the data source and permissions, and applying filters, if needed.

Let's review each of these elements' unique functionality and customization options.

### Calendar

The Calendar element allows you to view records by dates, providing a convenient way to schedule events, plan tasks, and track timelines. You can customize the appearance of the calendar and choose which fields to display, allowing users to easily navigate and interact with their data in date-based contexts.

For the Calendar element, you can add it to the canvas, set the source table, and configure data and appearance settings such as start and end dates, color coding, and initial view. Users can interact with the calendar to view events, search for specific records, and click on events to see more details.

### Gallery

The Gallery element focuses on visual representation, particularly when there are attachment fields in the table. It gives users a thumbnail preview of attachments along with other field information. Key features include thumbnail-size adjustments, configurable appearance settings, and highlighting records based on specific field values.

With the Gallery element, you can choose a table as the source and set permissions. You can configure filters and customize appearance settings such as thumbnail images, title fields, and conditional coloring.

### Grid

The Grid element provides a spreadsheet-like interface where data can be displayed tabularly. It closely resembles the Grid view in Airtable but offers greater control over the displayed fields and record details. Users can sort, filter, and search within the Grid element, optimizing their data viewing experience.

The Grid element gives a spreadsheet-like viewing experience with options to limit access to certain data. You can choose a table as the source, set permissions, and configure fields, sorting, and grouping options. Grid elements are useful for displaying and managing data in a customizable interface.

### Kanban

The Kanban element is ideal for project management and agile workflows. It enables you to organize and visualize tasks or projects on a board with movable cards. Users can customize the appearance of the Kanban cards, color-code them based on specific field values, and configure filters to focus on relevant data.

Kanban elements are designed for tracking and managing projects in an agile way. They can be added to the canvas and configured with a source table, permissions, filters, and record details toggle. Appearance settings allow customization of cards on the Kanban board.

### List

The List element is specifically designed for creating, editing, and managing hierarchical data. It allows users to easily organize tasks, projects, campaigns, or any other type of hierarchical information based on important categorizations such as status, deadline, or priority.

The key difference of the List element, like the List view, is that you'll need to start by navigating to the table that will represent the lowest level of the view you are creating. Then add linked record fields that will connect each of the tables together.

### Timeline

Lastly, the Timeline element allows you to visualize chronologically ordered records. You can set each item's start and end dates and display them dynamically on a timeline. Features like adjustable snapshot types (day, week, month), filtering options, and customizable appearance settings make it easy to showcase events and timelines in a visually appealing way.

When designing an interface using these elements, consider how each one caters specifically to certain types of data or workflows. By leveraging their unique functionalities and settings, you can create interfaces that perfectly suit your needs and streamline your data management and visualization.

## Discrete Elements

The six interface view elements are larger and tend to represent individual records. The different discrete elements detailed next can be used as tools—to filter, for example, or to represent data more simply, such as the Number element.

## "Button" element

By using the Button element, you can enable users to perform actions by simply clicking on a button. This saves time and effort as users don't need to navigate through menus or remember complex commands. Instead, they can access necessary functionalities with just a single click. From updating information to deleting records, buttons provide a convenient way to interact with the data within an interface.

You can customize various attributes of the buttons, such as labels and colors, allowing for intuitive navigation and clear communication of the button's purpose.

## "Chart" element

After dragging the chart element from the "Add element" menu, we have a unique set of options in our right-hand pane. We can choose from four charts: line, pie, donut, and scatter. You may notice these are the same charts available in the Airtable "Chart" extension.

As we've seen with other elements, we want to choose the table as our source for this element. There are two unique sections in this data tab of options for the chart element. First, we have options for the x-axis. We can choose a field, whether we want to order it by the x value or the y value, if we want it to be in an ascending or descending direction, and whether or not we want to include any empty records in the chart.

We also have options for the chart element for the y-axis, similar to the Number element. The y-axis can count records but also adds the ability to group them by "Start at zero" or begin with the first lowest value.

The other group of options for the y-axis in the chart element is "Field summary." For this y-axis option, we choose a field and, like the Number element, choose how we want to aggregate it. We can aggregate it by the number of distinct records if it is a text field. Or if it is a Number field, we have five additional options: sum, average, median, minimum, and maximum. Furthermore, another field can group these fields.

The other section for the chart element is appearance. Depending on which of the five chart types you've chosen, you can choose a color scheme, create a legend, and place the legend around the chart wherever you'd like. You can also title the chart and the x- and y-axes, as we saw in the earlier example of creating a chart to track ticket sales.

## Record picker element

The Record summary layout hinges on the Record picker element. This element allows you to choose a record from a table, and it can be used in combination with other elements such as the Text element to build your own specialized layouts, wherein the Record picker element dictates which record's information another element displays.

### Filter element

As we've seen, Interfaces can give users limited functionality to explore data in your base while minimizing the chances that they will break something. The Filter element is one simple and controlled way to give users the option to explore data with less risk.

From a single Filter element, we can have many filters, and those filters can connect to many elements.

### Number element

When we looked at the Dashboard layout example, we saw that the Number element is a read-only element that summarizes records or values.

### Text element

Interface Designer's simplest and most utilitarian element is the Text element. You can drag and drop a Text element from the "Add element" pop-up box in the lower left-hand corner of the Interfaces screen.

These text elements can be a good place to add context or instructions for your users. The text inside of these elements can be formatted in bold, in italics, or as a header.

## Interface Designer Permissions

Interface Designer is powerful because it enables you to build interfaces that filter and display only the relevant data for specific users. You can define different permission levels when sharing an interface, such as viewer, commentor, or editor, as seen in Table 12-1. These permissions determine what actions collaborators can take within the interface, from simply viewing information to making edits or adding new records.

There are some important dependencies and considerations when using Interface Designer. For example, it replaces the need for hidden fields since collaborators only see the fields that creators have shared with them. By granting access thoughtfully, you can tailor interfaces to meet the needs of different users and ensure that sensitive information remains protected.

*Table 12-1. The different levels of permissions and access for users.*

| Interface Designer actions | Interface-only viewer | Interface-only commenter | Interface-only editor | Base viewer | Base commenter | Base editor | Base creator | Non-Airtable user/external colleague |
|---|---|---|---|---|---|---|---|---|
| Can view interfaces | ✓ | ✓ | ✓ | ✓ | ✓ | ✓ | ✓ | ✗ |
| Can comment on interfaces | ✗ | ✓ | ✓ | ✗ | ✓ | ✓ | ✓ | ✗ |
| Can edit interface records | ✗ | ✗ | ✓ | ✗ | ✗ | ✓ | ✓ | ✗ |
| Can create new records via form entry in interface containing form functionality | ✗ | ✗ | ✓ | ✗ | ✗ | ✓ | ✓ | ✗ |
| Can access the full base | ✗ | ✗ | ✗ | ✓ | ✓ | ✓ | ✓ | ✗ |
| Can add or update interface and interface pages | ✗ | ✗ | ✗ | ✗ | ✗ | ✗ | ✗ | ✓ |
| Can share access to interface at their permission level | ✓ | ✓ | ✓ | ✓ | ✓ | ✓ | ✓ | ✗ |
| Billable (Pro plans) | ✗ | ✓ | ✓ | ✗ | ✓ | ✓ | ✓ | ✗ |

As we've seen, we can create an interface for almost any need. We can also shape an interface to fit a particular team member's needs or to serve a specific business workflow. In the next chapter, we will look at examples of third-party platforms we can use with Airtable.

# CHAPTER 13

# Platforms That Extend Airtable

Airtable's unique value proposition as an easy-to-use web-based database has prompted many developers to start companies that make tools explicitly for use with Airtable. This chapter will look at two major categories of applications you can use to extend your Airtable bases—connectors and app builders.

Connectors allow us to create automation workflows based on and interacting with our Airtable data. Chapter 11 examined Airtable Automations, which allows for multistep workflows fully based on no-code logic. Before Automations was released in 2020, the no-code community went to tools like Zapier and Make.com to connect third-party apps to Airtable. We will look at both Make and Zapier in this chapter, comparing the capabilities of each with Airtable Automations.

In Chapter 12, we looked at Airtable Interfaces, which allow Airtable users to create internal interactive applications based on data in their Airtable databases. Before Interface Designer was released, users optimized other platforms to build dynamic database-driven websites on top of their Airtable bases, such as Softr and Stacker. In this chapter, we'll look at key differences between Airtable Interfaces and app builders. For example, app builders offer compelling cost savings if you have many users, and both Softr and Stacker have capabilities for building an app intended for outside users.

The first chapter of this book noted that Airtable is a product that reflects many years of iteration and improvement and that many high-profile customers can vouch for its stability and reliability. The four platforms described in this chapter were similarly developed and have comparable reputations. Thousands of companies are actively using these platforms in mission-critical scenarios.

# Connectors

Interest in connecting different software through no-code automation has exploded over the past decade and will likely continue. Let's take a look at the two most prominent connector platforms that are commonly used to build workflows between Airtable and other software.

## Zapier

Zapier is a powerful and versatile platform that allows users to create custom integrations between different applications and automate repetitive tasks. Zapier is similar to Airtable's Automations, allowing users to connect the applications they use most to eliminate manual work and avoid human error. Zapier was first released around the same time as Airtable's launch and is considered the leader in platforms that connect software-as-a-service (SaaS) applications like Salesforce, Gmail, QuickBooks, HubSpot, and many others.

As we saw in Chapter 11 with Airtable Automations, Zapier uses triggers and actions that begin a workflow and execute the steps in that workflow. Zapier is similar to Airtable Automations because it uses a linear, top-to-bottom sequence that starts the trigger and has actions that follow, as seen in Figure 13-1.

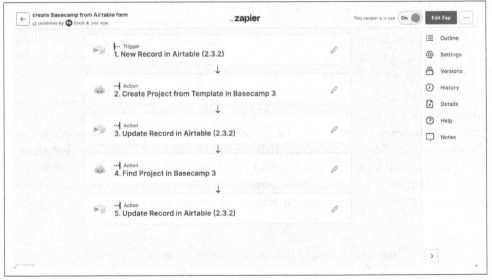

*Figure 13-1. The steps of a Zapier automation flow.*

### Advantages of Zapier

Getting started with Zapier is easy, and the user experience is tailored toward shepherding a new and often nontechnical user through the steps to get their first Zap

---

(the nickname for a Zapier trigger and actions) up and running. The learning curve is comparable to Airtable Automations. However, Zapier's connection with Airtable is less direct; as a result, users can experience a lag between changes to an Airtable base and Zapier's recognition of those changes. Therefore, building Zaps can be more cumbersome and confusing than working inside Airtable Automations.

The number of apps that Zapier allows users to connect to Airtable is unparalleled. Over 5,000 applications are readily available in Zapier's catalog.

Airtable Automations only supports roughly a dozen of the most popular applications, so Zapier's more extensive selection could be relevant to you for several reasons. After all, plenty of web-based applications are not for broad mainstream use but are targeted toward specific industries. So, for example, if you are using appointment-setting software for hair salons, you'd likely find this kind of niche application in Zapier's selection.

## Make

Like its app connector contemporaries, Make allows users to create automation workflows between various applications, providing an ecosystem for integrating Airtable with other tools.

Make has a visual layout that can show you all of the different steps in a workflow that can occur from a single trigger, as shown in Figure 13-2.

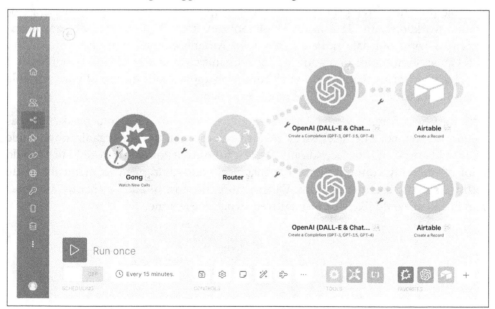

*Figure 13-2. The different components in a Make flow.*

### Advantages of Make

Make provides advanced routing capabilities that enhance the flexibility and customization of workflows. Users can create multiple routes within a single scenario, enabling branching logic based on specific conditions. These routes can act as decision points, allowing you to direct automation flows according to dynamically changing variables. Additionally, Make offers error handlers, empowering users to define action protocols in case of errors or exceptions during execution.

Data manipulation is another strength of Make. Aside from supporting basic operations like data transformation, Make provides built-in transformers, enabling you to modify data without the need for external tools. Moreover, it offers aggregators and iterators, which prove immensely valuable when handling bulk data and repeating actions across your dataset.

Make's robustness and flexibility, while being its strengths, can also introduce a notable learning curve for newcomers. Users unfamiliar with automation or those transitioning from simpler platforms might find it challenging initially. Moreover, the platform's capability of designing intricate workflows can sometimes lead to overwhelming complexity, especially for those who are not well versed in automation intricacies.

# App Builders

Airtable provides three primary tools for working with your data: a database, automation workflows, and Interfaces. These tools are helpful when internal team members work with your data and are part of your Airtable count. But what if you want to build an application for users outside your organization on top of your Airtable data? There are platforms that allow you to build web applications on top of your Airtable data without coding, just like the Airtable experience.

Let's start by considering why Airtable Interfaces may not meet your needs. First, as we just mentioned, Interfaces isn't ideal for users external to your organization. While you could create an Interfaces dashboard just for one customer, you would need to do a lot of unwieldy configurations. For instance, you would need to manually create settings-specific user permissions. Furthermore, the cost of adding that user to your Airtable plan would likely be prohibitively expensive at scale.

The most critical capabilities that tools for building applications on top of Airtable must have are automatic deployment, automatic sign-up, and an affordable price for each user/collaborator.

 There are other reasons to consider using a third-party app builder on top of your Airtable data. You may want to remove any Airtable branding, have customized design elements, and have other functionalities from modern web apps, such as allowing users to log in with one-click "magic links" instead of using a password.

Softr and Stacker are app-building tools that can easily integrate with Airtable for client portals, internal tools, or building public-facing web applications to make it easier to start building an app. In addition, both services have templates geared toward the most common use cases for turning Airtable data into web-based applications. Both tools meet our three criteria of being able to automatically have new user accounts with each user's specific data (i.e., configuration), enable self-serve sign-up, and be cost-effective for adding lots of users.

With Airtable data feeding into your application via one of these services, changes to your Airtable data can be reflected soon after they occur (though not in real time). As these app builders have progressed with enhanced functionality, it's now possible to edit and create records in your Airtable base from the application's frontend interface in Softr and Stacker.

Both Softr and Stacker are robust platforms with many features; a book could be written on each. But let's compare the primary advantages of each platform and understand where they excel.

## Softr

Softr and Stacker both have templates for commonly needed applications like client portals, team intranets, and CRM systems. However, Softr has more flexibility to create an application from scratch using its building blocks feature.

Softr users can access over 100 building blocks to create an application. In addition to basics like photo galleries and tables for your Airtable data, Softr also has blocks to create charts and calendars, the ability to plot data on a geographic map, and much more, as shown in Figure 13-3.

*Figure 13-3. Softr has a variety of blocks that add functionality to a Softr application.*

It's easy to use the building blocks in Softr. A block spans the horizontal width of a page, and blocks are stacked on top of each other. For example, we might have a small photo gallery with a map below it and a footer bar at the bottom of the page.

These building blocks can be static or have dynamic content from Airtable. We covered the ideas of static and dynamic content when we discussed the data passed between steps in Automations in Chapter 11. Softr's building blocks follow the same concept. A static block can be modified to have text or images, for example, but a dynamic block can change the number of items in a list based on how many items are in the table it is referencing.

To give some examples of static data, you might have an FAQ that doesn't change very often or a pricing page that might be easier to update inside the Softr editor instead of laying it out in an Airtable table and linking that data to Softr. (Conversely, for dynamic data, pages in your Softr application can reflect new records, or changes to records, as they are made in Airtable.)

While there are many different features to compare the Softr and Stacker platforms, it's fair to say that Softr has the upper hand when it comes to design and customization. Let's next look at how Stacker differs from Softr.

## Stacker

While Softr has limitless options to configure a web application, Stacker is more limited. Stacker is more geared toward creating multiple applications. It has a relatively unified look and feel, with layouts similar to how your Airtable is shown in the Grid view. In this way, Stacker is closer to Airtable Interfaces. So why not just use Airtable Interfaces?

As mentioned at the beginning of this chapter, there's a real economic cost to adding users to Airtable, especially if they just need to interact with data in an interface or two (it's free to add read-only users in interfaces).

It's anyone's guess whether Airtable will introduce interface-only users that can interact with data in Airtable interfaces. So, for now, it is generally prohibitive to have dozens or hundreds of clients, for example, logging in to Airtable to work with data relevant to them in an interface. Stacker, on the other hand, is built for having lots of users that need to add and modify data, just like Softr.

Similar to Airtable Interfaces, Stacker starts with a handful of templates. For instance, Stacker has templates for a client project portal, a CRM employee directory, and more. Unlike Softr, these templates come out of the box with a clean enterprise software aesthetic, as shown in Figure 13-4.

*Figure 13-4. The utilitarian layout and design of a Stacker application.*

Stacker automatically assumes you're interested in putting all the fields from a table into your Stacker application. You can toggle fields on and off, toggle on and off permissions to edit those fields, and do other things you would do in Airtable Interfaces, such as creating a button to interact with your Airtable data.

Stacker also has the ability to create a custom page layout. However, it only offers a relative handful of static and dynamic elements, called widgets. The dynamic widgets include a table displaying data as cards or a simple data display as rows.

While Softr has dozens and dozens of options for customizing your Airtable-based application, Stacker is known for creating applications that have a more standardized look and feel without the bells and whistles that you might have in a typical web application for outside users. Suppose you're looking to have the kind of functionality you get building Airtable Interfaces and a standardized look and feel. In that case, Stacker may be the best choice, especially if you're dealing with dozens, hundreds, or even thousands of users.

## Summary

So which is better for your needs, Stacker or Softr? Make or Zapier? The answer, of course, depends on your needs. For example, Zapier is a bit more expensive than Make but easier to get started with. However, with Make, it's easier to create more complex workflows and actions closer to the power of actual software development. In terms of complexity, the application builders are similar. As we've noted, Softr has more design flexibility and is better suited for an external SaaS application, but Stacker makes it easy to build enterprise applications right out of the box based on your Airtable data. So you'll need to investigate how each of these platforms can meet your particular needs. Although no-code programs don't require any code, they do require time.

If there's one thing that's true about no-code tools like Airtable, they are made to work with other no-code tools. Zapier, Softr, Make, and Stacker are no exceptions. Of course, there are differences in what you can do to send data to or from these platforms, but they can be connected together. Ultimately, they're very capable of being connected to Airtable in different ways.

It's worth remembering that these four platforms are not the only no-code platforms that connect to Airtable. A very large portion of the no-code community considers Airtable to be the leading no-code database. So before Airtable Automations and Interfaces were introduced, many applications offered the ability to connect to Airtable (via its REST API). There will continue to be more startups with new ideas of how to extend Airtable for specific use cases using their own no-code products, expanding the options for nondevelopers using Airtable.

# The Web API and Blocks SDK for Nondevelopers

We covered many topics to help you use Airtable as an integrated no-code system for storing, sharing, and analyzing your data. You should now understand how to set up and import data into your base, write and use formulas, make the most of tools like Automations and Interfaces, and extend your Airtable base with third-party connectors and app builders.

However, Airtable's full capabilities go beyond what you can accomplish independently as a user with little to no coding experience. And if you're not a developer but are working with a developer, you should know it's possible to extend your Airtable base using the Airtable Web API and the Blocks SDK.

If you're developer, the concepts here will be familiar to you already. Airtable has a site for developer docs (*https://airtable.com/ developers*).

In this chapter, we'll take a brief conceptual overview of these two components of the Airtable universe and what they can offer when leveraged by a developer. This isn't meant to be a full introduction for someone planning to write code and use the Web API or Blocks SDK directly; far from it. It's an opportunity for a nondeveloper to get more familiar with what these tools are so they can work with developers on creating custom tools for their Airtable bases.

Let's review some terminology and concepts you'll need to understand.

# The Airtable Web API

It's important to understand that a developer can use the Airtable Web API to connect your data directly to other services using code (e.g., JavaScript, Python) instead of through a third-party service like Zapier. Let's start by reviewing the basics of what an API is.

## What's a REST API?

Before we dive into the specifics of the Airtable REST API, let's briefly touch on what an API actually is. API stands for application programming interface. It's like a bridge between different software systems, allowing them to share information and work together seamlessly. An API determines how software components should interact and how data can be transferred between them.

In practical terms, think of an API as a set of rules and methods that define how different applications can request and exchange data. It enables applications to talk to each other without needing to know the internal complexities of each system.

## How Does the Airtable REST API Work?

To interact with the Airtable REST API, you will need to use a programming language like JavaScript or Python. A key difference between using Airtable's Web API and other ways of interacting with Airtable data using code (e.g., the Scripting extension) is that the actual code for using the Web API lives outside of Airtable. If you're using the Web API, you're running code in one of a myriad of programming languages, and that code is running somewhere outside of Airtable.

Almost every contemporary web application with an API is offering a REST API. The Airtable REST API follows a widely used protocol called REST (representational state transfer). RESTful APIs are built around a set of principles that enable systems to exchange information in a simple and standardized way using HTTP requests. HTTP requests are made using different methods. Each method corresponds to a specific action: fetching data (GET), creating new data (POST), updating existing data (PUT), or deleting data (DELETE).

When you make a request to the Airtable REST API, you are essentially communicating with the data in your bases sitting on Airtable's servers. You send an HTTP request specifying the desired action, such as fetching data, creating a new record, or updating an existing record.

This standardization of REST APIs ensures consistency while also making it easier for developers to work with a new REST API they haven't encountered yet. In other words, a skilled developer will be able to look at Airtable's API documentation and quickly have a grasp of what's available and possible.

# What Can You Do with the Airtable REST API?

With the Airtable REST API, you can perform a wide range of operations on your Airtable data. Here are a few examples:

*Read and retrieve records*
> You can fetch data from your Airtable base, filter records based on specific criteria, and retrieve specific fields for further analysis or processing.

*Create and update records*
> You can programmatically create new records in your Airtable base or update existing records. This allows for seamless integration with other systems that generate or manipulate data.

*Perform bulk operations*
> If you need to perform actions on multiple records simultaneously, such as updating all records that match specific criteria or deleting a group of records, the Web API provides endpoints for bulk operations.

*Integrate with external services*
> One of the most powerful capabilities of the Web API is its ability to connect Airtable with other software services. For example, you can automatically create tasks in project management tools like Asana or trigger actions in customer relationship management (CRM) platforms like Salesforce based on changes in your Airtable data.

These are just the most basic examples of what you can achieve by building custom software integrations with the Airtable Web API. The possibilities are vast and depend only on your imagination and the skills of your development team.

# Developing Custom Airtable Extensions with the Airtable Blocks SDK

Next, we'll explore the Airtable Blocks software development kit (SDK) and its significance in extending the functionality of Airtable. Although we won't dive into the technical details, we'll aim for a conceptual understanding of the Blocks SDK and why it matters. The goal is to equip you with the knowledge you need to communicate effectively with software developers about building custom Extensions for your Airtable bases.

Before Airtable extensions were called extensions, they were called blocks. Although the name changed in Airtable's main interface, the SDK for creating extensions continues to be called the Blocks SDK. There's a risk of confusion, so just remember that extensions are formerly known as blocks but are one and the same.

# What Are Extensions?

Before we delve into the Blocks SDK, which is used to make custom Extensions, let's briefly recap what Airtable Extensions are. Extensions are mini apps or plugins that extend the capabilities of Airtable. They allow you to enhance and customize your bases by adding new features and integrations, such as the Page designer Extension, which creates customized PDF layouts.

There are many tried-and-true Extensions in the Extensions Marketplace from Chapter 10. However, sometimes these prebuilt options might not fully meet your specific needs, which is where the Blocks SDK comes into play.

# The Power of the Blocks SDK

The Airtable Blocks SDK empowers software developers to create custom Extensions tailored to your unique requirements. It allows them to leverage their coding expertise to build specialized functionality that goes beyond what's available in prebuilt Extensions.

Using the SDK, developers can access your Airtable's data and connect it with other services or platforms. They can create seamless integrations with external tools, add interactive visualizations, automate complex workflows, or build entirely new interfaces on top of your Airtable data. For example, let's say you need an advanced chart visualization that isn't provided as one of the built-in views. With the Blocks SDK, a developer can create a custom Extension that generates interactive charts based on your data.

By providing developers with this level of customization and flexibility, Airtable enables you to create powerful solutions for your specific use cases. Whether you need a custom analytics dashboard or a unique Calendar view, the Blocks SDK gives developers a direct path to customizing the experience of Extensions in the Data section of Airtable.

# How Does the Blocks SDK Work?

The Blocks SDK is a toolkit developers use to build custom Extensions. It provides a set of tools, libraries, and APIs (not to be confused with the Web API) to interact with Airtable and build the desired functionality.

At its core, the Blocks SDK allows developers to build Extensions by writing code in popular programming languages like JavaScript and React. This code enables a custom Extension to fetch data from your bases, update records, or perform other actions.

The Blocks SDK also provides standardized UI components and styling options that developers can use to create a consistent look and feel within their Extensions. This ensures that custom Extensions seamlessly integrate with the rest of Airtable's interface, providing a cohesive user experience.

Once the custom Extension is built using the Blocks SDK, it can be shared with other users within your Airtable workspace. Users can install these Extensions and easily add them to their bases, expanding the functionality of their workflow without requiring any coding knowledge. This collaborative approach allows teams to leverage the expertise of software developers while providing nontechnical users with new tools to enhance their productivity.

In conclusion, the Airtable Web API and Blocks SDK enable developers to extend and customize the functionality of Airtable. By leveraging the Web API, developers can connect Airtable with other services, automate tasks, and perform advanced data operations. The Blocks SDK empowers developers to create custom Extensions that add specialized features and integrations to your Airtable bases. Understanding these tools allows you to communicate ideas and requirements to developers better and unlock the full potential of Airtable for your organization.

# Formula Functions and Operators

This list of formula operators and functions includes those used in the examples in Chapter 8, as well as the rest available for use in Airtable formulas. You will see a quick description of each text function, along with the format in which to use it and a simple example.

## Text Operators

### &

The & operator is used to join, or concatenate, two or more text strings together:

```
"First name" & "Last name" => "First name Last name"
```

### '\n'

Creates line breaks when placed between other text within formulas:

```
'\n'
```

```
({Musicians} & '\n' & {Comments})
```

## Text Functions

### CONCATENATE()

Joins together two or more text strings into one. This is especially useful when you need to combine separate pieces of information, like first and last names or city and state:

```
CONCATENATE(string1, string2, ..., stringN)

CONCATENATE("New ", "York ", "City") => "New York City"
```

# RIGHT()

Extracts a specific number of characters from the end of a text string. This is particularly useful when you need to isolate specific data, such as the last four digits of a credit card number or the domain of an email address:

```
RIGHT(string, howMany)

RIGHT("slow red fox", 6) => "ed fox"
```

# LEFT()

The LEFT() formula function in Airtable works in a parallel way to the RIGHT() function, except it operates on the opposite side of a text string. This function is handy for when you need to extract or isolate specific data from the beginning of a string:

```
LEFT(string, howMany)

LEFT("John Doe", 4) => "John"
```

# LEN()

Counts the number of characters in a text string. This is particularly useful when you need to measure the length of a text entry, such as counting the number of words in an essay or determining the character length of a tweet:

```
LEN(string)

LEN("blueberry pie") => 13
```

# LOWER()

Changes all uppercase letters in a given piece of text to lowercase:

```
LOWER(string)

LOWER("Goodbye!") => "goodbye!"
```

# TRIM()

Removes any extra spaces at the start or end of text:

```
TRIM(string)

TRIM(" Goodbye! ") => "Goodbye!"
```

# SEARCH()

Allows you to find specific text within a larger string of text. It's useful when you need to find the position of a particular word or character in a field.

Searches for occurrences of `stringToFind` when a `whereToSearch` string starts from an optional `startFromPosition`. (By default, the `startFromPosition` is 0.) If occurrences of `stringToFind` are not found, you'll receive an empty result.

This function is similar to the FIND() function, but FIND() returns a 0 rather than just being empty if occurrences of `stringToFind` are not found:

```
SEARCH(stringToFind, whereToSearch,[startFromPosition])

SEARCH("blue", "deep blue sea") => 6
```

# ENCODE_URL_COMPONENT()

Transforms a text string into a format that can be safely used within a URL. This is particularly handy when you're dealing with text that includes special characters or spaces, which can cause problems in URLs:

```
ENCODE_URL_COMPONENT(component_string)

ENCODE_URL_COMPONENT("Hello, World!") => "Hello%2C%20World%21"
```

# SUBSTITUTE()

Replaces specific text within a string with other text. This is especially useful when you need to change a certain word in a set of data, such as replacing "Mr." with "Ms." in a list of names, or changing city names from their English to Spanish counterparts:

```
SUBSTITUTE(string, old_text, new_text, [index])

SUBSTITUTE("I love ice cream", "ice cream", "gelato") => "I love gelato"
```

# FIND()

Searches for a specific text string within another text string and returns the position where the first occurrence starts. This function is crucial when you want to locate certain information within a larger body of text, like finding a specific word in a paragraph or a product code in an inventory list:

```
FIND(stringToFind, whereToSearch,[startFromPosition])

FIND("sun", "The sun rises in the east.") => 5
```

# LOWER()

Changes all uppercase letters in a given text to lowercase:

```
LOWER(string)

LOWER("Goodbye!") => "goodbye!"
```

# UPPER()

Converts all letters in a text string to uppercase:

```
UPPER(string)

UPPER("Goodbye!") => "GOODBYE!"
```

# REPT()

Repeats a string a certain number of times:

```
REPT(string, number)

REPT("Bye!", 3) => "Bye! Bye! Bye!"
```

# MID()

Extracts a specific subset of characters from a text string, starting at the position you specify. You can define both the starting point and the length of the substring you want to extract:

```
MID(string, whereToStart, count)

MID("fast black cat", 8, 7) => "black"
```

# T()

Returns an argument if it is only text and otherwise blank:

```
T(value1)

T("goodbye") => "goodbye"
T(42) => blank
```

# REPLACE()

Substitutes a specific segment of text within a string with a different segment of text. It finds the specified text in a larger string and changes it to the text you've provided, accurately maintaining the rest of the original string. (If you want to replace more than one occurrence of text, check out SUBSTITUTE().)

```
REPLACE(string, start_character, number_of_characters, replacement)

REPLACE("fast black car", 6, 5, "blue") => "fast blue car"
```

# LEN()

Determines the length of a text string by counting the number of characters it contains. This is especially handy when you need to verify data, such as ensuring a phone number or ID number has the correct amount of digits:

```
LEN(string)

LEN("The Berlin Wall fell in 1989.") => 30
```

# Date and Time Functions

## DATESTR()

Converts datetimes into strings (formatted as YYYY-MM-DD):

```
DATESTR([date])

DATESTR("6/01/23") => 2023-06-01
```

## DATETIME_DIFF()

Calculates the difference between two dates or times, expressed in a unit of your choice. This is useful for estimating project timelines, tracking task durations, or comparing dates for other analytical purposes:

```
DATETIME_DIFF([date1], [date2], 'units')

DATETIME_DIFF("2022-04-10", "2022-04-01", "days") => 9
```

## DATETIME_FORMAT()

Converts a date or datetime value to a string according to a specified format. This can be especially helpful when you want to display dates in a specific style, such as "January 1, 2020" instead of "01/01/2020":

```
DATETIME_FORMAT(datetime, format)

DATETIME_FORMAT("2022-03-14", 'MMMM D, YYYY') => "March 14, 2022"
```

## DATEADD()

Add specific amounts of time, such as days, months, or years, to a given date. This is useful for scheduling or forecasting activities—for instance, establishing deadlines by adding a specific number of days to today's date:

```
DATEADD([date], [#], 'units')

DATEADD("06/01/23", 10, "days") => 2023-06-11

DATEADD("06/01/23", 1, "years") => 2024-06-01

DATEADD("06/01/23 02:02:01", 60, "seconds")=> 2023-06-01 2:03am
```

## DATETIME_PARSE()

Transforms text into a date or time. Consequently, it enables monitoring and evaluating of the data as Airtable-readable dates and times that can now be used in formulas, rollups, and more. It's critical to Airtable's system of notation for date and time correctly in the 'input format' portion so that it can be correctly converted. (There is also an advanced option to return the result based on how dates are formatted in a certain locale.)

```
DATETIME_PARSE(date, ['input format'], ['locale'])

DATETIME_PARSE("5 Apr 2023 22:00", 'D MMM YYYY HH:mm') => 4/5/2023 10:00pm
```

## HOUR()

Allows you to extract the hour from a time value in a 24-hour format (e.g., 0 for midnight, 14 for 2 p.m.):

```
HOUR([datetime])

HOUR("2022-04-29T15:30:00.000Z") => 15
```

## IS_BEFORE()

Compares two dates and determines if the first is earlier than the second. Returns 0 if no and 1 if yes:

```
IS_BEFORE([date1], [date2])

IS_BEFORE("2022-03-01", "2022-03-15") => TRUE
IS_BEFORE({Due Date}, TOMORROW())
```

## IS_AFTER()

Compares two dates and determines if the first is later than the second. Returns 0 if no and 1 if yes:

```
IS_AFTER([date1], [date2])

IS_AFTER("2022-06-01", "2022-05-01") => True

IS_AFTER({Due Date}, TOMORROW())
```

# IS_SAME()

Compares two dates and determines if, up to a specified unit (e.g., day, hour), they are the same. Returns 0 if no and 1 if yes:

```
IS_SAME([date1], [date2], [unit])

IS_SAME({Date 1}, {Date 2}, 'day') => 0
```

# DAY()

Allows you to extract the day of the month as a number ranging between 1 and 31:

```
DAY([date])

DAY("03/18/2023") => 18
```

# MONTH()

Allows you to extract the month as a number ranging from 1 (January) to 12 (December):

```
MONTH([date])

MONTH("03/18/2023 8:31") => 3
```

# SET_LOCALE()

Allows you to set a specific country or region setting for its data. Depending on the locale, this can change the order of the components in a date, such as day and month, for example. (As shown in the following formula, this function is used in combination with DATETIME_FORMAT.)

```
SET_LOCALE([date], [locale_modifier])

DATETIME_FORMAT(SET_LOCALE("2022-03-01", "fr") => "1 mars 2022")

DATETIME_FORMAT(SET_LOCALE("07/11/23", 'el'), 'LLLL') =>
        Τετάρτη, 11 Ιουλίου 2023 12:00 ΠΜ
```

# MINUTE()

Gives a datetime's minute as a number ranging from 0 to 59:

```
MINUTE([datetime])

MINUTE("03/18/2023 7:32") => 32
```

## SECOND()

Gives a datetime's second as a number ranging from 0 to 59:

```
SECOND([datetime])

SECOND("03/18/2023 7:32:26") => 26
```

## SET_TIMEZONE()

Allows you to adjust the time zone for a datetime. Useful to standardize time with a team that's distributed across different geographical locations. (As shown in the following formula, this function is used in combination with DATETIME_FORMAT.)

```
SET_TIMEZONE([date], [tz_identifier])

DATETIME_FORMAT(SET_TIMEZONE("08/11/23 13:00", 'Australia/Sydney'),
        'M/D/YYYY h:mm') => 8/11/2023 11:00
```

## NOW()

Although similar to the TODAY() function, NOW() gives you both the current date AND time.

The function automatically updates if a formula is recalculated or a base is loaded, or about every 15 minutes if a base is open. However, if a base is closed, this function automatically updates about every hour, but only if the base has either time-dependent actions/automation triggers or sync dependencies:

```
NOW()

NOW() => 2023-07-10 4:18pm
```

## WEEKDAY()

Gives the day of the week as a number ranging from 0 (Sunday) to 6 (Saturday):

```
WEEKDAY([date])

WEEKDAY("2022-03-11") => 4 (for Thursday)
```

## TIMESTR()

Allows you to format a datetime as a time-only string (HH:mm:ss):

```
TIMESTR([date/timestamp])

TIMESTR("03/18/2023 8:32:26") => 8:32:26
```

# WORKDAY()

Gives you the date that is `numDays` working days after a given `startDate`. However, working days exclude weekends as well as an optional list of national holidays that are formatted as comma-separated strings of ISO-formatted dates:

```
WORKDAY(startDate, numDays, [holidays])

WORKDAY('10/16/23', 10, '2023-10-16, 2023-10-19') => 2023-11-02
```

# WEEKNUM()

Determines the week number of the year for a specific date. This function is especially helpful when you need to organize or track information based on the week of the year, such as planning weekly meetings or tracking sales performance:

```
WEEKNUM([date])

WEEKNUM("2022-10-15") => 41
```

# WORKDAY_DIFF()

Calculates the number of workdays between two given dates, excluding weekends and optionally specified holidays. This can be helpful for project management, as it gives a clear, business-day count of the time taken or to be taken for a task:

```
WORKDAY_DIFF(startDate, endDate, [holidays])

WORKDAY_DIFF('10/16/23','11/02/2023', '2023-10-16, 2023-10-19') => 12
WORKDAY_DIFF("2022-01-01", "2022-01-31", "2022-01-17") => 20
```

# YEAR()

Gives you a datetime's four-digit year:

```
YEAR([date])

YEAR("2023-06-10") => 2023
```

# TODAY()

Although similar to a NOW() function, the TODAY() function gives you the current date. (But this function will not return the current time, if formatted, so the time will return as 12:00 a.m.). Plus, the function updates if the formula is recalculated, if a base is loaded, or about every 15 minutes if a base is open. However, when the base is closed, the function updates approximately every 60 minutes if the base has time-dependent actions/automation triggers or sync dependencies:

```
TODAY()

TODAY() => 2023-07-10 12:00am
```

## TONOW()

One of three counting functions. Counts the number of days between a current date and another date in the past:

```
TONOW([date])

TONOW("2023-08-02") => 21 days
```

## FROMNOW()

Calculates the time difference between a specified date and the current date:

```
FROMNOW([date])

FROMNOW("2023-08-02") => 21 days
```

# Numeric Operators

```
+

-

*

/
```

# Numeric Functions

## AVERAGE()

Gives the mean value of a set of numbers:

```
AVERAGE(number1, [number2, ...])

AVERAGE(2,3,4,5,6) => 4
```

## COUNT()

Allows you to total the number of records that contain any numeric value within a specific field. (It will not count nonnumbers or empty values.)

```
COUNT(number1, [number2, ....])

COUNT(2,3,4,"","four") => 3
```

# MAX()

Identifies the largest number in a set of given numbers:

```
MAX(number1, [number2, ...])

MAX({Field1}, {Field2})
MAX(12, 20, 25, 9, 34) => 34
```

# MIN()

Identifies the smallest number in a set of given numbers:

```
MIN(number1, [number2, ...])

MIN({Field1}, {Field2})

MIN(21, 14, 7, 2, 19) => 2
```

# SUM()

Adds a set of numbers together. This function is equivalent to listing each number with a "+" in between each (e.g., 2 + 3 + 4):

```
SUM(number1, [number2, ...])

SUM({Field1}, {Field2})
SUM(9, 15, 6) => 30
```

# ABS()

Provides the absolute value:

```
ABS(value)

ABS(-6) => 6
```

# COUNTA()

Counts how many non-empty values exist. It counts numeric as well as text values:

```
COUNTA(textOrNumber1, [number2, ....])

COUNTA(2,3,"40", " ", "four") => 5
```

# CEILING()

Gives you the nearest integer multiple of significance greater than or equal to a given value. However, if a significance is not provided, the function assumes a significance of 1:

```
CEILING(value, [significance])

CEILING(1.01) => 2
CEILING(1.06, 0.1) => 1.1
```

# EVEN()

Gives the smallest even integer that is greater than or equal to a specified value:

```
EVEN(value)

EVEN(2.3) => 4
EVEN(7) => 8
```

# COUNTALL()

Counts all elements, including blanks and text:

```
COUNTALL(textOrNumber1, [number2, ....])

COUNTALL(2,3,4,"","four") => 5
```

# FLOOR()

Calculates the nearest integer multiple of significance less than or equal to a given value. However, if a significance is not provided, the function assumes a significance of 1:

```
FLOOR(value, [significance])

FLOOR(1.88) => 1
FLOOR(1.88, 0.1) => 1.8
```

# EXP()

Calculates Euler's number (e) to a specified power:

```
EXP(power)

EXP(1) => 2.71828
EXP(3) => 20.08554
```

# LOG()

Calculates the logarithm of a given value in a specified base. However, the base defaults to 10 if it is not specified:

```
LOG(number, [base])

LOG(1024, 2) => 10
LOG(1000) => 3
```

# INT()

Gives you the largest integer that is equal to or less than a specified value:

```
INT(value)

INT(1.98)=> 1
INT(-1.98) => -2
```

# MOD()

Calculates the remainder after dividing a first argument by a second argument:

```
MOD(value, divisor)

MOD(10, 5) => 0
```

# POWER()

Calculates a specified base to a specified power:

```
POWER(base, power)

POWER(2, 3) => 8
POWER(8, 2) => 64
```

# ODD()

Rounds up a positive value to the nearest odd number and, likewise, rounds a negative value down to the nearest odd number:

```
ODD(value)

ODD(1.2) => 3
ODD(-1.2) => -3
```

# MAX()

Determines the largest of a set of given numbers:

```
MAX(number1, [number2, ...])

MAX({Field1}, {Field2})
MAX(11, 101) => 101
```

# ROUND()

Rounds a value up or down to a set number of decimal places. (More specifically, the ROUND function rounds to the nearest integer at a specified precision; ties are broken by rounding up toward positive infinity.)

```
ROUND(value, precision)

ROUND(4.5, 0) => 5
ROUND(3.2, 0) => 3
```

## ROUNDUP()

Rounds up a value to a specific number of decimal places, always rounding up (that is, away from zero). However, you must always give a value for the precision (number of decimal places); otherwise, the function does not work:

```
ROUNDUP(value, precision)

ROUNDUP(4.6, 0) => 5
ROUNDUP(4.3, 0) => 5
```

## ROUNDDOWN()

Rounds down a value to a specific number of decimal places, always rounding down (that is, toward zero). However, you must always give a value for the precision (number of decimal places) or the function does not work:

```
ROUNDDOWN(value, precision)

ROUNDDOWN(3.6, 0) => 3
ROUNDDOWN(4.4, 0) => 4
```

## SQRT()

Gives the square root of nonnegative numbers:

```
SQRT(value)

SQRT(64) => 8
```

## VALUE()

Transforms a text string to a number. However, a few exceptions apply. For instance, if strings have certain mathematical operators (like – or %), then results may not return as expected. In these limited scenarios, you should use a combination of the VALUE and REGEX_REPLACE functions to remove nondigit values from strings:

```
VALUE(REGEX_REPLACE(YOURSTRING, "\\D", ""))

VALUE(text)

VALUE("$2000") => 2000
```

# Logic Functions

## AND()

Allows you to create a condition that requires one or more statements to be true. It will return as true if all of the arguments are true (1); otherwise, it returns as false (0):

```
AND(expression, [exp2, ...])

AND({{Field 1}, {Field 2})
AND("red" = "green", 2 + 2 = 4) => 0
AND("blue" = "blue", 2 + 2 = 4) => 1
```

## BLANK()

Returns an empty value, which helps to distinguish between a field that has been left empty intentionally and one that simply hasn't been filled in yet:

```
BLANK()

IF({Discount Applied} = BLANK(), "No Discount", "Discount Applied")
```

## FALSE()

Returns value that is false, represented as 0. This can be helpful for noting where a certain condition isn't met:

```
FALSE() => 0

IF({Field1} > {Field2}, "Field1 is greater", FALSE())
```

## IF()

Returns the first value if a logical argument is true and returns the second value if the logical argument is false. Nested IF() functions allow you to create complex conditions, providing outcomes based on multiple "if this, then that" scenarios. Plus, it can be used to check on whether a cell is blank or empty:

```
IF(expression, ifTrue, ifFalse)

IF({Hours Worked} > 40, "Overtime", "Regular")
IF({Order Total} > 100, "Large Order", "Small Order")
```

## NOT()

Used to reverse the logical value of a condition. It's useful because it helps you easily identify the opposite or inverse of a specific condition or scenario in your data:

```
NOT(expression)
```

## OR()

Evaluates one or more logical statements and returns true if at least one of the statements is true. This function is useful when you have multiple conditions to meet and only one needs to be true for the action to proceed:

```
OR(expression, [exp2, ...])

OR({Status} = "Complete", {Status} = "In Progress") => 1
        (if the 'Status' field is either 'Complete' or 'In Progress', or 0 if not)
```

## SWITCH()

Examines a given expression, evaluates possible values for that expression, and determines the value that the expression should have in that unique case. Plus, it can take a default value if the expression does not correspond to any of the defined patterns. SWITCH() can often be used instead of nested IF() formulas, in many cases:

```
SWITCH(expression, [pattern, result ... , default])

SWITCH({Discount},
15, {Amount} * .15,
25, {Amount} * .25,
30, {Amount} * .30
)
```

## XOR()

Will return true when an odd number of arguments are found to be true:

```
XOR(expression, [exp2, ...])

XOR(TRUE(), FALSE(), TRUE()) => 0
XOR(TRUE(), FALSE(), FALSE()) => 1
```

## TRUE()

States that a logical value is true. A true value of true is numerically represented by a 1:

```
TRUE() => 1

IF(insertCondition, TRUE(), FALSE())
```

# Logic Operators

## !=

Checks if a first given value does not equal a second given value:

`4 != 3=>` True (represented by a 1)

## <

Checks if a first value is less than a second value:

`4 < 3 =>` False (represented by a 0)

## <=

Checks if a first value is less than or equal to a second value:

`1 <= 2 =>` True (represented by a 1)

## =

Checks if a first value equals a second value:

`6 = 6=>` True (represented by a 1)

## >

Checks if a first value is larger than a second value:

`4 > 3 =>` True (represented by a 1)

## >=

Checks if a first value is larger than or equal to a second value:

`>= 4 >= 4 =>` True (represented by a 1)

# Regex Functions

Airtable's formulas are not limited to basic operations and simple calculations. With the addition of regex (regular expressions) functions, users can perform complex pattern matching and manipulation on text data. Regex is a powerful tool used to search for and manipulate specific patterns of text within larger bodies of text.

While Airtable's regex functions provide powerful capabilities, it's important to note that regular expressions themselves are a vast topic with numerous intricacies. This appendix aims to introduce these regex functions within the context of Airtable, but readers looking to dive deeper into regex should seek additional resources online.

Airtable provides several regex functions that can be used in formulas to perform tasks such as finding and replacing specific patterns, extracting certain parts of text, and validating input. These functions include `REGEX_MATCH`, `REGEX_REPLACE`, `REGEX_EXTRACT`, and `REGEX_TEST`.

For example, the `REGEX_MATCH` function allows users to check whether a string matches a specified pattern. This can be useful for validating user input or verifying the format of data. The `REGEX_REPLACE` function enables users to replace specific patterns in a string with new values. This can be handy for cleaning up messy data or formatting text in a particular way.

These regex functions give users the flexibility to create dynamic formulas that can handle various scenarios involving text manipulation. By combining regex functions with other operators and functions, users can have precise control over how their data is formatted and extracted in their Airtable bases. Whether it's extracting email addresses from a list of strings or validating phone numbers based on specific patterns, Airtable's regex functions provide powerful tools for efficient data processing.

## REGEX_EXTRACT()

Gives you the first substring that matches a given expression:

```
REGEX_EXTRACT(string, regex)
```

```
REGEX_EXTRACT("Goodbye Summer", "S.*") => "Summer"
```

## REGEX_REPLACE()

Replaces all matching substrings with substitute string values:

```
REGEX_REPLACE(string, regex, replacement)
```

```
REGEX_REPLACE("Goodbye Summer", " S.*", " Winter") => "Goodbye Winter"
```

## REGEX_MATCH()

Tells you if input text corresponds with a regular expression:

```
REGEX_MATCH(string, regex)
```

```
REGEX_MATCH("Goodbye Summer", "Goodbye.Summer") => 1
```

# Array Functions

Airtable's array functions are designed to manipulate arrays—a convention of programming—which are collections of values (e.g., text, numbers, dates). They allow us to store and organize multiple pieces of data in a single variable: the array. In Airtable, arrays are enclosed in square brackets [], and each value within the array is separated by a comma:

 Array functions can only be used with values that are first aggregated by a Rollup field or when the values are referenced from a Lookup field. You can't create an array that an Airtable formula will understand by putting values into a text field, for example.

These array functions provide powerful tools for manipulating and organizing data in Airtable. By understanding arrays and how to use these functions effectively, users can streamline their workflows and create more sophisticated formulas in their bases.

## ARRAYJOIN()

Combines an array of strings into a single string, separated by a specified delimiter. This is handy when you want to take separate pieces of data and join them together into one, like creating a full address from separate city, state, and zip code fields:

```
ARRAYJOIN([item1, item2, item3], separator)

values = [4,5,6]

ARRAYJOIN(values, ""; "") => 4; 5; 6
ARRAYJOIN({"New York", "NY", "10001"}, ", ") => "New York, NY, 10001"
```

## ARRAYCOMPACT()

Helps the user remove empty strings or null values from an array. However, it maintains "false" and any strings with blank characters:

```
ARRAYCOMPACT([item1, item2, item3])

values = ["apple","", "banana", null, "cherry"]

ARRAYCOMPACT(values)=> ["apple", "banana", "cherry"]
```

## ARRAYFLATTEN()

A nested array is an array that contains other arrays. This function takes a nested array and returns a new flat array with all the values from the nested arrays combined into a single level of values:

```
ARRAYFLATTEN([item1, item2, item3])

values = [[4,5,6],[true]]

ARRAYFLATTEN(values)=> [4,5,6,true]
```

## ARRAYUNIQUE()

Will only return unique items in an array. If there are multiple occurrences of the same value within the input array, ARRAYUNIQUE() will remove all but one of them. This helps us remove duplicate values from an array and returns a new array with only unique elements:

```
ARRAYUNIQUE([item1, item2, item3])

values = [4,5,6,6,5,4]

ARRAYUNIQUE(values)=> [4,5,6]
```

# Record Functions

Airtable's record functions provide information about records in a table that's valuable for building sophisticated formulas.

Like the Last Modified field type, LAST_MODIFIED_TIME() returns the date and time when a record was last modified. Similarly, CREATED_TIME() retrieves the creation date and time of a record, much like the Created field type. Lastly, RECORD_ID() generates a unique identifier for each record, facilitating referencing and linking records in formulas.

## LAST_MODIFIED_TIME()

Gives you the date and time of recent modifications made by users in noncalculated fields in a table. If you are only concerned about modifications to particular fields, you can incorporate field names (one or more), and the LAST_MODIFIED_TIME() function will only give you the date and time of the most recently made changes in any of the specified fields:

```
LAST_MODIFIED_TIME([{field1},{field2}, ...])

LAST_MODIFIED_TIME()
 => 6/10/2022 2:39 a.m.

LAST_MODIFIED_TIME({Field1})
 => 4/17/2022 7:56 p.m.
```

## CREATED_TIME()

Gives you the date and time that a particular record was created:

```
CREATED_TIME()

CREATED_TIME()  => 6/8/2022 2:38 a.m.
```

## RECORD_ID()

Gives you the ID of a certain record:

```
RECORD_ID()

RECORD_ID() => recDu9IZ2ZDO6FsHp
```

# Error Functions

Airtable provides error functions that can be used to handle and identify errors in formulas. The ERROR() function is used to generate an error message within a formula. For example, if we want to display an error message when a certain condition is not met, we can use the ERROR() function like this:

```
IF({Quantity} < 0, ERROR("Invalid quantity"), ...)
```

The ISERROR() function, on the other hand, allows us to check if a formula contains an error. It returns a Boolean value of true if there is an error and false otherwise. Here's an example:

```
ISERROR({Total Sales})
```

This formula will return true if there is an error in the calculation of the "Total Sales" field.

These error functions are useful when dealing with complex calculations or when ensuring data accuracy in our formulas. They allow us to handle errors gracefully by displaying custom error messages or by executing alternative actions based on whether an error is present or not.

## ERROR()

Will return a generic error value (#ERROR!):

```
ERROR()

IF({Amount} < 0, ERROR(), "Larger than zero!")
```

## ISERROR()

Will return as true if an expression causes an error:

```
ISERROR(expression)
ISERROR(2/0) => 1 (true because divide by zero error)
```

# Index

## Symbols

!= operator, 348
" (quotation mark) operator, 142, 144, 146
& (ampersand) operator, 146, 333
'\n' operator, 333
* (multiplication formula operator), 165
** (double asterisks), 258
+ (plus symbol), 143
12-hour format, 28
24-hour format, 28
; (semicolon), 180
< (less-than symbol), 143
< operator, 349
<= operator, 349
= operator, 349
> (greater-than symbol), 143
> operator, 349
>= operator, 349
@ (at symbol), 260
– (minus symbol), 143

## A

ABS() function, 343
actions, 275
"Add records" option, 292
agile workflows, 314
AI, generative, 199
Airtable
    advantages of, 9-10
    as combination spreadsheet and database,
        3-4
    community, 9
    components of, 4-8
        Automations, 4, 7
        bases, 5
        Data section, 4
        fields, 6
        Interfaces, 8
        records, 5
        tables, 5
        views, 6
    defined, 1
    design elements, 10
    funding and growth of, 10
    no-code movement and, 2
    pricing, 9
    production databases versus, 10
Airtable Automations
    actions, 275
    advantages of, 232
    disadvantages of, 232
    if/then logic of, 233
    overview of, 231
    simple automation example
        choosing field to monitor, 235
        choosing trigger, 243
        running the action, 242
        setting up the action, 236, 245
        setting up the trigger, 234, 243
        static and dynamic data, 237-240
        testing the action, 241, 245
        testing the step, 236
        testing the trigger, 244
    triggers, 272-275
Airtable Blocks SDK, 329-331
Airtable mobile app
    phone calls with, 26
    scanning barcodes with, 31

Airtable REST API, 328
Airtable Scripts extension, 193
Airtable Web API, 328-329
ampersand operator (&), 146, 333
"and" conjunction, 58-59
AND() function, 166, 179, 347
API key, 192, 224
APIs (application programming interfaces)
    connecting to, 192
    defined, 328
Arithmetic Rollup functions, 178
array functions, 145, 350-352
ARRAYCOMPACT() function, 180, 351
ARRAYFLATTEN() function, 351
ARRAYJOIN() function, 181, 351
ARRAYUNIQUE() function, 181, 352
Asana, 329
at (@) symbol, 260
"At a scheduled time" trigger, 247, 273
Attachment field, 70, 108
    overview of, 30-31
    "Reverse Attachment Order" script, 199
audio, 30
autocompleting names, 32
automated web scraping, 212
automatic sync, 90
Automations (see Airtable Automations)
Autonumber field, 21, 35
AVERAGE() function, 166, 178, 342

# B

backups, 192
bar charts, 203-205, 297
Barcode field, 31
Barrett, Justin, 199
Base Schema extension, 44, 188
bases
    defined, 5
    naming, 11
Batch update extension, 189-190
bell icon, 38
binary variable, 29
blank values, 162, 180
BLANK() function, 347
blocks (see extensions)
bold text, 258
Boolean values, 86
branding, 323
bucketing values, 209

building blocks feature, Softr, 323
bulk data, 322
bulk operations, 329
Business plan
    automation allowances on, 232
    maximum records with, 11
    pricing of, 9
    storage allowance with, 30
    Sync limitations with, 88
Button field, 31-34, 97
buttons
    adding, 303
    configuring action for, 304

# C

Calculated fields, 35-38
    Autonumber field, 35
    "Created by" field, 37
    "Last modified by" field, 37
    "Last modified time" field, 36
    User field, 37
Calendar view, 6, 28, 111-116, 289
Cascading Style Sheets (CSS), 212
CEILING() function, 343
Chart extension
    bar charts, 203-205
    in Dashboard layout, 310
    donut charts, 210
    line charts, 206
    overview of, 185, 203
    pie charts, 210
    scatter plot charts, 208-210
Checkbox field, 29, 86
    sorting, 62
    when to use instead of triggers, 272
Chrome extension, 211
"Click into record details" option, 292
cloud services
    using On2Air Backups extension for, 192
    uploading files from, 82
collaboration, 10
    benefits of using Airtable for, 2
    with Blocks SDK, 331
    Locked views, 78
    shared reference of time for, 29
    tracking changes, 37
    viewing Personal views, 77
collapsing grouping, 73
colors

reassigning, 26
for records, 70, 115
columns, 1, 6
(see also fields)
commas, 87, 149
commentor permissions, 316
community forum, 9, 198
CONCATENATE() function, 143, 147-148,
158, 180, 333
condition groups
conjunctions and, 58-59
nesting, 60
conditional form fields, 104-106
conditional logic, 262, 276
conditions
adding to Lookup field, 49
automation triggered by records matching,
244
in Calendar view, 115
filtering, 56
if/then logic of automations, 233
setting for Rollup field, 175
Convert URLs to attachments script, 194
Count field, 51, 137
count option, Summary extension, 186
COUNT() function, 143, 342
COUNTA() function, 343
COUNTALL() function, 344
"Create record" action, 275
"Created by" field, 37
"Created time" field, 36
CREATED_TIME() function, 352
creating, reading, updating, deleting (CRUD), 2
creator permissions, 233, 283
CRM (customer relationship management)
platforms, 329
cross-referencing, 45
CRUD (creating, reading, updating, deleting), 2
CSS (Cascading Style Sheets), 212
CSV files, importing, 80, 127
curly brackets, 142
Currency field, 28, 239
currency, importing, 84
Custom Extensions API, 193
customer relationship management (CRM)
platforms, 329

**D**

Dashboard layout

adding filters, 296
bar charts, 297
creating, 293-296
scatter plots, 298
data and time functions, 337-342
data corruption, 190
Data Fetcher extension, 192
data manipulation, 322
Data section, 4
data types, 84
databases (see relational databases)
date and time functions, 145
Date field, 28
DATEADD() function, 337
dates
Calendar view, 6, 111-116
importing, 85
summary functions for, 70
Timeline view, 116-119
DATESTR() function, 337
DATETIMEDIFF() function, 337
DATETIME_DIFF() function, 159
DATETIME_FORMAT() function, 157, 256,
337
DATETIME_PARSE() function, 338
DATETIME_TIME() operator, 248
DAY() function, 339
decimal numbers (floating-point numbers), 144
Decrement By action, 190
Dedupe extension, 186
DELETE method, 328
deleting
extensions, 228
records, 90
delimiters, 180
Dependencies field, 120
descriptions, trigger action, 237
desktop applications, 3
destinations, 87, 91
disabling extensions, 228
Divide By action, 190
dollar symbol, 84
donut charts, 210
dotted lines, 121
double asterisks (**), 258
double quotes, 147
Dropbox, 82
duplicate records, 186
duplicate values, 35, 68, 181

Duration field, 27, 28, 86
dynamic elements, 216, 237

## E

editing fields, 8
editor permissions, 233, 316
email domain
    extracting, 260
    restricting form access by, 104
    securing shared data via, 98
Email field, 25
emails, validating, 195
empty summary function, 67
ENCODE_URL_COMPONENT() function, 335
Enterprise Scale plan, 9
error codes, 169
error functions, 353
error messages, 170
ERROR() function, 353
European date format, 28
EVEN() function, 344
exact matching, 187
Excel, importing data from, 81-83
EXP() function, 344
Expanded view, 19
expanding grouping, 73
extensions, 33, 330
    Base schema extension, 188
    Batch update extension, 189-190
    Chart extension
        bar charts, 203-205
        donut charts, 210
        line charts, 206
        overview of, 185, 203
        pie charts, 210
        scatter plot charts, 208-210
    Data Fetcher extension, 192
    Dedupe extension, 186
    Manage Extensions dashboard, 229
    NoBull extension, 192
    On2Air Backups extension, 192
    Page designer
        available fields and records in, 217
        drawbacks of, 223
        overview of, 215
        positioning elements on the page, 219-222
        printing from, 223

static and dynamic elements, 216
    table fields and, 215
Scripting extension
    Convert URLs to attachments script, 194
    finding scripts, 198
    installing custom code into, 197
    installing scripts, 197
    overview of, 193
    putting code into, 199-202
    Validate emails script, 195
Summary extension, 185
third-party, 191-193
Translate extension
    configuring, 224
    creating translations, 224-227
    overview of, 224
    setting up, 224
utility extensions, 186
for visual display, 185
Web Clipper extension
    advanced options, 214
    Chrome extension for, 211
    data that can be captured by, 212
    overview of, 211
    setting up, 212
    using, 213
external APIs, 8

## F

Facebook pages, 8
"Facebook Pages: Create a new post" action, 279
false negatives, 188
false positives, 188
FALSE() function, 347
favorites section, 76
fetching data, 328
fields, 17, 22-38
    (see also names of specific fields)
    allowing users to edit, 8
    Calculated fields, 35-38
    Count field, 51
    defined, 6
    importing data and changing type of, 81
    input fields, 25-31
    Lookup fields, 45-50
    managing in multisource syncing, 95
    naming, 11
    overview of, 17, 22-24

primary, 20-22
   referencing in formulas, 143
filled summary function, 67
Filter element, 309
filtering
   in Calendar view, 114, 291
   in Grid view, 56-61
      condition groups and, 59-59
      conjunctions and, 58-59
      linked records, 50
      records, 8
"Find records" action, 261-265, 276
"Find records" option, 292
FIND() function, 151-154, 335
Finsweet, 192
floating-point numbers (decimal numbers), 144
FLOOR() function, 344
Form view, 7
   conditional form fields, 104-106
   managing access, 103
   overview of, 98
   setting up form, 99-103
formatting text, 25, 113
formulas
   examples of, 146-148
   Formula editor, 144
   Formula field, 6, 21, 140-142
   functions in
      categories of, 145
      date and time functions, 155-162
      logic functions, 166-170
      numeric functions, 162-165
      overview of, 143
      text functions, 149-154
   inability to import, 87
   numbers in, 144
   operators in, 143, 145
   overview of, 139
   referencing fields in, 143
   text/string data in, 144
fractions, 28
Free plan, 9
   automation allowances on, 232
   storage allowance with, 30
   Sync limitations with, 88
FROMNOW() function, 342
frontend web design, 212
full-page layouts, Interface Designer
   "Add records" option, 292

"Click into record details" option, 292
"Find records" option, 292
global preferences for, 290
views, 284-290
functions, 145
   (see also specific functions by name)
   array functions, 145, 350-352
   categories of, 145-145
   date and time functions, 145, 155-162
   error functions, 353
   logic functions, 145, 347-348
      creating conditional logic with IF(), 153
      in insurance buying example, 166-170
      used in Rollup fields, 179
   numbers in, 145
   numeric functions, 162-165
   overview of, 143
   record functions, 145, 352
   regex functions, 145, 349-350
   Rollup functions
      Arithmetic Rollup functions, 178
      array functions, 180-181
      CONCATENATE function, 180
      logic functions, 179
   text functions, 145, 149-154
fuzzy matching, 187

## G

Gallery view, 6, 108, 288
Gantt view, 6, 28, 120-123
generative AI, 199
geographic routing, 135
GET method, 328
GitHub, 4, 8, 92
"GitHub Issues: Create issue" action, 279
"GitHub Issues: Update issue" action, 279
GitHub repository, 198
"Gmail: Send email" action, 258, 268-270, 278, 305
GMT time, 147
Google, 3
"Google Calendar: When event canceled" trigger, 274
"Google Calendar: When event changed" trigger, 274
"Google Calendar: When event created" trigger, 274
Google Cloud platform, 224
Google Cloud Translate service, 224

Google Drive, 82, 92
"Google Forms: When a new response arrives" trigger, 275
Google Sheets, importing data from, 81-83
"Google Sheets: Append a new row to a spread-sheet" action, 278
"Google Sheets: When a row is created" trigger, 274
Google Workspace suite, 8
grammar, with formulas, 148
greater-than symbol (>), 143
Grid view, 1, 6
    coloring records in, 70
    configuration options, 55
    filtering in, 56-61
        condition groups and, 59-61
        conjunctions and, 58
    formulas in, 140
    grouping records in, 71-74
    hiding fields in, 64-66
    overview of, 54
    row height in, 66
    sorting in, 61-64
    summary bar, 67-70
grouping records, 71-74, 110
groups, repeating, 277

**H**

"has none of" operator, 57
Hide fields button, 19
hiding fields, 64-66, 95
hierarchical data, 314
histogram, 70
"Hootsuite: Schedule post" action, 279
HOUR() function, 338
HTML (Hypertext Markup Language), 212
HTTP requests, 328

**I**

icons
    bell, 38
    lightning bolt, 91
    magnifying glass, 134
    rating with, 29
identifiers, 10, 21
IF() function, 153-154, 347
    using AND() function with, 166
    leaving out third element with, 161
    nesting, 167, 169

if/then logic, of automations, 233
if/then statement, 145
images
    adding to calendar events, 113
    in Gallery view, 108
    previewing, 30
importing attachments, 30
importing data
    columns as Multiple select field, 86
    converting spreadsheet columns into check-box field, 86
    currency, 84
    dates, 85
    Google Sheets and Excel data, 81-83
    inability to import formulas, 87
    numbers, 84
    overview of, 79
    synchronizing data
        multisource sync, 95-97
        overview of, 87-89
        security when, 97
        from source outside Airtable, 92-95
        trade-offs, 91
        views, 89-91
    tabular data from CSV Files, 80
    using Form view
        conditional form fields, 104-106
        managing access, 103
        overview of, 98
        setting up view, 99-103
Increment By action, 190
input fields, 25-31
    Attachment field, 30-31
    Barcode field, 31
    Checkbox field, 29
    Currency field, 28
    Date field, 28
    Duration field, 28
    Email field, 25
    Multiple select fields, 26-27
    Number field, 28
    Percent field, 28
    Phone number field, 25
    Rating field, 29
    Single select fields, 26-27
    text fields, 25
    URL field, 25
INT() function, 345
integers (whole numbers), 144

Interface Designer, 185
  advantages of, 282-283
  dashboard interface
    bar charts, 297
    creating, 293-296
    filters, 296
    scatter plots, 298
  full-page layouts
    "Add records" option, 292
    buttons in, adding, 292
    "Click into record details" option, 292
    "Find records" option, 292
    global preferences for, 290
    views, 284-290
  interface components, 283
  interface elements
    discrete elements, 314-316
    view elements, 313-314
  interface layouts
    Dashboard layout, 309
    Form layout, 311
    full-page layouts, 284-292, 311
    overview of, 306
    "Record review" layout, 307
    "Record summary" layout, 308
  interface with multiple tables and buttons
    adding buttons, 303
    adding fields, 303
    automation for interface button, 305
    functionality, 300-302
  overview of, 281
  permissions, 316
interface-only users, 325
invalid dependencies, 121
"is empty" operator, 57
"is not empty" operator, 57
ISERROR() function, 353
ISO 8601 format, 147
ISO specification format, 28
IS_AFTER() function, 338
IS_BEFORE() function, 338
IS_SAME() function, 339

## J

JavaScript, 34, 193, 330
Jira, 92
Jotform, 98

## K

Kanban view, 109-111

## L

"Last modified by" field, 37
"Last modified time" field, 36
LAST_MODIFIED_TIME() function, 352
LEFT() function, 152-154, 334
LEN() function, 334, 337
less-than symbol (<), 143
lightning bolt icons, 91
line breaks, 25
line charts, 206
lines, dotted, 121
Linked record field, 39, 120-123
linked records, 39-51
  aggregating data from, 45-51
  creating Fall Tour Tracker base with,
    127-138
    Regions table, 136-138
    relationships between tables, 129-133
    Shows table, 133-135
  reasons for using, 40-42
    defining relationships, 40
    reducing repetitive manual entry, 41
    single source of truth, 41
  relational database relationships, 42-45
  rolling up values from, 177
  setting up to use DATETIME_DIFF() func-
    tion, 159
linked relationships, 20, 125
List layout, 285-288
List view, 124-126
Locked views, 78, 273
LOG() function, 344
logic functions, 145, 347-348
  creating conditional logic with IF(), 153
  in insurance buying example, 166-170
  used in Rollup fields, 179
logic operators, 348
Long text field, 25
Lookup fields, 45-50
  adding conditions to, 49
  creating, 47-49
  linked records as, 134
  putting conditions on, 49
  referencing in formulas, 143
Loom screencast service, 191
LOWER() function, 334, 336

## M

"magic links", 323

magnifying glass icon, 134

Manage Extensions dashboard, 229

many-to-many relationships, 43

Markdown, 25, 258

Marketplace, 33, 183, 197

mathematical operators, 69

MAX() function, 175, 179, 343, 345

measurement units, 222

meta information, 35

Microsoft Teams, 8, 278

MID() function, 336

milestones, 116, 121, 123

MIN() function, 179, 343

minus symbol (–), 143

MINUTE() function, 339

mixed data types, 84

MOD() function, 345

MONTH() function, 339

Multiple select field, 26-27, 86
    filtering with conditions, 57
    sorting records, 62

multiplication formula operator (*), 165

Multiply By action, 190

multisource sync, 95-97

## N

NaN (not a number) error code, 169

native integrations, 7

nested condition groups, 60

nested IF() statements, 167, 169

no-code movement, 2

NoBull extension, 192

not a number (NAN) error code, 169

NOT() function, 347

NOW() function, 249, 340

Number field, 28

numbers
    in formulas, 144
    in functions, 145
    importing, 84
    summary functions for, 69

numeric functions, 342-346

numeric operators, 342

## O

ODD() function, 345

On2Air Backups extension, 192

one-click "magic links", 323

one-to-many relationships, 43

one-to-one relationships, 42, 129

operators, 57, 143, 145
    (see also specific operators by name)
    categories of, 145
    functions versus, 143
    logic operators, 348
    numeric operators, 342
    text operators, 333

"or" conjunction, 58-59

OR() function, 179, 348

order of options, 64

"Outlook Calendar: When event changed" trigger, 274

"Outlook Calendar: When event created" trigger, 274

"Outlook Email: Send email" action, 278

"Outlook Email: When email is received" trigger, 274

## P

Page designer
    available fields and records in, 217
    drawbacks of, 223
    overview of, 215
    positioning elements on the page, 219-222
    printing from, 223
    static and dynamic elements, 216
    table fields and, 215

pages, interface designer, 283

parenthesis, 143

passwords
    for Form layout, 311
    restricting form access with, 104
    sharing data using, 98
    third-party app builders and, 323

PDF creation, 224

percent empty summary function, 67

Percent field, 28

percent field summary function, 67

Percent unique function, 68

permissions
    creating and modifying Automations, 233
    creator permissions, 283
    external Interface users needing, 322
    Scripting extension and, 193
    for syncing, 98

in views, 77-78
Personal views, 77
Pexels, 33
Phone number field, 25
pie charts, 210, 298
plus symbol (+), 143
POST method, 328
POWER() function, 345
precision, 84
pricing, 9
    automation allowances and, 232
    extension availability based on, 183
    storage allowances and, 30
    Sync limitations with, 88
primary field, 20-22, 158
printing records, 223
project management, 314, 329
punctuation, 87
PUT method, 328

## Q

QR codes, 31
quotation mark operator ("), 142, 144, 146

## R

Rating field, 29
    sorting records, 62
    when to use instead of triggers, 272
React, 330
read-only users, 325
record functions, 145, 352
record ID, 21, 267
"Record picker" element, 308
"Record review" layout, 307
"Record summary" layout, 308
records, 18-19
    checking quota of, 30
    defined, 5
    filtering, 8
    linked, 39-51
    printing, 223
    sorting by creation, 37
RECORD_ID() function, 353
regex functions, 145, 349-350
REGEX_EXTRACT() function, 350
REGEX_MATCH() function, 350
REGEX_REPLACE() function, 350
Regions table, in Fall Tour Tracker, 136
relational databases

Airtable as combination of spreadsheets
    and, 3-4
    relationships, 42-45
        many-to-many relationships, 43
        one-to-many relationships, 43
        one-to-one relationships, 42
    rules in, 2
repeating groups, 277
REPLACE() function, 336
REPT() function, 336
REST API, 328
"Reverse Attachment Order" script, 199-201
RIGHT() function, 334
Rollup field, 249
    adding to Fall Tour Tracker base, 177
    choosing field of linked records, 174
    choosing Rollup function, 175
    functions, 178
        (see also specific functions by name)
        Arithmetic Rollup functions, 178
        array functions, 180-181
        CONCATENATE function, 180
        logic functions, 179
    overview of, 173
    setting conditions for, 175
ROUND() function, 165, 345
ROUNDDOWN() function, 346
ROUNDUP() function, 346
routing, 322
rows, 1
    formulas in, 140
    height of, 66
"Run a script" action, 276

## S

SaaS (software-as-a-service), 320
Salesforce, 329
scale, rating, 29
scatter plot charts, 208, 298
Scripting API, 193
Scripting extension, 34
    Convert URLs to attachments script, 194
    finding scripts, 198
    installing custom code into, 197
    installing scripts, 197
    overview of, 193
    putting code into, 199-202
    "Run a script" action and, 276
    Validate emails script, 195

search query, 65
SEARCH() function, 335
SECOND() function, 340
security, when syncing data, 97
semicolon (;), 180
"Send a Slack message" action, 270-272, 277
"Send an email" action, 256-258, 275
    running the action, 242
    setting up the action, 236
    static and dynamic data, 237-240
    testing, 241
"Send MS Teams message" action, 278
SendGrid, 33
separators, 181
sequential numbers, 35
Set to Number action, 189
Set to Random Number Between action, 189
SET_LOCALE() function, 339
SET_TIMEZONE() function, 340
Share option, 55
Shows table, in Fall Tour Tracker, 133-135
side sheets, 301
Single line text field, 25, 132
single quotes, 147
Single select fields, 26-27, 62, 272
Slack messages, triggering, 245, 253
Slack notifications, triggering, 7
software development, 2, 330
software-as-a-service (SaaS), 320
sorting data, 61-64
spaces, 149
Specific fields option, 36
spreadsheets, 3-4, 140
SQRT() function, 346
static elements, 216, 237
static snapshots, 81
storage, 30
string data, in formulas, 144
subgroups, 72
submitting forms, 102
SUBSTITUTE() function, 149-151, 335
SUM() function, 178, 343
SUM(values) aggregation, 249
summary bar, 67-70, 73, 119
Summary extension, 185
SWITCH() function, 167, 348
synchronizing data
    to external calendars, 115
    for Fall Tour Tracker base, 128

multisource sync, 95-97
overview of, 87-89
security when, 97
from source outside Airtable, 92-95
trade-offs, 91
views, 89-91

# T

T() function, 336
tables
    Base Schema extension showing connections between, 188
    defined, 5
    entity representation in, 17
    linked records and, 41
    managing and enhancing multisource synced tables, 96
    naming, 11
    Page designer layout based on, 218
    primary field in, 20
    relationships between, creating, 129-133
tabs, 291
Team plan
    automation allowances on, 232
    maximum records with, 11
    pricing of, 9
    storage allowance with, 30
    Sync limitations with, 88
Teams, Microsoft, 8, 278
text data, in formulas, 144
text fields, 25
text functions, 145, 149-154, 333-337
text operators, 333
third-party APIs, 33
third-party app integration, 8, 321
thumbnails, 313
time data, 86
time duration, 28
time zones, 28
Timeline view, 6, 28
timestamps, 36
TIMESTR() function, 340
TODAY() function, 341
TONOW() function, 342
toolbar, control, 54
Translate extension
    configuring, 224
    creating translations, 224-227
    overview of, 224

setting up, 224
triggering
    actions with Button field, 31
    advantages of Airtable, 232
    automations, 7
    conditional form fields, 104
    Page designer and, 224
    Scripting extension, 34
triggers, 234, 272-275
TRIM() function, 334
TRUE() function, 348
true-or-false data types, 86
12-hour format, 28
24-hour format, 28
Twilio, 33
"Twitter: Post Tweet" action, 279
Typeform, 98

## U

Unique function, 68
UPC codes, 31
"Update Record" action, 265-268
uploading attachments, 30
UPPER() function, 336
URL field, 25
URLs
    Airtable structure of, 11
    converting to attachments script, 194
    importing files via, 30, 82
    security when syncing, 97
    sharing data from view with, 88
US date format, 28
User field, 37
utility extensions, 186

## V

Validate emails script, 195
VALUE() function, 346
venture capital funding, 10
video attachments, 30
viewer permissions, 316
views, 4
    advantages of using, 2
    benefits of, 53
    Calendar view, 111-116
    configuring, 54
    creating, 74
    defined, 6
    Gallery view, 108

    Gantt view, 120-123
    Kanban view, 109-111
    List view, 124-126
    locked, 78
    naming, 11
    permissions, 77-78
    personal, 77
    synchronizing data in, 89-91
    Timeline view, 116-119
    types of, 53, 107
visualizations
    coloring records, 70
    histogram, 70
    of linked record connections to base, 44
Vorderbruggen, Kuovonne, 199

## W

warnings
    scripting extensions and, 201
    translation costs, 225
Web API, 193
Web Clipper extension
    advanced options, 214
    Chrome extension for, 211
    data that can be captured by, 212
    overview of, 211
    setting up, 212
    setting up trigger in, 244
    using, 213
web services, connecting to, 192
web-based applications, 3
web-based forms, 7
Webflow, 192
webhooks, 273
WEEKDAY() function, 340
WEEKNUM() function, 155, 341
"When a form is submitted" trigger, 273
"When a record enters a view" trigger, 273
"When a record is created" trigger, 272
"When a record is updated" trigger, 235, 243, 272
    overview of, 234
    setting up the trigger, 234
"When a webhook is received" trigger, 273
"When record matches condition" trigger
    setting up, 243
    testing, 244
white spaces, 149
whole numbers (integers), 144

widgets, 325
WORKDAY() function, 341
WORKDAY_DIFF() function, 341
wrapping text, 25

## X

XOR() function, 179, 348

## Y

YEAR() function, 341

## Z

Zapier, 232
Zendesk, 92

## About the Author

**Elliott Adams** is a founder, technologist, and educator. He taught the first university course on building with no-code tools, ran startup programs for Techstars in San Francisco, led technology-focused economic development efforts for the State of Louisiana after Hurricane Katrina, and served as CTO of online music pioneer CD Baby. Elliott is the founder of TwoTabs.io, which builds business solutions using Airtable and other no-code and low-code platforms. He teaches at Stanford University and UC Berkeley.

## Colophon

The animal on the cover of *Learning Airtable* is a stripe-necked mongoose (*Urva vitticollis*). It is native to Sri Lanka and the southwest coast of India, where it lives in forests and shrublands, usually close to water. Its fur is reddish-brown to gray, and it is named for the black stripe running along both sides of the neck.

The stripe-necked mongoose is the largest of the Asiatic mongoose species, with a body length of up to 20 inches and a tail length of about 12 inches. Individuals weigh about 3 to 6 pounds, with males generally being larger and heavier than females. The stripe-necked mongoose feeds on crabs and small vertebrates, including rodents, hares, mouse deer, frogs, birds, and reptiles. They prefer to hunt during the day and have been known to prey on animals larger than they are.

Because of its large populations in the wild, the stripe-necked mongoose is considered a species of least concern. Many of the animals on O'Reilly covers are endangered; all of them are important to the world.

The cover illustration is by Karen Montgomery, based on an antique line engraving from *Sketches of the Natural History of Ceylon*. The series design is by Edie Freedman, Ellie Volckhausen, and Karen Montgomery. The cover fonts are Gilroy Semibold and Guardian Sans. The text font is Adobe Minion Pro; the heading font is Adobe Myriad Condensed; and the code font is Dalton Maag's Ubuntu Mono.